The Parables

Also available in the Biblical Explorations series

Journey to the Empty Tomb
Journey to the Manger

BIBLICAL EXPLORATIONS

The Parables

Paula Gooder

CANTERBURY
PRESS
Norwich

© Paula Gooder 2020

Published in 2020 by Canterbury Press
Editorial office
3rd Floor, Invicta House,
108–114 Golden Lane,
London EC1Y 0TG, UK
www.canterburypress.co.uk

Canterbury Press is an imprint of Hymns Ancient & Modern Ltd
(a registered charity)

Hymns Ancient & Modern® is a registered trademark of
Hymns Ancient & Modern Ltd
13A Hellesdon Park Road, Norwich,
Norfolk NR6 5DR, UK

Scripture quotations, unless otherwise marked, are from the New
Revised Standard Version of the Bible, Anglicized Edition, copyright
© 1989, 1995 by the Division of Christian Education of the National
Council of the Churches of Christ in the USA. Used by permission.
All rights reserved.

British Library Cataloguing in Publication data

A catalogue record for this book is available
from the British Library

978-1-78622-153-7

Typeset by Regent Typesetting
Printed and bound by
CPI Group (UK) Ltd

Contents

A More Detailed Table of Contents

There is a biblical references index at the back of this book, but should you find it easier to locate the parables by their titles, these are included here. You will find both what I have called them in the book and their more usual titles in brackets. 'The parable of ...' is assumed in each title.

Part 1 The Land and All That Lives on It

1 Weeds and Wheat, Sowing and Growing

2 On Vines, Vineyards and Fruit Trees

3 Fishing

4 Shepherds, Sheep and Goats

Part 2 Houses and Their Occupants

5 Everyday Objects

6 Buildings and Their Owners

11 Money: Lacking It

Part 4 Odds and Ends

12 Parables That Don't Fit Easily Elsewhere

Introduction

He told them many things in parables ... (Matthew 13.3)

If you think, for a moment, about Jesus' teaching, what comes most readily to mind? For many people it will be one of his parables: maybe the parable of the good Samaritan or of the prodigal son; perhaps the lost sheep or the parable of the mustard seed. Indeed there is a good argument for claiming that parables are one of the most characteristic features of Jesus' teaching. This is not to say that he taught only in parables: Jesus is well known for his aphorisms, his questions, his disputes and other kinds of explanations. Nor does it forget the importance of his life and actions in understanding his teaching. It also doesn't claim that he was the first, or only, person to teach in parables: parables were in widespread usage in most ancient cultures. It simply notices that parables are an essential part of Jesus' teaching; that many of the best-loved strands of his teaching are parables and that his use of them is, arguably, wider and more varied than the use of parables by many other people.

There is something about the parables that, for me at least, captures the essence of Jesus. They are playful and thought-provoking. They cannot be easily tied down. So often when I think of the parables I imagine Jesus with a twinkle in his eye or a raised eyebrow, waiting, as we reflect on them, for us to discover the sting in the tail, that moment of discomfort that means we have to think again about ourselves, or God, or the world in which we live – or even all three. In the parables Jesus dances one step ahead of us, challenging us to leave the comfort of what we know we know and instead venture into a new world in which the familiar becomes strange and we have to think, and think, and think to unravel how we might make sense of what is laid before us.

One of the most remarkable features of Jesus' parables is their variety: Jesus told long, complex, allegorical-type parables (like the parable of the sower); he painted rich but sparse narrative worlds (like those in the parable of the prodigal son); he used short, quick-fire images (such as the parable about the mustard seed) and even made brief comparisons (such as the children in the marketplace calling to one another). So rich and varied is Jesus' use of parables that it is not easy either to define or interpret them. Indeed there is only one thing we can say about Jesus' parables with any level of certainty: no one statement is true of all the parables. In other words, any definition you might try to offer or any interpretation you might propose will fit a few of Jesus' parables but not all of them.

No one statement is true of all the parables

While many parables are best not explained, some are better if explained – and we know this because they were explained by Jesus in the Gospels (the parables that were explained were the parable of the sower, the parable of the wheat and the weeds and the parable of the fishing net). There are also others that clearly are meant to be understood as referring to something particular (even if they aren't explained as such). For example, the parable of the tenants was 'understood' by the scribes and Pharisees to be told against them – and we certainly understand it that way.

There are other parables – like the lost sheep or the lamp on a lampstand – that shift their meaning from Gospel to Gospel and have a slightly different meaning in each. Then there are those that have traditionally been understood in one way but on further reflection might be interpreted in other ways. Or there are those that are so tricky to understand it is hard to tie them down at all.

All we can say with any certainty is that no one statement is true of all parables, and after that we need to take them on a case-by-case basis and see what emerges as we do.

The challenge of parables

Over the years, the sheer variety of Jesus' parables has caused problems for those studying them. People who have sought a single definition or a single method of interpretation have struggled to find a solution that works in every case, or have had to wrestle to squeeze certain parables into a definition that worked in one case but not so easily in another. One way around this is to explore only some of the parables – the most famous or most similar parables – and to omit those that really do not fit with the rest.

This approach has a lot going for it: it provides greater clarity and allows incisive points to be made about Jesus' teaching. The disadvantage, however, is that it implies a greater coherence between the parables than is possible if you explore them all. This book has attempted to include the widest possible range of parables, exploring all those that are commonly identified as parables – as well as a few others too – and by doing so to illustrate the range of parables found in the Gospels.

There are around 55 parables in all and the quantity of them communicates something vital about Jesus' teaching. They reveal something we already know but that we so easily forget: Jesus was a storyteller par excellence, an evoker of worlds, a suggester of ideas, a conjurer for the imagination. He didn't tell us things when instead he could leave us to reflect and explore them for ourselves. He asked more questions than he made statements. He wove more stories than he gave commandments. In this book I am going to be exploring the vast range of parables we find in the Gospels and, in doing so, attempt to bring us closer to this tantalizing, riddling, storytelling Jesus.

In recognizing the unique gift of the parables, we need to recognize a fundamental challenge for any book on the parables. Many parables – a little like jokes – are best *not* explained. The minute we try to tie them down and explain what they mean, they lose some of their power. It is the fact that some parables shift and change, inviting us to think new thoughts and to explore new avenues, that makes them so evocative and effective.

The point of many of the parables is that they are open – they invite us into a different world: one that asks questions, explores possibility but that rarely ends in a clear, single answer. The problem we face, however, as twenty-first-century readers, is twofold. The first is that the parables use everyday examples from rural first-century Galilee and Judea to explore a range of ideas. Jesus used these because he knew that everyone in their everyday lives either did, or saw other people doing, the things he described: scattering seed as you walk; herding sheep; queuing for employment in a vineyard or wheat field; relating as a slave or servant to an absentee master. These 'everyday' events are no longer everyday in our twenty-first-century lives. They are examples that no longer resonate with the way we live our lives. As a result, we struggle to enter the world Jesus depicts in his stories because it is so alien to us. Jesus' original hearers would have understood the emotions evoked by the stories: the horror and shame, for example, of being shut out of the wedding by the bridegroom (Matthew 25.1–13) or the terror that a despotic absentee landlord might elicit (Matthew 25.14–30). Unlike Jesus' original audience, *we* need explanation in order to be able to engage in the simple act of imagination, of entering the stories as Jesus intended.

The other problem is even more complex. While some of the images Jesus used would have made sense and been expected, others of them would have been startling, unlikely and unsettling. Our difficulty is that they aren't any more. Many Christians are so used to Jesus' references to mustard seeds, yeast or fish that they barely register them – let alone wrestle to make sense of them in their everyday lives. In order to engage properly with the parables today we need both to *re-familiarize* ourselves with the 'everyday' references they make and *de-familiarize* ourselves with the images Jesus used – we need to 're-strange' the parables so that they can surprise us again, and as they surprise us, help us hear afresh Jesus' words of comfort and challenge.

Defining parables

Any attempt to come up with a single, authoritative and convincing definition of parables that can be applied to every single parable is doomed to failure. As we have already noted, no one statement is true of all parables.

Some of the previous attempts to define parables have begun with the word itself, which in Greek is *parabolē*. The etymology of this word suggests something 'thrown alongside' (it comes from the verb *ballō*, meaning to throw, and the preposition *para*, meaning alongside). Thus, some have argued that a story 'thrown alongside' an idea was a parable and hence an illustration. The problem with this definition is that there is no evidence that the word 'parable' was ever used to mean illustration. Indeed the uses of it in the Gospels suggest something altogether more opaque and harder to comprehend (see, for example, Mark 4.11–12, where Jesus says that for those 'outside, everything comes in parables' so that they might look and not perceive etc.). In the same kind of way, the other popular definition of parables – that they are earthly stories with heavenly meanings – does not ring true. Parables are nearly always about the nitty-gritty of earthly life rather than what is going on in heaven.

The Hebrew word **mashal** *and Jesus' parables*

The Hebrew word that would most likely be translated as 'parable' would be *mashal* where it is used, occasionally, in the way we might expect as some kind of vivid image that needs deep reflection (see, for example, Ezekiel 24.3, 'And utter an allegory [*mashal*] to the rebellious house and say to them, "Thus says the Lord God: Set on the pot, set it on, pour in water also ..."'), but it is most often used to mean a proverb (for example, 1 Kings 4.32 says of King Solomon that he 'composed three thousand proverbs [*meshalim*], and his songs numbered a thousand and five'; it is also used in the plural as the title for the book of Proverbs). *Mashal* can also be a verb when it means 'to be like' or 'to use a proverb'.

As a result, although *mashal* does overlap with how Jesus used parables, the overlap is small and Jesus' usage was much wider and more varied.

Parables are far more than illustrations, similes or metaphors. They often present an imaginary world, but it is a world based on reality and not on fantasy. They begin with the known but point us to the unknown. They challenge us to think and think again until we begin to get a sense of the truth that lurks just beyond our reach. They are a tantalizing, expansive invitation into seeing our same old world with new eyes. They are visual (asking us to see them in our mind's eye) not conceptual; allusive not concrete. They are hard to tie down and often leave loose ends trailing. They are frustrating in the extreme and at the same time deeply satisfying. They cannot easily be defined and yet we often know a parable when we see one, except for when we don't (there are some that leave us wondering whether it is in fact a parable or not, and others that provoke us to wonder whether if *that* particular one is, perhaps others like it should be included too).

John and the word paroimia

It is probably worth adding here that while *parabolē* is used for parables in Matthew, Mark and Luke, a different word is used in John. John's Gospel does not really have many parables such as we find in Matthew, Mark and Luke, but it does from time to time have vivid images that describe Jesus as being the light of the world, the gate or the vine. They are not full stories in the way, for example, the parable of the good Samaritan is, but they are rich and evocative. They may not be actual 'parables' but exploring them alongside those in Matthew, Mark and Luke brings them to life in a new and interesting way.

There are two key differences, however, between John's 'parables' and those in the other Gospels. The first is that in Matthew, Mark and Luke many of the parables are used to compare the kingdom of God/heaven; John's focus is on Jesus himself. The second is the word used to describe them: John never used the word *parabolē*; instead he used *paroimia* (see John 10.6 and 16.25, 29), which means a proverb or a figure of speech and is much closer in meaning to the Hebrew word *mashal* (see discussion above). Nevertheless, excluding the *paroimia* from the definition of 'parable' somewhat limits how we view parables.

All in all, parables are hard work. They require us continually to ask questions, and to receive only a few answers in return. The more I have worked on the parables the less certain I have become about defining them. There are passages that are very clearly parables. There are passages that are very clearly *not* parables. But there are far more passages than is comfortable that could be defined as a parable, but equally could be declared not to be. We should not underestimate the importance of these passages as we wrestle to understand Jesus' parables. During his lifetime Jesus defied those who attempted to pigeonhole him and his teaching, so we should not be surprised that 2,000 years on he still defies our attempts to tie him down.

Interpreting the parables

If defining the parables is complex, interpreting them is even more so. It is tempting to imagine that because some parables appear to be allegories, in which each detail of the parable links to something outside of it (as in the parable of the sower where Jesus declared what each one of the features of the story was; see Mark 4.1–20), they all are. This clearly cannot be the case, however, as some parables are too short or too allusive to allow a one-to-one correlation with anything.

Parables as allegories

An allegory is a story that can be interpreted to reveal a hidden meaning, and often in an allegory there is a one-to-one correlation between characters or other features of the story and the world outside it.

Probably the most famous allegorical interpretation of a parable is the one given by Jesus of the parable of the sower (Matthew 13.3–23, Mark 4.1–20; Luke 8.5–15; see pp. 3–11 for more on this). In his interpretation of that parable Jesus suggested an interpretation for each feature of the story.

Seed	= The word
The path	= Those from whom Satan takes the word immediately
Rocky ground	= Those who have no root and endure for a while
Thorns	= Those distracted by the cares of the world
Good soil	= Those who bear much fruit

One of the issues that arises in scholarly discussion about this parable (and about the parable of the wheat and the weeds (Matthew

---

13.24-30 and 36-43), and the parable of the fishing net (Matthew 13.47-50), and pp. 12-18 and pp. 51-4) is the question of who interpreted them. Are these the words of Jesus or the later words of Matthew and/or Matthew's community? Ultimately these questions are unanswerable; few clues are given to help us form a view. As a result, it is not an issue that will be pursued in this book.

Even though, in principle, we know that allegorical interpretations will not work with every parable, the idea lurks firmly in our minds, suggesting with each parable that God must be found somewhere in the story. Is God perhaps the unjust judge in the parable of the persistent widow (Luke 18.1–8), or in the woman seeking her coins in Luke 15.8–10? Some will answer yes, others no, but there is great danger in assuming that God (or, indeed, we ourselves) need to have a role in every parable just because it is possible to trace such roles in some parables. We need to allow each parable to speak for itself, not insisting that what was true of another parable is equally true of this one.

In some ways this approach is unsettling. It is much more reassuring to imagine that if we apply this or that formula to the text in the same way each time, then we can be sure to have an accurate interpretation each time. The parables resist this and in doing so challenge us to think again about our interpretation of the Bible as a whole. Biblical scholars have, rightly, for years been encouraging readers of the Bible to recognize the genre of what they are reading and to interpret it accordingly – for example, to recognize that you don't interpret Leviticus as you might the book of Psalms, or the Gospels as you might the letters of Paul. Interpreting the parables requires two or three more steps along this same road into recognizing that you cannot even interpret literature of the same genre (in this case, parables) in the same way every time. We need to take our lead from the text itself and allow it to guide us in interpretation. Sometimes reading a parable as an allegory will be the right way to do it; sometimes a partial allegory will work, in which it is possible to identify God/Jesus and other key characters; sometimes the text will resist such categories and ask us to think again. Exploring the parables requires advanced-level skills in biblical interpretation or, at least, the ability to be relaxed and not to assume that because this is a good way to interpret this parable it will work on every other parable in exactly the same way.

Order and context in the Gospels

It is also important to notice where the parables occur in the Gospels and how their context affects them. Many of those in Matthew, Mark and Luke occur in all three Gospels; some occur in just two of them and some in only one. Some appear in John's Gospel alone; none of them occur in all four Gospels. This proves challenging for working out how to order them in a book like this. We could go through each Gospel in turn, but if we do we end up either with great repetition or the need to omit parables that have occurred in other previously explored Gospels. As a result, I have decided to split the parables up by subject area. The advantage of this is that you get a vivid illustration of the down-to-earth, everyday nature of the parables, with their topics of agriculture, household items, family and household relations and so on. The big disadvantage relates to the order of the parables.

It is quite clear that Jesus told his stories more than once and that, when he did so, he sometimes changed the key point of the parable (see, for example, the parable of the lost sheep, which ends up with a slightly different meaning in Matthew 18.10–14 than it does in Luke 15.1–7). Add to this the fact that each Gospel writer collected the parables together in different orders and we become aware that context as well as content can shape the suggested meaning of the parable. Ordering the parables by subject-area sometimes masks this additional meaning. As a result, in what follows I will draw attention to those places where context particularly affects meaning in an attempt not to lose sight of it.

Where the same parables occur in Matthew, Mark and Luke, I will use Mark's text and draw attention to any differences that occur in Matthew and Luke. Where they occur in just Matthew and Luke, I will choose on a case-by-case basis which to use as the base text; where the parables differ strikingly in two Gospels, I provide both texts. As there are no parables that John tells that also appear in Matthew, Mark and Luke (though there are some interesting overlapping strands, which a thematic organization draws out), John's parables will always be explored on their own.

I have provided my own translation for each parable explored. For each translation I have attempted to hold three key principles together: being as close to the original Greek as possible; using modern and inclusive language wherever possible (and especially where the original suggests it); and illustrating the use of unusual words or surprising grammar by leaving them in the text even if this makes the translation clunky. The translation is not there to be used on its own as a definitive translation but to illustrate points that arise in the Greek. Where there are particularly interesting points to observe I have highlighted them in the sections called 'Interesting words ...' under each translation. When I cite a Greek word I use the first-person-present singular form (for verbs) and the nominative singular (for nouns and adjectives), not the grammatically correct form found in the relevant verse. This is to try to minimize confusion for those who don't know Greek.

The singular 'they'

In order to avoid using 'he' as the pronoun, especially when Greek has used *anthrōpos*, which means a 'person' not a 'man', I have opted to use the singular 'they'. I am aware that this is controversial and will annoy some people. I would, however, argue that it is legitimate (the *Oxford English Dictionary* traces the usage of the singular 'they' back to the fourteenth century) and I think it is a better solution than other attempts to avoid using 'he'.

The notes in what follows are designed to leave the text as open as possible, explaining what needs explaining either to re-familiarize or de-familiarize it to the modern eye but attempting to do so in such a way that there is still much work to be done in seeing and perceiving, and listening and understanding. The purpose of this book is not to tell you what each parable means but to give you the tools to reflect on each one more deeply than would have been possible without them, and in doing so to catch a glimpse of the Jesus who told the parables: the Jesus who asked questions, told riddles and stories as a way to call us to follow him.

What counts as a parable?

One of the intriguing conundrums of the complexity of defining parables is what to include in a book that seeks to cover as many as possible. It is easy for books on the parables to establish a self-defining circle in which passages we think are parables are 'in', and then use those parables to decide which ones are 'out'. The problem here is that this requires us to exclude passages – and those like them – that are explicitly given the title 'parable' (either *parabolē* or *paroimia*) in the Gospels. For example, the lesson of the fig tree in Luke 21.29–33 is not what *we* would normally categorize as a parable as it is really a simile. Nevertheless, Jesus terms it a 'parable' and therefore it should be included. Likewise, in John, Jesus calls the image of Jesus as the shepherd who calls the sheep a *paroimia* (John 10.6), which suggests that both it and the other 'I am' sayings like it that use narrative imagery should be included (though I have not included either 'I am the resurrection and the life' or 'I am the way, the truth, and the life' as they are more abstract and less concrete). The technique for choosing is unscientific in the extreme. We begin with those passages that are called parables. Then we add in others that are not called parables but are like those that are. The challenge is how 'like' is 'like enough'? And where do you stop?

The grey areas at the edges of the definition of parables are complex and, ultimately, require arbitrary decisions that will include some and exclude others. I have tried to cast the net of definition quite widely. As a result, I have included some of the 'I am' sayings but not others; I've included the camel and the eye of the needle but not Jesus' teachings about the lilies of the field and the birds of the air (because they are not sufficiently likened to something or built into enough of a narrative world). Having said that, the decision was a tricky one and I'm not sure that I would agree with all the choices I ended up making. On another occasion I might make different ones. This is worth bearing in mind and, as you read, it is good to ask yourself the question of what you would include if you were to undertake a similar project.

Three criteria for identifying whether something is a parable

Given the complexity of defining parables it is hard to offer any criteria that include or exclude passages. Two to bear in mind, however, are:

1 The image set out is compared to something else. The phrasing differs. Some things are *like*. Some are *likened* or *compared to*. Some have *become like*. In this sense, parables are similar to similes, while at the same time different. Similes present something that is genuinely like something else ('Her smile was radiant like the sun on a summer's day'), whereas parables often are less obviously like that which they are compared to. It really takes some thought to imagine how the kingdom might be like a mustard seed.
2 A good number of parables begin with the phrase 'A certain person …' This alerts us to their not being an 'actual' person but a fictional exemplar for us to reflect on.
3 Some parables take the form more of an extended narrative than a simple image, with characters, a conversation and a conclusion.

There are parables that don't fall into any of these categories, but the majority of them fit one or another – or sometimes more than one of them.

How to use this book

While some people will want to read the whole book, many will use it to dip in and out of to explore particular parables. While you do that I would encourage you to cast your net a little wider and read a few extra parables while you are at it. Our view of parables has become a little skewed by reading just a few regularly. This has meant that we have only a few 'types' of parable that we think about – particularly the longer narrative ones and the shorter 'the kingdom of God is like …' parables – and have ignored the rest. Exploring some of the less well-known parables paints a richer and deeper picture of Jesus' use of parable than the usual few do.

My own experience of working closely with the parables over a long period of time is that they have changed me. I see the Gospels differently. I see the world differently. I see myself differently. They have taken up residence inside me. I have even found myself solving problems by telling myself a parable: 'A certain person decided to do x but then found that y got in the way ...' Oddly, it works! I simply can't encourage you enough to spend time with the parables – all of them – as in their quirky, surprising, suggestive ways they unravel the world around us and offer a new way of looking at it. They annoy you into thinking new things about God's kingdom. They prod you to new ways of being. They are far from comfortable to read but they are very much worth the effort.

I would stress that parables are designed to make you think. Sometimes they will throw you a little and cause you to re-evaluate how you view the world. As I've said already, this book won't answer all your questions about the parables; it is designed to help you ask more questions for yourself. Rather than asking 'What does this parable mean?' I would suggest you ask 'What does this parable make me think and feel, about the kingdom, about the world, about God, about myself?' Give yourself time to reflect and allow the parable to act on you and grow within you.

Another key question when reflecting on the parables is 'Where is God in this parable?' As you will see throughout the book, there are numerous parables where we assume a certain character is God and then that character acts with a surprising, sometimes even shocking, moral compass that appears out of character with God. For me the question 'Where is God?' is a key one to ask again and again, and once you ask it often enough you begin to see God in the most surprising of places. It is vital not to shoehorn God into the parables without thought, as doing so can do violence to our sense of who God is.

Some people might want to use the book in a study group. If you do, I would suggest that, for each session, you pick either one or more particular parables or choose a theme (like sheep, or families).

- If you feel you know the parables well to begin with, you might like to think about starting with telling the parables as a group *without* looking at the text, then read the parable in any translation (mine or another or, even better, more than one) and notice what jumps out at you.
- Spend some time talking about the cultural context and what you

need to know in order to get the parables to make sense (you'll find a lot of answers to this kind of question in the book).

- Then go on to talk about what they make you think and feel. Did you feel comfortable or uncomfortable? Can you work out why?
- You might like to end by 'translating' the parables into modern life – if you were to tell this story today using everyday experiences from the twenty-first century, how would you do it?
- At the very end, invite each person to share what they will take away to think about more.

The four parts of the book

When organizing the book I split it into four main parts:

Part 1 The Land and All That Lives on It
This part covers all those parables that are about plants and trees and animals. It begins with wheat and other crops; then moves on to vines and fruit trees; and ends with fish and sheep.

Part 2 Houses and Their Occupants
This part is about households. It begins with everyday objects before looking at buildings and their owners, and then the relationships that take place within households – particularly family relationships and masters and slaves. It ends with special events such as banquets and wedding feasts.

The vast majority of the parables are in Parts 1 or 2.

Part 3 Money – Having It and Lacking It
Part 3 explores money, looking in turn at those who have it and keep it for themselves, and those who have none.

Part 4 Odds and Ends
Inevitably there are some parables that don't quite fit thematically with the rest, and you will find these here.

One of the fascinating features that emerges from organizing the parables thematically is looking at them next to one another (for example, the parable of the lost sheep alongside Jesus as the good shepherd). This kind of thematic structure gives a depth to the parables that we might otherwise miss. What comes out most clearly from this structure is how far the world of Jesus – and the world evoked in the parables – is from our own. Stories of everyday agriculture, of everyday objects and of everyday relationships all emphasize how wide a gap there is between the world of the first century and the world of the twenty-first century. Stories that would have been easily recognizable vignettes of everyday living in the first century are to us strange narratives that require mental effort to comprehend. We simply need to acknowledge this as we read the parables, noting that translation requires more than simply having the parables in our own language. The task of translation – of making the parables live again in the twenty-first century – is the task of everyone who reads them, and here I try to offer the tools to help with this.

At the end of each parable I have proposed a question for further reflection. I have tried to make them both a little quirky and relevant to life today. Only use them if they are helpful. At the end of each chapter I have taken a little time to reflect more widely on the themes that have emerged for me in the chapter – and you might like to do the same before moving on.

For further reading

This book is, intentionally, very introductory and I took the decision, as with the other books in this series, not to provide footnotes or references, since so many people find them dispiriting and offputting. If you would like to know more about the subject, though, there is a wealth of books on the parables to choose from. My favourites are listed below; those with an * by them are the ones I particularly recommend:

*Bailey, Kenneth E., *Poet and Peasant: Literary-Cultural Approach to the Parables in Luke* (combined edition, Grand Rapids, MI: Eerdmans, 1983).
Blomberg, Craig L., *Interpreting the Parables* (Downers Grove, IL: IVP Academic, 2012).
Capon, Robert Farrar, *Kingdom, Grace, Judgment: Paradox, Outrage, and Vindication in the Parables of Jesus* (Grand Rapids, MI: Eerdmans, 2002).

Crossan, John Dominic, *The Power of Parables: How Fiction by Jesus Became Fiction About Jesus* (New York: HarperOne, 2012).

Herzog, William R., *Parables as Subversive Speech: Jesus as Pedagogue of the Oppressed* (Louisville, KY: Westminster John Knox Press, 1994).

Hultgren, Arland J., *Parables of Jesus* (Grand Rapids, MI: Eerdmans, 2002).

*Levine, A.-J., *Short Stories by Jesus* (New York: HarperOne, 2014).

*Schottroff, Luise, *The Parables of Jesus* (Minneapolis, MN: Fortress Press, 2006).

Snodgrass, Klyne R., *Stories with Intent: A Comprehensive Guide to the Parables of Jesus* (Grand Rapids, MI: Eerdmans, 2008).

Young, Brad H., *Parables: The Jewish Tradition and Christian Interpretation* (Peabody, MA: Baker Academic, 2008).

PART I

The Land and All That Lives on It

The world in which Jesus lived was largely agricultural. Everyday life was dominated by questions of how to grow wheat success-fully or ensure that your small flock of sheep found food. It is not surprising, therefore, that many of Jesus' parables feature subjects that reflect this existence: experiences that explore the growing of wheat; growing of fruit on trees; and how shepherds look after their flocks. These are all subjects that would have been very familiar to Jesus' original audience.

It is interesting to notice, however, that Jesus' parables don't just imagine a life in which people struggle to get by. In some, though not all of these parables, the central character is wealthy enough to employ servants and to own vineyards or large flocks of sheep. We might imagine Jesus to have been speaking to an audience made up of people struggling to get by – and for the most part he probably was – but the parables he tells don't just reflect this experience. Sometimes they expect us to feel sympathy for wealthy landowners as well as for struggling farmers. As we read our way through them it is worth keeping this in mind and asking what they might have sounded like to those listening to them for the first time.

1

Weeds and Wheat, Sowing
and Growing

Introduction

The parable of the seed and the soil plays an important function in the Gospels of Matthew, Mark and Luke. Although the parable has a slightly different context in each Gospel, they all contain a commentary on parables and their function, so that it is not just a parable about sown seed, it is a parable about parables themselves. It makes most sense, therefore, to start a book on parables with it, since it gives us some idea (though perhaps not as much as we might like) about what Jesus thought parables were for.

The rest of this chapter explores the parables that, like the seed and the soil, refer to things grown in fields, whether wheat or less welcome crops.

1 The seed and the soil (Mark 4.1–20; Matthew 13.3–23; Luke 8.5–15)

One of the intriguing features of this parable is that it is one of only two parables in Matthew's Gospel (the other one being the parable of the weeds, 13.36) that is given a title in the Gospel itself (13.18) – in this instance, the title given is the 'parable of the sower'. This might be the title given in the Gospel – and it is certainly the title we now know the parable by – but the parable isn't really about the sower at all. The 'sower' only appears once, right at the start of the story. The story's real focus is on the seed sown by the sower and how it does (or does not) grow.

Mark 4.1–20

[1]*Again he began to teach beside the sea, and a huge crowd gathered around so that he got into a boat on the sea to sit down. The crowd was beside the sea on the land.* [2]*And he taught them in many parables and in his teaching he said to them:* [3]*'Listen! A sower went out to sow.* [4]*And in the sowing some seed fell by the path, and the birds came and ate it.* [5]*Other seed fell on stony ground where there was not much earth and straight away it sprang up on account of not having much depth of earth.* [6]*And when the sun rose it was burnt up and, on account of not having much root, it withered.* [7]*And other seed fell into a patch of thorns, and the thorns rose up and choked it, and it produced no fruit.* [8]*Others still fell into good earth and produced a crop, growing and increasing, with one producing thirty and one sixty and another one hundred.'* [9]*And he said, 'Let the person with ears to hear, hear'.*

[10]*And when he was by himself, those around him – together with the twelve – asked him about the parables.* [11]*And he said to them, 'To you has been given the mystery of the kingdom of God. But to those outside everything is in parables.* [12]*So that seeing they might see but not perceive and hearing they might hear but not understand, lest they turn back and be forgiven.'*

[13]*And he said to them, 'Surely you understand this parable? How then will you understand all the parables?* [14]*The sower is sowing the word.* [15]*These ones are the ones on the path where the word is sown: whenever they hear, right away Satan comes and takes the word that was sown in them.* [16]*In the same way, these are the ones sown on stony ground: whenever they hear the word right away they receive it with great joy,* [17]*and they have no root in themselves but they last for a short time; then pressures or persecutions because of the word arise and right away they stumble.* [18]*And others are those sown into a patch of thorns. These are those who hear the word* [19]*and the anxieties of this age, and love of wealth and cravings for other things come in and choke the word and they become unproductive.* [20]*And the ones sown on good earth, those ones are the ones hearing the word and receiving it and bearing fruit, one thirty, one sixty and one a hundred.'*

Interesting words ...

- v. 17: the word for 'last for a short time' is *proskairos*, which can mean 'occasional' or 'extraordinary' but also 'temporary' or 'transient'. In other words, they have no staying power.
- v. 17: the word for 'stumble' is *skandalizō*, which means to be 'made to stumble' or 'to take offence'.
- v. 19: 'cravings' (*epithumia*) is normally translated as 'desires', with the implication that these desires are sexual. While the word would include sexual desire, it refers to anything you yearn for; therefore 'cravings' might be a better translation.

The sermon in a boat?

Mark's opening to this parable – and his first significant section of teaching by Jesus – takes place in a boat. The location is noteworthy. Matthew and Mark both have motifs that they often use to mark when a story is significant. For Matthew it is mountains and for Mark it is boats (Luke's motifs are less obvious but journeys do seem to be important – whether the long journey to Jerusalem or shorter ones such as that to Emmaus). In both Matthew and Mark, the slightly formal – and therefore stilted – opening alerts us to the fact that we should take particular note of what is about to happen.

Compare, for example, the opening of this parable in the NRSV:

> Again he began to teach beside the lake. Such a very large crowd gathered around him that he got into a boat on the lake and sat there, while the whole crowd was beside the lake on the land. He began to teach them many things in parables, and in his teaching he said to them ... (Mark 4.1–2)

with the opening of the Sermon of the Mount:

> When Jesus saw the crowds, he went up the mountain; and after he sat down, his disciples came to him. Then he began to speak, and taught them, saying ... (Matthew 5.1–2)

Indeed you could say that Mark 4 is the equivalent of Matthew's Sermon on the Mount and Luke's Sermon on the Plain – it is the

Sermon in a Boat. The key difference, of course, is that Mark's 'sermon' is made up almost entirely of parables and discussions about parables, and not of sayings as Matthew and Luke's versions are. He certainly seems to draw our attention to the importance of this chapter, as Matthew does to the Sermon on the Mount.

The impression that this is Mark's Sermon in a Boat is only heightened by the way the parable opens: 'Listen!' or 'Hear', which mimics the opening of the *Shema* (the Hebrew word *shema* means 'hear'): 'Hear, O Israel: The LORD is our God, the LORD alone. You shall love the LORD your God with all your heart, and with all your soul, and with all your might' (Deuteronomy 6.4–5). As the *Shema* is the preamble to the Ten Commandments, the use of the word 'hear' suggests that some important teaching is about to be given.

The parable in context

This parable occurs in all three Gospels (Mark 4.1–20; Matthew 13.3–23; Luke 8.5–15). The placing of the parable in each Gospel provides a slightly different emphasis depending on context. In Mark's Gospel it is followed by the parable of the lamp on the lamp-stand (4.21–22) and then two further parables about growing (the seed growing secretly, 4.26–29; and the mustard seed, 4.30–32).

In Matthew the parable is followed by six other parables – two more about growing (the wheat and the weeds, 13.24–30, which like this parable was then explained in verses 36–43, and the parable of the mustard seed, 13.31–32); also before the explanation of the parable of the wheat and the weeds comes the parable of the yeast. Then after the explanation of the parable of the wheat and weeds we find the parable of the treasure in the field, the pearl of great value, and the net, with its explanation of the householder who brings out treasure old and new. These six parables all focus on the kingdom and are found in a section of Matthew (9.35—16.10) that recounts Jesus' frequent rejection by those he came to serve.

Luke's Gospel simply has this parable, with explanation, followed by the lamp on the lampstand. What is interesting about the placing of the parable in Luke's Gospel is that it is embedded in a section in which the disciples have been sent out to proclaim the kingdom. As a result, the focus in Luke falls closer to an explanation of why, sometimes, the message that the disciples proclaim will fall on deaf ears and sometimes it won't.

Mark's context focuses attention strongly on growth: the seeds in this parable, the seed that grows secretly and the growth of the mustard seed; whereas in Matthew the focus is more on the kingdom (and those who reject it) since all the parables, except for this one, are likened to the kingdom. Even the explanation in Matthew has, as an addition, that the seed is the 'word of the kingdom', not just 'the word' as in Mark or 'the word of God' as in Luke. Luke's context makes it more of an explanation to the disciples. None of these contexts is wildly different but the slight differences are, nevertheless, interesting.

The parable of the seed and the soil?

One of the interesting features of this parable is that although Matthew gives it the title of the parable of the sower in the explanation of the parable ('Hear then the parable of the sower', 13.18), it is not really about the sower at all. Without Matthew's title we might, with more justification, call this the parable of the seed or the parable of the soil, since that is its focus. The sower is a vague shadowy figure who exists simply to sow the seed and then to melt away. Even when the parable is explained, the sower is neither named nor identified. As a result, whereas we might imagine that the sower was meant to be Jesus, in reality the sower becomes anyone who shares the word (this is particularly true of the context in Luke's Gospel), as the focus is not on who proclaims the word but on who receives it.

On sowing seed

One of the most discussed features of this parable is the method the sower used to sow the seed. He appears to be wasteful, throwing the seed about and leaving it to fall where it lands. Modern farming methods suggest that this is not the most judicious use of a precious commodity and have raised questions about whether it would really have happened in the ancient world. As a result, a great debate has emerged among scholars about whether, in the ancient world, ploughing preceded sowing (as it does in modern practice) or followed it. If it followed it, the seed would be sown and then the ground ploughed up around it, so that, for example, that which fell on the path would no longer be the path since it was now ploughed up into the field.

Scholars remain divided on the issue, with some arguing that ploughing both preceded *and* followed the sowing, but the argument seems to have lost sight of the point of the parable (and possibly to be pressing its details too far). The point of the parable *is* that seed fell in different places – and if those places were then ploughed so they all became the same, the point of the parable would be lost. Whether they ploughed before sowing or after sowing, or both, ancient practices demanded that seed was thrown and therefore would land in expected places as well as unexpected places.

It is also worth noting that the story does not necessarily imply that three-quarters of the seed was lost (this is something often masked in English translations). In Mark's Gospel (though fascinatingly not in Matthew, where the seeds are plural throughout), in the first three cases (the path, verse 4; the rocky ground, verse 5; and the thorny ground, verse 6) the seed is referred to in the singular, whereas in verse 8 the seed that fell on good soil is referred to in the plural. So one fell on the path, one on rocky ground, one on thorny ground, and the rest on good soil. In Mark, then, the wastage was normal and natural for a pre-mechanized world: three were lost out of an unknown total.

The parable ends with a classically kingdom image of overwhelming generosity. The expected yield in this period would be somewhere between 5:1 and, at best, 15:1. In this parable, even the least productive of the seeds that fell on good soil yielded 30:1 and the others 60:1 and 100:1 respectively. The vision is intended to be lavish (and reminds us that we shouldn't have been taking this parable too seriously in every detail). The economy of the kingdom is not one of wastage but of generosity. Part of the point of the parable is that seeds do fall without a pre-judgement having been made about what kind of soil will receive them and whether that soil will produce a good seed or not, but where the seed is productive the results are overwhelming. So it is in the kingdom. The kingdom of God is a place of overwhelming and constant generosity. The word falls where it falls – no pre-judgement is made before it is sown about whether the soil will be 'good' or not.

The purpose of parables

One of the most troubling elements of Jesus' teaching is his statement in Mark 4.10–12 (mirrored in Matthew 13.10–16 and Luke
8.9) that the purpose of parables for those 'outside' was to prevent
them from seeing and perceiving, or hearing and understanding. This
seems to be the opposite of Jesus' desire to proclaim the kingdom
and to encourage his followers to do the same.

A little careful probing provides some illumination – even if not
quite as much as we would like. Jesus addressed the disciples and
told them that they had been given the 'secret of the kingdom of God'
whereas for those 'outside' 'everything comes in parables'. The implication of what he said is that the secret of the kingdom of God reveals
to them what they need to know, unlike for those 'outside', who have
no help in understanding. In doing so Jesus set up a category of
'insiders' (the disciples) and one of 'outsiders' (the others). The irony
is that only four chapters later this distinction collapses in on itself,
when Jesus said to the disciples: 'Do you still not perceive or understand? Are your hearts hardened? Do you have eyes, and fail to see?
Do you have ears, and fail to hear? And do you not remember?' (Mark
8.17–18). Here it turns out that the 'insiders' with the secret of the
kingdom of God are outsiders after all – they don't understand either.
The neat categories of chapter 4 have fallen apart already.

Alongside that in Mark 4–8, Jesus had multiple encounters with
'outsiders' (the Gerasene demoniac, the Syrophoenician woman, the
woman with a haemorrhage – to name but a few) who all did perceive
and understand far better than the 'insiders'. Perhaps, then, all is not
as it seems at first glance. And Jesus' saying needs as much reflection as his parables do. Perhaps the secret of the kingdom of God is
to be found in encounter with Jesus – and that very encounter is what
helps to reveal whether we are 'insiders' or 'outsiders'; the key to the
parables is the person of Jesus and our response to him.

The soils explained

One of the powerful elements of the explanation of this parable is how immediately recognizable each of these categories is:

- Those who have the word taken from them because the ground is so hard it can only lie on the surface and has nowhere to go beyond that hard surface.
- Those who have no roots (we might want to say 'depth') and so have nowhere for the seed to take root.
- Those so overwhelmed by life that their concerns and desires choke the word.

As we noted above, whereas Matthew's and Mark's contexts seem to focus our attention on the question of why Jesus' own message was not received well in Galilee, Luke's context begs the question of why the word more generally is not received – whether Jesus is proclaiming it or one of his followers (then or now). Either way, the point is that the 'fault' is not with the message but with the soil. Neither the disciples nor indeed any other follower is to read from lack of acceptance that the message needs improvement. Instead they should acknowledge that circumstances mean that sometimes the hearers simply cannot hear the word in such a way that it grows within them.

The evil one

In each of the Gospels some of the fault for the loss of the seed that fell on the path is laid at the door of 'Satan' (Mark); 'the evil one' (Matthew) or the 'devil' (Luke). Matthew's use of the words 'evil one' (*ho ponēros*) for the devil occurs more than once in his Gospel – most notably in his version of the Lord's Prayer, in which we pray for delivery from 'the evil one', not just evil in general as in Luke. While each Gospel has a clearly personified expression of evil and rebellion against God, it is noticeable that no one title is used to describe this 'person'. This is true elsewhere in the Gospels too, where Beelzebub/ Beelzebul is also used as a title. This communicates that while the idea has formed that evil can be personified, no agreement has yet been reached as to what title that character should have. It remains fluid in this period, slipping between different descriptions and titles. The implication of Satan/the evil one/the devil taking the seed is striking. While the word does fall on the soil - as it does in all the other cases - it cannot do anything other than sit on the surface because it is so hard that it is impenetrable. As a result, Satan/the evil one/the devil can easily snatch it away. Soil that was more receptive would make the word/seed harder to steal. This is a rich concept, ensuring that we are not so 'hard' on the outside that the word cannot sink below the surface, take root and grow; it is a message as relevant today as it was during the time of Jesus.

Whose interpretation is it?

One of the live questions about the interpretations offered for the parables in Matthew is: whose interpretations are they? Are they original to Jesus or were they offered later by a member or members of the early Christian community? This is not an easy question to answer. Some scholars argue strongly that the only possible author of the interpretations was Jesus; others argue equally strongly that the interpretations must have been added at a later date.

One possible way of deciding is to ask whether the interpretations fundamentally cohere with, or alter, the original meaning of the parable. If the original parable shifts in its meaning in the interpretation, this could point to the interpretation being added later. On the other hand, it could simply illustrate that parables were told multiple times with slightly different emphases (see, for example, the parable of the lost sheep below). It is impossible to adjudicate easily on such a fierce debate but it is worth asking the question for each parable that is interpreted (the seed and the soil; the weeds and the net) how authentic the interpretations feel to the original weighting of the parable.

A final point worth noting is that the image of the wheat implies the passing on of the word. Wheat doesn't grow for its own benefit - it grows to provide nourishment for others and also to be sown for further crops. The idea of the seed that falls on good soil is that it produces 30, 60 or 100 times its original seed, not so that the wheat can feel good about itself but so that there is plenty more seed to nourish/sow for others.

To think about ...

What would you identify in your life as the fruit produced by hearing the word and receiving it?

---

2 The wheat and the weeds (Matthew 13.24–30, 36–43)

The popular title for this parable is the 'parable of the tares' or the 'wheat and the tares'. The word 'tare' in English refers to vetch, which is a herbaceous plant of the pea family often cultivated for fodder or silage. In the Bible it refers instead to a weed – *zizania* – that resembles wheat when it begins to grow. As it is not a widely used word, weed seems a better and more recognizable title.

Matthew 13.24–30, 36–43

²⁴*He laid before them another parable: 'The kingdom of the heavens has become like a man who sowed good seed in his field* ²⁵*but while people were sleeping, his enemy came, sowed zizania among the grain and went away again.* ²⁶*When the grass began to grow and produced fruit, then the zizania appeared.* ²⁷*The slaves of the master of the house went to him and said: "Lord, surely you sowed good seed in the field? Where has this zizania come from?"* ²⁸*He said to them: "An enemy did it." But the slaves said to him: "Do you want us to go away and gather it?"* ²⁹*But he said: "No, in case in gathering the zizania you uproot the grain too.* ³⁰*Leave them both to grow together until the harvest and at the time of the harvest I will tell the harvesters: Gather the zizania first and bind it into bundles to be burnt up, but gather the grain into my storehouse."'* ...

³⁶*Then he left the crowd and went into the house. And the disciples came to him and said: 'Make the parable of the zizania of the field clear to us.'* ³⁷*He answered and said: 'The one sowing the good seed is the Son of Man.* ³⁸*The field is the world, and the good seed are the children of the kingdom. The zizania is the children of the evil one,* ³⁹*the enemy who sowed it is the devil. The harvest is the completion of the age and the harvesters are the angels.* ⁴⁰*Therefore*

as the zizania is collected and burnt in the fire, so will it be at the completion of the age. [41]*The Son of Man will send his angels and they will collect out of his kingdom all those who cause people to stumble and those acting lawlessly.* [42]*And they will throw them into the furnace of fire. In that place there will be weeping and gnashing of teeth.* [43]*Then the righteous will shine like the sun in the kingdom of their Father. Let the person with ears to hear, hear.'*

Interesting words ...

- v. 24: while we are used to 'the kingdom of heaven' as a translation, the Greek actually says 'the kingdom of the heavens'.
- vv. 24, 25, 26: the good seed sown by the person who owned the field keeps on changing its name in this parable. The first time it is mentioned in verse 24 it is simply 'good seed' (*kalon sperma*). When the weeds were introduced by the enemy the good seed becomes *sitos*, a word that means grain and can refer to either wheat or barley. When it began to grow in verse 26 it was called *chortos*, grass or pasture.
- v. 25: zizania is probably a particular kind of weed – see box below, pp. 15–16.
- v. 26: fruit (*karpos* in Greek) is not used as it would be today to distinguish between different kinds of fruit and vegetables – here it just means what a plant produces.

Similarities with the parable of the seeds and soil

This parable, which only occurs in Matthew and not in the other Gospels, is similar to the parable of the seeds and the soil, which precedes it in Matthew 13, in two ways:

- It was later explained to the disciples by Jesus (apart from the parable of the seeds and the soil, the only other parable that was explained was the parable of the net, Matthew 13.47–49).
- In the explanation, just like the parable of the seeds and the soil, Jesus gave it a title: 'the parable of the weeds in the field'.

The parable in context

Whereas the focus of the whole of Mark 4 is on the kingdom as something that grows (see the comment on Mark 4.26–29 below), the comparable chapter in Matthew 13, through the placing of this particular parable, focuses the attention more on the evil that surrounds the growing kingdom but, at the same time, on the reassurance that, ultimately, this evil would not prevail against the kingdom.

What is the kingdom like?

Three parables (this one, Matthew 18.22 and 22.2) begin with the slightly unusual construction: 'the kingdom of heaven has become likened to ...' (aorist passive), which is probably better translated as 'has become like'. Three other parables, Matthew 7.24, 26 and 25.1, begin: 'the kingdom of heaven will be likened to' (future passive); some others begin 'the kingdom of heaven/God is likened to ...' (Matthew 11.16; Mark 4.30; Luke 7.31; 13.18, 20) (present active); others still begin 'is like' (Matthew 13.31; Luke 13.18, 19, 21, 33, 44, 45, 47, 52; Luke 20.1, and also Luke 6.47, 48, 49; 7.31, 32). This is something that is not easy to reflect in English translation.

It is hard to know how much we are meant to make of these very slightly different constructions. It might mean nothing at all; it might be very significant indeed. If there is anything to be made of the nuance of this opening wording then it probably refers to the experience of the kingdom in the present. There are some things that the kingdom is immediately similar to (even if we need to wrestle to understand in what way it is similar); there are some things to which the kingdom will be compared in the future; and yet other things to which it has become like. The field with the weeds is one of these latter cases. The kingdom has become like a field in which weeds and wheat grow side by side; the kingdom is already surrounded with evil but grows nevertheless.

A running feud?

The scenario painted by the opening parable is one of a running feud between neighbouring farmers, in which an enemy rose at night to sow weeds among the good wheat of the farmer's field. No explanation is given as to why this 'enemy' would choose to be so wilfully destructive and we are left to conclude that there was a running feud between the farmers that resulted in such action. Unless, of course, the interpretation of the parable governs the story from the beginning. If we are meant to see the 'enemy' as the evil one/the devil from the start then there is no need to enquire further about the motivation for destroying the farmer's crops so maliciously. This may suggest that the interpretation did not come later as some suggest, but actually drove the narrative from the start. If this is the case, the enemy who planted the weeds just sought to wreck the farmer's field and nothing more.

One of the striking features of the parable is that the social standing of the farmer appears to change halfway through. In the opening of the parable, we are introduced to 'someone' who sowed good seed in his field. Following on, as this parable does, from the parable of the sower, the wording brings to mind a lone – and probably poor – sower who went out to sow seed in his field. By verse 27 in Matthew 13, however, the scenario has changed. Here, in the NRSV translation, 'the slaves of the householder' (the Greek word, *oikodespotes*, has the stronger sense of 'master of the house') ask the 'someone' who sowed the seed at the start what they should do when the weeds began to grow. The sower of seed, we discover, is no subsistence farmer but a landlord and landowner who also owned slaves. As a result, it is unlikely that he actually sowed the wheat seeds himself, but instead sent others out to sow them at the relevant moment.

Zizania

The weed sown among the wheat is called in Greek *zizania*. The word is used only here so it is difficult to know precisely what it means. One option is that its name comes from the Hebrew root *znh*, which has a meaning of 'to be degenerate' – thus the 'weeds' would have been low-quality 'degenerated' wheat. Another, and very popular option, taken from the description in the passage more than the Greek name, is that the weed was *lolium temulentum* or bearded darnel, which looks just like wheat when it is young but when fully grown produces black seed and hosts a fungus that is toxic to humans.

There is even a Roman law against the sowing of darnel in a wheat field as an act of revenge against an enemy. This suggests that the scenario described here would have been all too familiar to its original hearers and would have evoked from them a familiar sense of outrage.

Darkness, furnaces, and weeping and gnashing of teeth

The phrase 'weeping and wailing and gnashing of teeth' is characteristic of Matthew (see 8.12; 13.42, 50; 22.13; 24.51; 25.30, and only in Luke 13.28 outside of Matthew's Gospel). The phrase always refers to the response of those who have been found wanting at the moment of judgement. Sometimes they are thrown into the outer darkness (8.12; 22.13; 25.30); at other times into the furnace of fire (13.42, 50). Only in Matthew 24.51 is the unfaithful slave 'cut into pieces' and 'put with the hypocrites', where there will be wailing and gnashing of teeth. In other words, the location changes (outer darkness; furnace of fire; with the hypocrites) but the reaction to the location remains the same: 'weeping and gnashing of teeth'.

The two key images (outer darkness and furnace of fire), of course, imply a very different quality of fate. Outer darkness has the sense of exclusion from a place where you would rather be. The image of darkness (as opposed to light) can be traced throughout the Old Testament as evoking a sense of misery and punishment (see, for example, 'For darkness shall cover the earth, and thick darkness the peoples' (Isaiah 60.2) or 'he has made me sit in darkness like the dead of long ago' (Lamentations 3.6)). The furnace of fire draws more from Daniel (see 3.6) and suggests suffering and destruction rather than simply punishment.

Gnashing or grinding of teeth suggests hostility and vexation. Although, to the modern mind, weeping suggests sorrow at what has happened and, in our minds, governs the gnashing of teeth that followed, in Hebrew tradition the gnashing of teeth more often expressed anger or aggression (see Job 16.9 or Psalm 37.12). The implication is that once people realized the outcome of the judgement made they would be overcome with anger and vexation.

One of the strands that comes out in Matthew's Gospel more clearly than in any other Gospel is that of the coming judgement. What is interesting, however, is that the images of what happens after the time of judgement vary, changing from darkness to fire to being with the hypocrites. This suggests that we shouldn't take these images too literally, nor should we try to work out how it can be fiery and dark at the same time.

The images are suggestive and evocative and do not tell us definitively what 'hell' will be like. Indeed, images of (what we might now call) hell are scattered throughout the Gospels, shifting and changing as they go. They do not present a coherent picture. All we do get is a sense of what Jesus thought would be people's reaction to the judgement, which seems, in this imagery at least, to be more anger than sorrow. When people finally realize the truth of the kingdom – and that they have been excluded from it by their actions – then anger will be the only possible response.

Explaining the parable

One of the major points of discussion in the interpretation of this parable is the question of what the field refers to. Historically, the field has been regarded as the Church and the parable as recommending that leaders of the Church must not be judgemental in rooting out evil in their congregations, but should allow them to wait patiently for God to judge everyone. A number of modern commentators, however, point out that this interpretation seems unlikely – not least because the interpretation itself identifies the field not as the Church but as the world. If the parable is understood like this, then its meaning is straightforward: the righteous should live alongside the unrighteous in the world and wait patiently for God to intervene in judgement at the end of times, and not attempt to pre-empt this by a precipitous judgement of their own. It is so very tempting to do God's 'judging' work for him – identifying who is acceptable and who not; who is worthy of the kingdom and who not; who is wheat and who weeds. This parable serves as a valuable reminder for what we all know but so easily forget – judging who should be 'in' and who 'out' is not ours to do. This is a role reserved for God and God alone. Any attempts to supplant God and do the job ourselves risk pulling good wheat up by the roots and damaging it.

To think about ...

What do you think it means to allow wheat and weeds to grow together in the kingdom? What should be challenged and what left to grow for God to judge?

---

3 The growing seed (Mark 4.26–29)

The parable of growing we find in Mark's Gospel is very much more benign than that in Matthew's. In this parable there is no enemy, no weeds, no separation or burning, just the simple act of growing. Although any gardener would tell you that seed planted and left to its own devices would not produce the best crop, the point of this parable is not the nuts and bolts of good farming but growth. Farming is a profoundly active exercise, but at its heart lies a mystery: the mystery of growth. Conditions – such as soil quality or the presence of weeds – will affect the quantity of production, but seeds do just grow. It is what they do. As any gardener will tell you, it is in the very nature of a seed to grow – all we have to do is let it.

Mark 4.26–29

[26]And he said: 'The kingdom of God is like if a person scattered seed on the earth, [27]and then slept and got up by night and by day, and the seed sprouted and then grew tall, they didn't know how. [28]The earth bears fruit by itself – first grass; then a head of grain; then full grain in the head of grain. [29]But when the fruit is ready, straight away the sickle is sent out because the harvest has come.'

Interesting words ...

• This whole parable is in the subjective or conditional tense – the kingdom is like if a person did this. Unlike many other parables this is cast as an entirely hypothetical scenario.

- v. 27: the word translated 'grew tall' is the Greek word *mākunō*, which means to lengthen or prolong.
- v. 28: 'by itself' is translated from the Greek word *automatos*, a word that means 'self-acting'.

> ### Someone
>
> Just like the parable of the wheat and the weeds in Matthew's Gospel, the kingdom is compared to 'someone' who sowed seed. The difference in this parable is that the status of this 'someone' does not change; no slaves appear halfway through the story. We begin by imagining a subsistence farmer and have no need to change our mental image halfway through. It is worth noting, however, that this is a hypothetical 'someone' who is more hypothetical than most other characters in parables.

A growing kingdom

This parable seems to suggest that the kingdom is just like seeds. Just as seeds grow, so the kingdom does too. It may not appear to grow. It may take a long time to do so, but it *does* grow. And the very worst thing we can do is continually pull it up by its roots to see whether it is growing. The kingdom grows – that's what it does – we just need to let it. There will come a time when the kingdom reaches its harvest time, but in the meantime – like the farmer in the parable – we have to sleep and get up and trust in the nature of the kingdom that it will grow.

> ### Hear
>
> One of the key words in Mark 4 is 'hear' (the word also runs through Matthew 13): Jesus invites anyone with ears to hear to hear twice (there is not the same distinction in Greek between hearing and listening); the parable of the sower talks about the different people

who hear the word and the whole chapter ends with the statement that he spoke parables to them 'as they were able to hear it'.

The repetition of 'hearing' throughout the chapter stresses that Jesus is not just talking about the physical hearing of sound but the hearing, listening, understanding and changing of how we live that makes up the whole act of 'hearing'. The importance of the word in the chapter calls to mind the opening of the Ten Commandments ('Hear, O Israel: The LORD is our God, the LORD alone' (Deuteronomy 6.4), also known as the *Shema* – the Hebrew word that means simply 'hear'.) Here, as in Deuteronomy, the act of hearing is a whole life action that expects a change in behaviour.

4 The mustard seed (Matthew 13.31–32; Mark 4.30–32; Luke 13.18–19)

The parable of the mustard seed is found in Matthew, Mark and Luke and is one of Jesus' most famous and well-loved parables.

Mark 4.30–32

[30]*And he said: 'How shall we liken the kingdom of God? Or with what parable shall we explain it?* [31]*It is like a grain of mustard, which, whenever it is sown on the ground is smaller than all the other seeds of the earth.* [32]*And when it is sown it grows up and becomes the greatest of all the garden vegetables and it makes massive branches so that the birds of the heavens are able to settle beneath its shade.'*

Interesting words ...

- v. 31: the word for 'mustard' (*sinapi*) is a relatively generic word and offers little help for those attempting to identify precisely what this plant was (see discussion below).
- v. 32: the word used in Matthew and Mark for the plants compared in size to the mustard plant is *lachanon*, which refers to garden plants or herbs.

What kind of seed?

One of the key interpretational debates about the parable of the mustard seed is what kind of seed the parable refers to. Many scholars take it to refer to black mustard (*brassica nigra*), which was grown extensively in this area and used for its pungent flavour. The problem with this theory is that, while black mustard does grow quickly to a height of 10 feet or so, it would not reasonably be considered to be a tree. An alternative theory, favoured by some scholars and which I find very attractive myself, is that the seed was *salvadora persica*, which has a pungent flavour, like mustard, and does grow swiftly into a large tree. Pliny the Elder (a Roman naturalist) said of the plant that it was 'extremely beneficial for the health. It grows entirely wild, though it is improved by being transplanted: but on the other hand when it has once been sown it is scarcely possible to get the place free of it, as the seed when it falls germinates at once' (*Natural History* 19:170).

The parable in context

Matthew and Luke place this parable next to the parable of the leaven or yeast (see below, pp. 93–4); Mark's Gospel does not have the parable of the yeast but, instead, the parable of the mustard seed follows immediately after the parable of the growing seed (see above, pp. 18–20). As a result, the context of each one of the Gospels emphasizes the remarkable growth of the mustard seed from the 'smallest of all the seeds' to the 'greatest of all the shrubs'. Matthew and Luke do so alongside yeast which, like mustard seeds, also grows exponentially; Mark does so alongside the seed that grows.

The challenge of this plant is that it can grow wild, and therefore may not qualify for the label of *lachanon* (see above, in 'interesting words', though Pliny does say it can be transplanted, and at that point it would then be cultivated).

If Jesus meant *salvadora persica* then the parable changes quite dramatically. Rather than being a 'simple' parable of growth, the parable refers to the kingdom as an invasive plant (something like mint in a Western garden) which, though cultivated, can quickly take over the whole plot. Such an interpretation is intriguing and a little tantalizing: 'the kingdom is like an invasive plant which, once planted, grows and grows and can rarely be eradicated.' It also attracts birds. While birds are a welcome visitor to a flower garden, they are less appreciated in a place where crops are grown. Flocks of birds such as are described as being attracted to the branches of the mustard tree could destroy a whole crop.

On this interpretation the kingdom becomes an unsettling, disruptive force in the world that can never be eradicated no matter how hard you might try. It also attracts outsiders and outcasts to its shelter, who will disrupt the neat expectations of the person sowing the seed. This interpretation would certainly ring true with the kind of kingdom that Jesus lived out in his life and teaching – a kingdom that discomforts the comfortable and unsettles the powerful, and that offers shelter to outsiders and outcasts.

If this interpretation is not correct and the mustard seed is *brassica nigra* instead, the parable remains powerful, reminding us that the kingdom grows and grows and grows whether we see it growing or not.

To think about ...

Where do you look for signs of the kingdom growing? Do you think you are looking in the right place?

Reflection

When time and circumstance allow I love to garden. I love the feel and smell of soil in spring; I love the thrill of tiny seedlings springing up through the soil; I love the joy of gathering in the harvest in autumn time. As a new and anxious gardener I read an article about vegetable planting and how you help your seeds to grow; in it the expert gardener said simply that it is in the very nature of seeds to grow, and all you have to do is to provide the right conditions to allow this to happen.

Every time I read one of the parables about wheat and growing, I am reminded of this advice. We might paraphrase it as 'it is in the very nature of the kingdom to grow'. We could just stop there, because it *is* exactly in the very nature of the kingdom to grow. The kingdom grows mysteriously and spectacularly. In the people who hear and receive Jesus' words, in the world around us, in our communities and society, the kingdom grows. It just does. It is so easy to imagine that the growing of the kingdom is down to me and my efforts. It is not. This is something that we should remind ourselves of on a regular basis. There is nothing we can do to make the kingdom grow – like seeds, it is in the kingdom's nature to grow.

One of the many paradoxes of the kingdom, however, is that while there is nothing we can do to make it grow, the right conditions (as with all seeds) encourage good productive growth and, conversely, poor conditions inhibit growth. The difference seems to be the growth of the kingdom in us. The kingdom will still be growing but its growth in individuals is dependent on the right soil and other conditions.

At the same time, while the kingdom grows, so evil grows too. Parables such as these examined here give us a realistic view of the world in which we live – we should expect to see the kingdom growing but not be surprised when we discover that evil is growing too. It is the nature of the world in which we live, a nature that will not change until the renewal of all things. The kingdom and evil grow side by side – and we should not forget this when it feels as though evil has taken over.

One of the potential images I love most, however, in these parables is the possibility that the mustard seed was a pernicious, spreading plant – that, once planted, could never be eradicated. Evil may exist in the world but the kingdom is like mint or Japanese knotweed – once planted you can never, ever get rid of it. It is stubborn, pernicious and ineradicable. The kingdom is here to stay and will grow and grow, no matter what we do.

2

On Vines, Vineyards and Fruit Trees

Introduction

In this chapter we move from wheat to parables about fruit trees and vines. They provide a fascinating snapshot of life in rural Galilee and Judea. Unlike the parables in the previous chapter about growing grains, which almost anyone at that time might have grown, from the poorest to the richest farmer, fruit trees and vines were more often grown by the wealthy. Wine is not an 'essential' foodstuff, and those in extreme poverty would have been unlikely to have been able to afford a vineyard even as a tenant farmer. As we will see in what follows, the wealthy owners of vineyards play a significant role in these parables.

5 Good and bad fruit (Matthew 7.15–20; 12.33–37; Luke 6.43–45)

The image of good and bad fruit was clearly an important one in Jesus' teaching as it occurs three times, though in slightly different forms. This is noteworthy. It is easy to believe that Jesus told his parables only once and, therefore, that each parable had one context and one meaning. The use of the same image twice in Matthew and once in Luke suggests that some images were used on more than one occasion, and that each time they were used it meant something slightly different.

Matthew 7.15–20

15Look out for false prophets. They come to you dressed up as sheep but inside they are rapacious wolves. 16You will know them from their fruits. Surely you don't gather grapes from thorn bushes? Or figs from thistles? 17In the same way all good trees produce fine fruit but worthless trees produce evil fruit. 18A good tree is not able to produce evil fruit, nor is a worthless tree able to produce fine fruit. 19Every tree that does not produce fine fruit is cut down and thrown into the fire. 20As a result you will know them by their fruit.

Matthew 12.33–37

33Either make the tree fine and its fruit fine, or make the tree worthless and its fruit worthless. For the tree is known from its fruit. 34You children of snakes, how are you able to say good things when you are evil? For the mouth speaks out of the fullness of the heart. 35The good person brings good things out of good treasure; the evil person brings out evil things from evil treasure. 36I say to you that every idle word that people speak needs to be accounted for on the day of judgement. 37From your words you will be vindicated and from your words you will be condemned.

Luke 6.43–45

43A fine tree does not produce worthless fruit, and again a worthless tree does not produce fine fruit 44for each tree is known by its own fruit. They do not gather figs from thorns nor do they harvest grapes from thorn bushes. 45A good person brings out good from the good treasures of his heart and an evil person brings out evil from the evil, for the mouth speaks from the fullness of the heart.

Interesting words …

- Matthew 7.16: one of the characteristics of Jesus' parables is that he asked questions expecting the answer to be 'yes' or 'no'. Matthew 7.16 is one of the occasions when we are clearly meant to answer 'no'.
- In all of these passages there are four words at play:
  - *agathos*, a word that is the general word for 'good';

- *kalos*, a word that has a little more moral charge to it, and can be translated 'fine', 'lovely' or 'noble';
- *sapros*, meaning 'rotten' or 'worthless';
- *ponēros*, which means evil, again with a more moral overtone.

Although it makes the translation more clunky I have kept these four words ('good', 'fine', 'worthless' and 'evil') with the same translation throughout so you can see where each word is used.

• Matthew 12.36: the word I have translated as 'idle' is the word *argon*, which means literally 'not working'.

On species and on quality

It is worth noting that, although they do get mixed up in Jesus' sayings here, there are two distinct images at play.

The first is a comment on the species of plants that can be found in both Matthew 7 and Luke 6. Here the contrast is made between grapes and figs, plants that were widely cultivated and desired, and between thorns and generic prickly plants (Matthew) or brambles (Luke), plants that grew wild and were hard to eradicate. In this image the type of fruit is dictated by the type of plant producing it. The second image is about the quality of the plant. A bad fig tree would produce no figs or poor ones but its fruit would still be figs. A good thistle would produce excellent thistles but they would still be thistles.

The passages in context

The context of each of these passages is slightly different. Matthew 7.15–20 appears towards the end of the Sermon on the Mount and, as a result, seems to be more generic in nature. There is nothing in the context that suggests that Jesus has any particular false prophets in mind – instead he is warning his listeners about false prophets in general.

In contrast, Matthew 12.33–37 appears in the context of Jesus' pronouncement about blasphemy against the Holy Spirit (the sin that cannot be forgiven) in 12.32. If these two passages are read together, then, this parable sheds light on the question of what the

---

blasphemy against the Holy Spirit was (at least in Matthew's Gospel). It was the utterance of words that come from an evil heart. So the context here focuses our attention on words meaning 'the fruit of a person' rather than on 'deeds'.

Luke's version sits halfway between Matthew 7.15–20 and Matthew 12.33–37: like Matthew 7, it is part of Luke's Sermon on the Plain; like Matthew 12, it focuses attention more on words than on deeds.

The key difference between the two different images is that a 'bad' plant with the right treatment can potentially become a 'good' plant; but a thistle will always remain a thistle. It is probably worth noting, though, that none of the uses of these images are about the intrinsic worth of the people involved, nor about whether they might or might not be saved. The images are about understanding people's words and/or deeds: what they say and what they do come out of who they are. If you want to know who someone is, look at what they say and do. It is a never-failing guide to who they really are.

This parable gives us a powerful but nevertheless helpful reminder of the importance of what we say and do. It is very tempting to dismiss cruel words or thoughtless deeds as 'not meaning anything'. These parables in their different versions remind us that they always mean something – they reveal what is in our hearts, who we really are. This is worth more than a little reflection.

To think about ...

Reflect on your words and actions this week. Would people conclude that you are a fig tree or a thistle?

6 The fruitful fig tree (Matthew 24.32–35; Mark 13.28–31; Luke 21.29–33)

The parable of the fig tree is as close to a simile as Jesus comes in his parables. The illustration is obvious and direct and needs little further interpretation.

Mark 13.28–31

²⁸*From the fig tree learn the parable, whenever the branch has become soft and sprouts foliage, you know that summer is near.* ²⁹*In the same way you, whenever you see these things happening, you know that he is at the doors.* ³⁰*I say to you – and this is true – that this generation will not pass away until all these things have happened.* ³¹*Heaven and earth will pass away but my words will never pass away.*

Interesting words ...

- v. 28: the word usually translated 'lesson' in English translations is in fact *parabolē* – this suggests that the word 'parable' implied a riddle or something to be learnt.
- v. 30: Jesus often said in his teaching, *amen legō humin*. *Legō humin* means 'I say to you' and *amen*, the word we use to close a prayer, indicates agreement. The word is Hebrew in origin and means 'true' or 'it is so'. I have opted to translate this phrase throughout as 'I say to you – and this is true'.

On fig trees

In Galilee and Judea, fig trees come into leaf in March and April and produce their first crop of fruit in May and June. Although summer can just mean the season of summer, it is most likely to refer to the season of harvest and of fruitfulness. In the context of Jesus' prophecies in Matthew 24, Mark 13 and Luke 21, it is probable that we are meant to understand him to mean 'harvest' here, since harvest is regularly used in Jesus' parables to refer to the time of judgement (see in particular the parable of the wheat and the weeds above, pp. 12–18).

Which harvest?

The question, however, is what event or events this 'harvest' refers to. While some see it as the end times when the Son of Man will return in glory, others regard the reference to the harvest as referring to the fall of Jerusalem in AD 70. This latter interpretation is certainly the easier one, not least because it did happen and almost – if not quite – within the generation to which Jesus referred. As a result, Jesus' prophecy came true in the time frame indicated. The former interpretation (that of Jesus referring to the end times) is trickier since the Son of Man has not yet returned, and certainly not while 'this generation' was still alive.

The question we each need to answer for ourselves is whether the easier interpretation is to be preferred because it is easier (and did in fact happen), or whether the harder interpretation that sees Jesus looking to a final 'end' within the lifetime of most of his hearers, an end that didn't take place as expected, is more likely to be what Jesus intended. The question is not easily answered. Scholars continue to be divided as to how best to interpret this passage, and there are no straightforward solutions to one of the most challenging questions in the study of the Gospels.

There is, however, a third option that is at least worth raising. In this, options 1 and 2 are both true: what if Jesus was, in fact, referring to the fall of Jerusalem, and at the same time also looking forward to a time in the future when heaven and earth will pass away in their entirety? Some people call this the 'bouncing bomb' theory of prophecy (though I can't say I like the imagery this suggests). In this theory a prophecy from the future could be true again and again: true each time the vision of the future fitted, and more true each time it happened, until – at last – it comes true in all its entirety. It is a solution I find very helpful but one that some people feel gets us off the hook of interpretation a little too easily.

Whatever interpretation we adopt, Jesus' simile here is a helpful reminder of how to live well in the world. Certain events come with inevitable consequences – when fig trees sprout leaves, summer is close. In the same way, certain actions and events almost always signal what will happen next. People who can interpret 'the signs of the times' (Matthew 16.3), who can read the significance of what is going on around us, are essential to wise living in complex times.

To think about ...

Reflect on recent events – global, national or local. Might someone who was alert have been able to read the signs of the times, like that of a fig tree about to come into fruit?

---

7 The fig tree that hasn't fruited ... yet (Luke 13.6–9)

This parable is often called the parable of the barren fig tree, but this seems far too pessimistic a conclusion to derive from the parable. The parable ends on a note of hope that, with the right treatment, the fig tree might produce fruit.

Luke 13.6–9

⁶Then he told this parable: 'Someone had a fig tree planted in his vineyard, and he came looking for fruit on it and found none. ⁷He said to the vine worker, "Look, for three years I have come looking for fruit on this fig tree and I have not found it. Cut it down. Why does it use up the earth?" ⁸But he answered him and said: "Lord, leave it for one year until I dig around it and throw on manure. ⁹It might produce fruit in the future, but if not chop it down."'

Interesting words ...

- v. 7: the word translated here 'vine worker' is the Greek word *ampelourgos* (from *ampelos*, which means 'vine' and *ergos*, which means 'worker'), but is often translated 'gardener' in English translations.

The cursing of the fig tree and the parable of the barren fig tree

Luke's parable of the unfruitful fig tree is strikingly reminiscent of Jesus' cursing of the fig tree in Mark 11.12–14 and Matthew 21.18–19. In that story it is Jesus who was looking for figs on a fig tree and he who cursed it, without allowing extra time as in this parable, so that it then withered. Nevertheless, the central theme of looking for figs and finding none connects the two accounts. The difference, however, is that this tree is offered a second chance, whereas the fig tree that was cursed was not.

This is where context becomes important. In the Mark and Matthew account the fig tree stands, in the narrative, in close proximity to the temple. In fact, in Mark, Jesus saw the fig tree and cursed it, went into the temple and 'cleansed it', and then came out and saw that the fig tree had withered. The implication of this is that just as the fig tree was not doing what fig trees should do – produce figs – the temple was not doing what the temple should do: be a house of prayer for all nations. Just as the fig tree was cursed and then withered, the temple had also just been cursed. The implication of the context of Mark is that we should watch to see whether the temple withers as the fig tree did (if Mark's Gospel was written after AD 70, after the Romans destroyed the temple, then his original readers would have known the answer to this question).

The fig tree in Luke, however, is different and not obviously connected to the temple. Fig trees and vines were a common symbol in the Old Testament of peace and prosperity (see, for example, 2 Kings 18.31), and Micah's vision of the new age of God included God's people sitting under their own vines and fig trees (Micah 4.4). Not only that, but unproductive plants were seen as a symbol of unfaithful nations or people (see, for example, Isaiah 5.1–5 or Micah 7.1–2).

Fig trees and vineyards

It was common practice in first-century Galilee to plant fig trees in vineyards. It is certainly the case that fig trees and vines are found together in the Old Testament on a regular basis (see, for example, 1 Kings 4.25 or Hosea 2.12), and sometimes also with pomegranates (see Deuteronomy 8.8). In Galilee, fig trees produce figs twice a year

– early figs in May and June and late figs in August to October. As a result, a fig tree would always have fruit on it, whether ripe now or ripening. A fig tree with no fruit on it at all would be problematic.

This parable is one of those stories that has the bare bones of a narrative around which we need to add more information for it to make full sense. It is most likely that the 'man' (that is, the person who 'had' a fig tree planted) was an absentee landlord (see box below) who knew nothing of farming and who visited once a year for three years only to find his fig tree with no fruit. The question for us is *why* it had no fruit.

Absentee landlords

Many of Jesus' parables feature absentee landlords, meaning people who own the land but don't live on it. They are such a common feature of Jesus' stories that it is clear that this was a well-known feature of Galilean life in his day. The majority of people living in Galilee in the first century were poor, and the best land, located in the plains, was owned by wealthy urban dwellers who visited their lands a few times a year at most. Local inhabitants who were able to own small, independent plots had their land in remote, less profitable areas.

The large estates were cared for by tenants and casual day-workers, both of whom often teetered on the brink of utter poverty: the day-workers because they were unable to find a reliable and regular source of income, and the tenants because they were expected to pay for their tenancy with the crops they produced. A bad harvest, therefore, would drive them into a debt they would be unable to repay.

Vineyards that were lucrative sources of income for their wealthy landowners were almost exclusively owned by absentee landlords. The cost of setting up a vineyard and waiting the four to five years for the vines to become productive was prohibitive for all but the wealthiest. Subsistence farmers would not have been able to wait long enough for their crops to produce income.

Absentee landlords were often experienced as remote and ruthless, visiting only to exact their dues. This is a theme that can be discerned in a large number of the parables.

One of the questions for us, which any reader of the parables should reflect on, is what it means to cast God as an absentee landlord. Does this cause more problems than it solves in interpretation?

> Is it possible to see God as an absentee landlord in a positive way? If not, how does this affect the way we read those many parables, including this one, that feature absentee landlords?

Some point out that figs should not be harvested for the first three years: not only because Leviticus 19.23–25 forbids it but also because a good gardener would remove the fruit in the first years of its life so that the tree could get fully established. If this is true, the absentee landlord reveals his ignorance both of Jewish law and of farming in his desire to get rid of the tree after only three years. Others point out that the age of the tree is not stated, and three years of lack of fruit could simply signify long-term unproductiveness.

What does it mean?

As one might expect, there has been a lot of discussion about the meaning of this parable. A key question is who the absentee landlord and the gardener were. A traditional interpretation of the parable presents God as the owner of the vineyard, Jesus as the gardener, and humanity as the unproductive fig tree. Here the gentle intercession of the gardener turns away the wrath of the owner from unproductive and sinful humanity. The challenge of this is how we understand the bare bones of the story before us. If the owner is not only absent and apparently uncaring about anything but the profits from his land, but also somewhat ignorant of the day-to-day realities of farming, then this would be a troubling depiction of God. It is possible to interpret this parable more positively as an owner who deserves to find fruit on his fig tree and is disappointed when he does not, but even then this raises questions about whether this is quite how we would want to depict God. Is God's character one that needs calming and encouraging in the direction of generosity and mercy?

Another option for interpretation is to recognize that, unlike the parable of the sower or the wheat and the weeds, this parable is not meant to have a simple one-to-one correlation of characters: the absentee landlord and the gardener are simply foils to the fig tree, which is given a reprieve and time to become productive. In other words, the fig tree is the key protagonist in the story, and not the owner or the gardener. They simply exist to focus our attention on the change needed in the fig tree. This is certainly an interpretation suggested by the opening of Luke 13, where the focus is firmly on repentance and change.

However we decide to interpret this parable the theme that comes out of it most clearly is the need for change. The fig tree needed to change and become productive, and so do we. We will be given time to do so, as well as the kind of care (the spiritual equivalent of fertilizer) that will help but, nevertheless, change *does* need to happen before it is too late.

To think about ...

What do you think the fruit symbolizes in this story? If some-one were looking for it in your life, would they find it?

---

8 The vine and the branches (John 15.1–8)

In this passage we move from fig trees to vines, but otherwise the imagery stays strikingly close to the parable of the unproductive fig tree. Yet again there is a plant – this time a vine. And, once again, the plant is not producing fruit – or at least part of it is not. Once again there is a gardener – though this time the 'vine grower' is clearly identified as God.

John 15.1–8

¹*I am the true vine, and my father is the farmer.* ²*He removes every branch which is not bearing fruit in me, and every one which is bearing fruit he prunes so that it bears more fruit.* ³*You are already pruned by the word that I have spoken to you.* ⁴*Remain in me and I in you. Just as the branch cannot bear fruit by itself unless it remains in the vine, neither can you unless you remain in me.* ⁵*I am the vine, you are the branches. The one remaining in me, and I in them, bears much fruit, because without me you are unable to do anything.* ⁶*If anyone does not remain in me, they are thrown out-side like a branch and wither. They gather it and throw it on the fire*

and it burns. ⁷But if you remain in me and my words remain in you, ask for whatever you want and it will happen for you. ⁸My father is glorified in this, that you bear much fruit and become my disciples. ⁹Just as the father has loved me, I also love you, remain in my love.

Interesting words ...

- v. 1: the word used to describe God here is *geōrgos*, which means 'farmer' or 'gardener'.
- v. 5: John's use of the verb 'bear' in this passage is a little unusual. In the Synoptic Gospels the verb used is mostly *poieō* – 'to make' or 'produce' – but the verb *pherō* is used by John and this has more of the sense of 'carry' or 'bear'. The emphasis is less on producing fruit than on having it on the branches.

Gardeners and vinedressers

The Greek word in Luke 13.7 (see above) commonly translated as 'gardener' is *ampelourgos* (literally 'worker with vines'), whereas the word used in John 15.1, often translated as 'vine grower' or 'vinedresser', is *geōrgos* – which is the normal word for a gardener or tenant farmer. English translators in published versions have clearly attempted to make sense of the words. In Luke 13.6–9, where the conversation is about fig trees, they have changed 'vine grower' to 'gardener'; in John, where the conversation is about vines, they have changed 'gardener' to 'vine grower'. What this loses is the emotional impact of God being described with the word often used of 'tenants'. Here God is described as the hands-on expert, the person who tills the soil, the ordinary worker who knows exactly what to do for the good of the plant. This seems important for understanding this image properly.

The passage in context

Although this is the first Johannine image in this book, John 15 contains the final 'I am' saying in his Gospel, and a very important one. Most scholars are agreed that although the whole passage runs from verse 1 to verse 17, it can be subdivided into verses 1-6 (the image itself) and 7-17 (a reflection on the image in the context of the Last Discourse in John). One of the key differences between these kinds of passages in John and the parables in Matthew, Mark and Luke is that all of John's images are explained (in contrast to only three in the other Gospels). In John's images we are left in no doubt at all about the identity of each of the key characters.

The 'true' vine

One of the important features of this passage is that Jesus identifies himself as the 'true' vine. As Israel is so often described as a vine (see Jeremiah 2.21 or Psalm 80.14–15), this is significant. Here Jesus is making it clear that he has taken on Israel's role as vine and has become the 'true' representative of God's own people. Thus the identification of God as the gardener focuses attention on the relationship between God (the carer and nurturer of the vine) and the vine itself (God's son). God is no distant owner, an absentee landlord who drops in from time to time, but instead the gardener who day-in, day-out cares for the vine and takes action to ensure its ongoing health.

The focus of this passage is found in the stress placed on the importance of good pruning to ensure the vine's health. Vines were normally pruned twice: once in February/March when the dead branches were removed, and once in midsummer after the leaves had sprouted – to encourage the fruit-bearing branches to produce as much fruit as possible. The image in verse 2 refers to both kinds of pruning – the full removal of dead branches and the pinching out to encourage more fruit.

A play on words

One of the features of this passage that makes it harder to read in English is that there is a play on words going on in the Greek. Branches that are cut off are taken away (*airō*), but those that remain are pruned (*kathairō*) and 'you' (that is, the disciples) have already been cleansed (*katharos*) by Jesus' words. This is why the word 'cleansed'

> suddenly appears as though from nowhere - it is a wordplay in Greek that cannot be replicated in English.

It is clear that the 'branches' refer to those who are in Christ – that is, members of the Christian community. This raises the question of what the 'fruit' is. It is tempting to assume that fruit equals good works, but there is no evidence in John's Gospel that this was a category he recognized at all. There is only one commandment that Jesus gave to his followers in John, and that is to love one another (John 13.34–35); this is a commandment that returns later in this very passage in verses 12 and 17. The fruit of those 'in Christ', therefore, appears to be love, and only love. Those who do not love are deemed to be dead branches, removed and burned.

On pruning

The nature of the pruning of the fruit-bearing branches is clarified in verse 3 – the word that Jesus has spoken is what prunes the vine to produce more fruit. Paying attention to his words, therefore, is what allows love to flourish and grow – though the implication is that his words are not always comfortable any more than pruning is.

The 'I am' sayings

It is interesting to notice that all but two of the 'I am' sayings use imagery ('I am the bread of life'; 'the light of the world'; 'the gate for the sheep'; 'the good shepherd'; 'the resurrection and the life'; 'the way the truth and the life'; and 'the true vine'). The odd ones out are 'I am the resurrection and the life' and 'the way, the truth and the life', which do not seem to fit so easily alongside the rest. As a result, these are the 'I am' sayings not explored in this book. It is nevertheless worth contemplating whether, in fact, they were meant to be read more like the other 'I am' sayings and to contain some level of imagery.

One of the most helpful elements of this image of pruning is the reminder again and again that fruit can only be produced in those who remain in Jesus. We are not expected to be able to love all by ourselves: those who remain in Jesus partake of the love between the Father and the Son and in doing so are drawn into greater and greater love themselves. In some ways this image is reminiscent of the Ephesians passage: 'that Christ may dwell in your hearts through faith, as you are being rooted and grounded in love' (3.17). It is through remaining in the source of all love that we can learn to love as he has loved us, and through that to produce the fruit of love in everything we do.

To think about ...

'Beloved, since God loved us so much, we also ought to love one another' (1 John 4.11). What does remaining in Jesus mean for who and how you love?

---

9 The tenants in the vineyard (Matthew 21.33–46; Mark 12.1–12; Luke 20.9–19)

Reading this parable shortly after the parable of the barren fig tree and John's 'I am the true vine' passage (see above) reveals fascinating nuances. It is easy, if you begin with the parable of the tenants, to assume that tenant farmers were the 'baddies' not to be trusted with the owners' property. This parable looks very different here in this sequence, following on from passages that talk about two different tenant farmers – one who begged the owner for mercy and the other, being God, who took the best care of the vine. Tenant farmers – just like anyone else – can be good or bad, faithful or unfaithful, and were so in the different parables Jesus told.

Mark 12.1–12

[1]*Then he began to speak to them in parables: 'A person planted a vineyard, he put a hedge around it, dug a winepress and built a tower. He hired it out to some farmers and went on a journey.* [2]*At the right moment he sent a slave to the farmers, to receive from the farmers a portion of the vineyard's fruit.* [3]*Seizing him they beat him and sent him away empty handed.* [4]*Again he sent another slave, that one they beat around the head and brought shame on him.* [5]*And he sent another – that one they killed – and many others too: some they beat and others they killed.* [6]*He had one more, a well-loved son, and he sent him last to them saying, "They will have respect for my son."* [7]*But those farmers said to one another, "This is the heir. Come, let us kill him and the inheritance will be ours."* [8]*And seizing him, they killed him and threw him out of the vineyard.* [9]*What, then, will the Lord of the vineyard do? He will come and destroy the farmers and give the vineyard to others.* [10]*Surely you have read the Scripture: "The stone which the builders rejected as unworthy, that stone has become the cornerstone.* [11] *This is from the Lord, and it is wonderful in our eyes."'*

[12]*They wanted to grab him, but they were afraid of the crowd because they knew that he spoke this parable with reference to them. So they left him and went away.*

Interesting words ...

- v. 2: the phrasing here is slightly odd: the landowner sent a slave so that he might 'receive from the farmers a portion of the vineyard's fruit'. It clearly suggests that payment was a portion of fruit, but for the first few years there would have been no fruit (see below, p. 43). Thus what is implied is rent.
- v. 4: the word for bringing 'shame' – *atimazō* – is a powerful one in Jesus' context. There were many ways of shaming people in this strongly honour/shame culture – from insults to treating with disrespect. It doesn't really matter what the tenant farmers did – whatever it was, it was shaming to the slave.
- v. 10: the cornerstone is literally 'the head of the corner', the most important loadbearing stone in the corner of a building.

The passage in context

In Mark's and Luke's Gospels the parable of the vineyard seems to be an odd interval between a string of controversies between Jesus and the chief priests, scribes and elders.

In Matthew, however, this parable forms the middle of three parables, each of which speaks of displacement. The first is the parable of the two sons, which ends with Jesus observing that the tax collectors and prostitutes would enter the kingdom of heaven ahead of the chief priests and the elders. The second is the parable of the tenants in the vineyard, and the third is the parable of the wedding banquet in which replacement guests are invited.

In Mark and Luke the focus is less on displacement than on the actions of the chief priests and elders (and, in the parable, the tenant farmers). Thus the controversies are cast as the chief priests and elders attempting to wrest Israel away from the Son; what happens afterwards is of less concern in Mark and Luke.

In terms of a spectrum from parables that were interpreted by Jesus with a one-to-one correlation or those left free-floating for a wide range of interpretations, this parable falls almost exactly in the middle. The parable itself is not interpreted, nor are we told who the tenant farmers are understood to be, but all three Gospels tell us that the chief priests, the scribes and (in Mark) the elders realized that Jesus 'told this parable against them' (12.12). So the parable's first hearers made that move for themselves even if Jesus did not go on to confirm that that was who he had in mind. This opens a window on to parable interpretation that we have not yet explored – parables offer to every hearer the opportunity to locate themselves within the narrative, to recognize that the parables speak to them, for them or – as here – against them. It is this invitation to locate ourselves in the narrative – either comfortably or uncomfortably – that makes them so abidingly powerful even 2,000 years later.

Wicked tenants?

It is probably worth noting that, despite English translations normally calling this parable 'the parable of the wicked tenants', the word 'wicked' is not used in the text. Indeed, the parable itself leaves open the question of why the tenants refused to acknowledge the ownership of the vineyard owner.

Isaiah 5.1–7: The song of the vineyard

As noted above, the image of Israel being a vineyard is a popular one but the iconic use of it can be found in Isaiah 5.1–7 which, in poetic form, tells the story of an owner's disappointment with a vineyard he planted. This, despite the care lavished on it, produced only wild grapes – rather than the cultivated grapes the owner hoped for. The Hebrew word for 'wild grapes' can also be translated as 'stinking' or 'worthless things'. This translation may be preferable here, because it isn't that the grape variety changed from cultivated to wild after planting, but that the cultivated vines planted produced worthless grapes. As a result, the owner allowed the vineyard to be turned back into wasteland again.

In its original context in Isaiah, the song of the vineyard was a clear prophetic message to God's people that continuing as they were could only have one outcome – that, like the vineyard, they would turn back into a wasteland.

Although there are differences between the description of the vineyard in Isaiah 5.1–7 and in this parable, the similarities are close enough (in particular the reference to the wine press and watchtower) for it to be clear that we are meant to call that passage to mind. In the light of that, the new inclusion of a set of tenant farmers to farm the owner's vineyard points firmly towards their being the current leaders of God's people.

Differences between Matthew's, Mark's and Luke's versions

There are a few differences between each version of this story:

- Matthew has the owner's slaves sent twice and they were variously beaten, killed and stoned. Mark has a string of slaves sent individually – the first was beaten and sent away; the second was beaten over the head and insulted; the third was killed; then others were sent who were either beaten or killed. Luke has three slaves sent in succession – the first was beaten and sent away; the second beaten, insulted and sent away; the third wounded and thrown out.
- The fate of the son also varies slightly: in Matthew and Luke the son was thrown out of the vineyard and then killed; in Mark he was killed and then thrown out of the vineyard.
- In the theme of displacement, mentioned in the box above, Matthew also has in his text: 'Therefore I tell you, the kingdom of God will be taken away from you and given to a people that produces the fruits of the kingdom' (21.43).

For the most part these differences make little real impact on our reading of the parable. They are more about narrative focus. The one exception is the order of the killing of the son and throwing him out of the vineyard. Scholars agree that Matthew's and Luke's reversal of the action (throwing out first, followed by being killed) suggest more closely Jesus' being led out of Jerusalem to be crucified than Mark's account does.

The conflict between the absentee landlord and the tenants

This parable reflects vividly an ongoing conflict in first-century Galilee (see box above, pp. 32–3 on absentee landlords). There were continual struggles between tenants and absentee owners about the terms of the tenancy and about who owned what from what the land produced.

One of the oddities of the story is the statement by the tenant farmers that if they killed the son of the owner, the inheritance would be theirs. There is no legal background to this claim: if they killed the son of the owner, the owner would still own the vineyard. One possibility is that a better translation of the Greek word *klēronomia* is 'possession'; thus the tenants said to themselves that if they killed the son they could take possession of the vineyard. This seems to be something they would have been more likely to say.

It is interesting to note where our sympathies are expected to lie in this parable. Newly planted vineyards, such as this one, would not – as we noted above – be expected to produce fruit for at least the first four to five years. The owner, therefore, was not sending his slaves to get his cut of the proceeds but to demand rent from tenants who did not at this stage have any income nor would be expected to have any for a few years to come. It is striking that this parable is clearly told in Jerusalem, where the majority of absentee landlords lived, and as a result seems to have been told with the intention of garnering the sympathy of fellow owners of vineyards, frustrated by regular conflicts with their tenants. That they should be cast as those troublesome tenants would have been doubly irritating.

Although it is clear that this parable has allegorical features in it, especially since the chief priests and scribes understood that it was told against them, the allegorical nature of the parable can't be pressed too far. The problem is the identity of the vineyard. This parable makes little sense if the vineyard is rigidly understood to be Israel – who would the new tenants be after the chief priests and scribes had been put to a 'miserable death' (Matthew 21.41)? Matthew's additional verse ('the kingdom of God will be taken away from you and given to a people that produces the fruits of the kingdom', 21.43) gives us a clue as to what is happening here.

The meaning of 'Israel' has shifted significantly in the telling of this parable, away from the Israel meant in Isaiah 5.1–7 to 'the kingdom of God' – that is, the realm cared for by God where God's rule of justice and righteousness is truly to be found. The vineyard, therefore, is no longer Israel itself but God's kingdom, and God's kingdom will be given to a people who produce the fruits that you would expect in that kingdom (for example, justice, peace, righteousness). It is easy to read this parable solely as a condemnation of the Jewish leaders of Jesus' day but to do so would be wrong. If the vineyard is indeed the kingdom of God and the tenants of the vineyard are expected to produce the fruits of the kingdom, then every tenant would do well to ask themselves whether, should the owner send messengers to receive the fruits of the kingdom, they would have much fruit to offer or whether they would resent the question and attack the messenger instead.

Supersessionism and displacement parables

Matthew's Gospel contains three 'displacement parables' (this one, the obedient and disobedient son, and the wedding banquet). Each of these, in their different ways, talks about taking the kingdom away from certain people, or others being allowed into the kingdom first. Parables such as these – as well as a range of other passages in the New Testament, for example 2 Corinthians 3.7–18 – have given rise to the concept of supersessionism. Supersessionism or replacement theology refers to the Christian belief that Christians are superior to, and have replaced, Jews as the new people of God. There are, of course, a range of views that all fall under the title supersessionism, some that simply observe that Christian theology might be fulfilled in Judaism, all the way through to a full-blown anti-Semitism that sees no good in Judaism at all.

What, then, do we do with parables such as this? The first thing we need to acknowledge is that Matthew was Jewish and remained so. It is a very different thing for a Jew to reflect on the relationship between their heritage and their following of Jesus than it is for Christians to do so with nearly 2,000 years of anti-Semitism in our history. Scholars have also observed over the years that Matthew's community (meaning the people for whom Matthew's Gospel was written) may have been in conflict with some of the Jewish communities around them, something that could have caused Matthew to write in the way he did.

There is no easy answer to the question of supersessionism: it would be odd if Christians did not believe that faith in Christ was the best of all options; at the same time we would be irresponsible and immoral to ignore the trail of devastation that such belief has wrought throughout Christian history. The fine balance we need to tread is between acknowledging that, for Christians, faith in Christ is the right and best option, and recognizing that this does not undermine the validity and profundity of the Jewish faith. Most of all we need to be very careful about our language and how we talk about the 'displacement' Matthew discusses here, recognizing that we might just as easily be 'displaced' as those to whom the parable was originally addressed.

To think about ...

If a messenger came to require the fruits of the kingdom from you – what would you have to offer? How defensive would you feel when they asked?

---

10 The workers in the vineyard (Matthew 20.1–16)

The parable of the workers in the vineyard is an odd and troubling parable. It appears to go against all our expectations of fairness and decency, which expect people to be paid 'the same' by hourly wage rather than 'the same' overall no matter how long they worked. It was clearly as troubling to Jesus' original audience as it is to us.

Matthew 20.1–16

¹*For the kingdom of the heavens is like the owner of a house who went out early in the morning to hire workers for their vineyard.* ²*He agreed with the workers a denarius for a day's work and sent them into the vineyard.* ³*And going out at the third hour he saw others standing idle in the marketplace.* ⁴*To them he said, 'You too go into the vineyard and I will give you what is fair.'* ⁵*So they went. Again he went out about the sixth and ninth hour and did the same.* ⁶*About the eleventh hour he went out and found others standing, and he said to them: 'Why are you standing idle all day?'* ⁷*They said to him 'Because no one has hired us.' He said to them, 'You also go into the vineyard.'* ⁸*When evening came the lord of the vineyard said to the manager, 'Call to the workers and give them their wages, starting with the last until the first.'* ⁹*And when those from the eleventh hour came, they each received a denarius.* ¹⁰*And those who were first thought that they would receive more and they each also received a denarius.* ¹¹*And receiving it they grumbled against the houseowner,* ¹²*saying 'These last ones did one hour's work and you have made them equal to those who bore the burden of the day and of the burning sun.'* ¹³*But he answered to one of them, 'Colleague, I have done you no wrong. Surely you agreed one denarius with me?* ¹⁴*Take what is yours and go. I want to give to this last*

person the same as you. ¹⁵*Aren't I permitted to do what I want with what is mine? Or is your eye evil because I am good?'* ¹⁶*Thus the last will be first and the first last.*

Interesting words ...

- v. 1: the word translated 'owner of a house' is *oikodespotēs* – literally, 'master of the house'; it can refer to a steward who manages the house for someone else or to the houseowner.
- v. 13: the word translated as 'colleague' is *etairos* and means something like 'comrade', 'companion', 'disciples', 'associate'.
- v. 15: 'Is your eye evil?' The question of the landowner to the worker he speaks to is not easy to interpret. It could suggest that he thought that this worker had cast an 'evil eye' on him because of his actions, but this seems unlikely in the context. 'Evil eye' can also mean 'a distorted view', so it may refer to the worker seeing things oddly because the landowner is good. Another possibility is that 'evil eye' here means envious; this would be an unusual usage of 'evil eye' but seems to make the best sense in the context.

The characters

The passage introduces a type of character we haven't met in our exploration of parables so far. The landowner is wealthy enough to be able to afford day labourers but not so wealthy as to leave everything to his tenants and to travel elsewhere. This kind of landowner falls in wealth between absentee landlord and tenant farmer – day labourers were the cheapest way of getting agricultural help, which suggests that, although he owned land, he was far from well-off. The day labourers mentioned in the parable were, arguably, among the worst-off members of ancient society. Slaves were the property of their master and it would be a bad investment to allow them to starve to death; day labourers had a precarious existence with, by definition, no guarantee of work from day to day. They were so badly off that Old Testament law required them to be paid each day at sunset (see Leviticus 19.13 and Deuteronomy 24.14–15) because they needed the money in order to survive.

The passage in context

One of the intriguing features of this parable in Matthew is that it has only the loosest of connections to the surrounding context. It doesn't really fit here – or, indeed, anywhere else in the Gospel. As a result, the context does not really help us in understanding how Matthew viewed the parable. The passage remains odd even when read in context.

It is interesting to note, however, that the final saying of the parable – 'the last will be first and the first last' (20.16) – does not really seem to match the parable itself (which is not so much about reversal as it is about generosity) and occurs in both Mark (10.31) and Luke (13.30) without this parable attached.

A third character also appears in the story – between the owner and the day labourers in terms of rank, is the person described in verse 8 as the 'manager'. The 'steward' (in Greek, *epitropos*) is the person to whom things are/can be entrusted. In this parable, he does not hire the labourers but is responsible for paying them at the end of the day.

The implicit background of this parable paints what would have been a very familiar scenario in first-century Galilee and Judea. The working day, beginning at around 6 a.m., lasted for 12 hours, and for a good number of months of the year would have involved working through scorching midday temperatures. Each day the day labourers would line up in the market square in the hope that employers would give them work. The parable hints at the labourers' desperation by pointing out that they were still there, waiting and available for hire, towards the end of the working day when all hope of work would normally have dried up.

The hours of the day

The NRSV translates the hours of the day into hours that make more sense in the modern Western world, but the actual hours are much more vague than the translation suggests. The timings given are *prōi* – early in the morning, verse 1; around the third hour (of the

---

working day), verse 3; around the sixth and ninth hours, verse 5; and around the eleventh hour, verse 6. Hours of the day were all counted from the first hour onwards, so what time these were depended on what time the day began.

On justice and generosity

The parable of the workers in the vineyard is not about fairness but about justice, and possibly also generosity (though one denarius is hardly very generous and certainly nowhere near the overwhelming divine generosity we find referred to elsewhere). The vineyard owner makes it very clear that he fulfilled the verbal contract that he made with each worker, regardless of when they began work and, in this, justice was served. But if he chose to make the same contract with a worker hired at the end of the day as he did with a worker hired first thing in the morning, then he was able to do that – in this he was free to be as generous as he chose to be.

A daily wage

Although the NRSV translates this as 'daily wage' (Matthew 20.2), the Greek text says that the landowner agreed with the day labourers that they would be paid a denarius for their day's work. One adult needed about half a denarius per day to survive (as an absolute minimum). A denarius might support a family at a stretch but, as the income was not guaranteed from day to day, it reveals quite how badly off these workers were. Overall, scholars estimate that day labourers would have needed around 200 denarii a year simply to survive as, in line with all agricultural workers, their work was seasonal and it would be highly unusual for anyone to find work every day of the year.

If this is a parable about generosity, it is generosity at subsistence level – no more than that.

Justice and generosity are surely hallmarks of the kingdom, but it is a particular kind of justice and one with which we struggle instinctively. Every fibre of our being cries out that fairness is comparative, and that I will know whether something is fair if I compare it to what *you* have and, according to my own rules, decide that it is comparable. This parable throws such ideas into the air and establishes a different definition of fairness. If person A agrees something with person B and then gives them what was agreed, the justice of that is not undermined by person A choosing to be more generous to person C. Justice is not diminished by generosity.

The justice lies in the fact that each person earned enough to live on. If those hired at the end of the day had been paid an hourly wage they would not have earned enough to survive that day. In some ways this parable might be best called 'the parable of not comparing yourself with others'. The actions of the landowner were only deemed to be unfair when the situations of the workers hired at different times of day were compared – if the situations had remained confidential, everyone would have thought they were treated entirely fairly.

Hardly surprisingly, one of the major points of discussion throughout Christian history has been to whom the different labourers refer. Many commentators opt to understand the parable as referring to God's generosity to sinners, which is the same no matter whether they converted on their deathbed or were lifelong Christians. While this is a possible interpretation, the problem with it is that the 'generosity' shown in this parable was very limited indeed – what was offered was no more than subsistence-level wages – and the workers did in fact deserve the wages they received in a way that 'sinners' do not. Grace is entirely undeserved and has not been worked for – even a little bit.

The point of the parable may, therefore, be more general than is often assumed. It is possible that the landowner is not God and the workers are not sinners. Instead, the point may simply be that the rules of the kingdom will almost certainly appear odd and incomprehensible to us. We may disagree with who is welcome in the kingdom. We may think that others are undeserving of the good things they receive. We may wonder why they were included. We may struggle to comprehend what the rules are at all. But the point is that we do not need to judge or to understand.

Each one of us has our own story – a story that may be comprehensible to others just as theirs may be to us. We are not invited to sit down and discuss whether they – whoever 'they' are – should be in the kingdom at all. Just as the landowner can make his own rules, which he negotiated with each worker in turn, so the rules of the kingdom invite each one of us in, but do not ask for our judgement on who else should be welcome and why. The landowner had his own rules, which he applied justly in each case, even though this seemed unfair to others. In the same way, we cannot hope to wrap our minds around the rules of the kingdom. We simply have to trust that the kingdom's rules will be just and generous to others as well as to us.

To think about ...

Reflect on justice and fairness and generosity in the light of this parable. What is justice in the kingdom? And fairness? And generosity?

Reflection

One of the themes that returns time and time again in the parables about vines, vineyards and fruit trees is fruitfulness. It is a theme that makes even the strongest heart quake. What does 'fruitful' look like? Am I being fruitful enough? How will I know? What do I need to do to be more fruitful?

At this point it is worth reminding ourselves that fruit trees produce fruit – it is what they do. Vines are not asked to produce figs; nor fig trees to produce grapes. They are expected to produce the fruit that they produce naturally. This is important. We are not asked, as citizens of the kingdom, to be anything other than we are. We are not being loaded with expectations that are impossible to fulfil. We are asked to be who we are. That is all. And in being who we are, we are expected to produce the fruit that comes naturally to us. Fruit that is in our nature to produce.

John's Gospel takes this one step further. If we remain in the true vine, then the fruit that does come naturally is love. We are not asked to love on our own, using our own willpower and effort. We love because God first loved us and, drawing on the rootstock of Christ, we bear the fruit of the love that flows through our veins (or 'branches' to keep with the metaphor).

This kind of fruitfulness is, surely, much easier to achieve.

3

Fishing

Introduction

One of the surprising features of Jesus' parables is that, despite the importance of fishing in the life of Galileans in general and of some of Jesus' disciples in particular (notably Peter, Andrew, James and John), there is only one parable about fishing. It is hard to know why. It might be because Jesus knew less about fishing than about other forms of agriculture (he did, after all, grow up away from Galilee and only moved to its shores as an adult). It might be simply coincidental and of no significance at all. But the virtue of laying out the parables by theme is that both overlaps and omissions are clearer than they would be otherwise.

11 The fishing net (Matthew 13.47–50)

The parable of the fishing net is not only unusual because it is the only parable about fishing. It is also unusual in that it is a short comparison parable similar in many ways to those that precede it in Matthew – the parables of the mustard seed, the yeast, the treasure in the field and the pearl of great price. What makes it stand out, however, is that, unlike all of those parables, it comes with its own explanation, which is very like that given for the parable of the wheat and the weeds.

Matthew 13.47–50

[47]*Again the kingdom of the heavens is like a dragnet thrown into the sea and gathering all types of fish.* [48]*When it was full it was pulled up again on to the shore and, sitting down, they collected*

the fine [fish] into a bucket and the rotten [fish] they threw out. [49]*So it will be in the completion of the age. The angels will come and will separate the evil out from among the righteous.* [50]*And they will throw them into the furnace of fire and there will be weeping and gnashing of teeth.*

Interesting words …

- v. 47: the net Jesus describes here is a *sagēnē* or 'dragnet'. For more on this, see discussion below.
- v. 47: 'all types' translates the word *genos* – which means 'class' or 'kind'; when used of people it means 'race' or 'kin'.
- v. 48: the words for good and bad fish (*kalos* and *sapros*) are the same as for 'good' and 'bad' fruit ('fine' and 'worthless') above (see pp. 25–6). No word is provided for 'fish' here, so it needs providing.
- v. 50: see above (pp. 16–17) for the significance of 'gnashing of teeth'.

The fishing net

The fishing net Jesus talks about in this one parable about fishing is a *sagēnē* – a large dragnet (with corks on the top and lead weights on the bottom) that would have been pulled along between two boats or dropped into the sea and then hauled to land using ropes. The idea of it was that once dropped in the sea it would catch absolutely anything in its path – including rubbish – without discrimination.

The passage in context

This parable can be found towards the end of Matthew chapter 13 – which begins with the parable of the sower, followed by other growing parables (the wheat and the weeds and the mustard seed), and then parables about yeast, treasure and the pearl. This fishing parable ends this run, and of all of the parables feels most like that of the wheat and the weeds. The other parables in the chapter are about the present kingdom, whereas both the wheat and the weeds and the fishing net are more focused on the future.

One feature worth noting is that this parable – the last in the chapter – shares some words in common with the scene set right at the start of the chapter, though this is not at all clear in the English translation: both have a form of the verb 'to gather' (crowds gathered in verse 2, and the fish were gathered – that is, caught – in verse 47); both use a form of the word 'sit' (verses 2 and 48) and both have the word 'shore' (verses 2 and 48, and which only occurs in these two verses in Matthew). The question, then, is whether this was intended to form an inclusio or wrap-around to focus our attention on this section, stretching from the present kingdom to the coming of the future kingdom and back again, or whether these parallels are coincidental.

There were around 24 different types of fish in the Sea of Galilee and the net would have caught them all. The sorting that took place would certainly have been to remove spoiled or inedible fish, but that is probably not what 'bad' fish refers to here. Jewish law only permitted the eating of fish with scales and fins. The 'bad' fish would probably refer to the kind that could not be eaten by law.

Parallels between the fishing net and the wheat and weeds

For comment on the parable of the wheat and the weeds, see pp. 12–18 above.

There are some striking overlaps between these two parables. Both describe the decision made as identifying the good (in Greek, *kalon*) fish or seed as 'the righteous' (13.43 and 49). Those doing the separating will be the angels and the action is described as 'gathering'.

Having said that, no one has made the 'bad fish' in the parable of the fishing net 'bad' – the evil one plays no role here – they are just present; equally, there is no waiting time after the gathering and before the decision.

This (partial) repetition of themes draws our attention backwards and forwards from the present (with the other parables) to the future (with these two). Their placing serves to remind us that in the kingdom, future decisions are as important as present realities.

What does it mean?

There are the usual wide range of ideas about what this parable refers to – from the Church and those in it, to the kingdom including every one of every kind. As is often the case, there are extensive proposed interpretations for what the net stands for or who the different kinds of fish might represent. As with many of the parables we have looked at so far, the simplest explanation might be the best. This parable probably provides the answer to the question as to why there is evil in the kingdom. Surely if the kingdom is present, then evil will have been vanquished? The answer is clearly no. Good and evil exist side by side but will not do so for ever. The kingdom gathers and will separate. The parable exists both as a reassurance and a warning that separation *will* take place at some point.

To think about ...

Why do you think we are so keen – despite being warned against it numerous times by Jesus – to judge what is good and what is bad or who is in and who out?

Reflection

Although on one level the parables of the wheat and the weeds and of the fishing net seem abstruse and hard to understand, on another level they answer one of our deepest questions: why does evil exist alongside good? Why, when good grows, does evil flourish too? The answer offered by both parables is simply because it does. It is how the world is at the moment but it won't always be like this.

And because it is like this, we shouldn't try too hard now to identify what is good and what is evil; who is good and who is evil. Darnel looks very like wheat when it's growing; fish all swim together in the same Sea of Galilee. The job of declaring good and evil and of separating us is not ours now, nor will it be when the moment finally comes. We need to learn to live with the reality that evil does exist in the world and will continue to do so until the great future harvest – or, as this parable casts it, the great future sort out. It isn't, perhaps, the answer we would like to be offered but, when you think about it, it does ring true.

4

Shepherds, Sheep and Goats

Introduction

Some of the best-known parables and images of Jesus include shepherds, sheep and goats. One of the key themes that comes through each of these passages is the intensity of relationship between shepherds and the flocks they care for. Unlike in modern-day industrial-size farms, the shepherd knew each sheep or goat, and the sheep and goats knew the shepherd. They would follow the shepherd's voice when called, but only their own shepherd and not any other. I lived in the Holy Land for a while and will never forget the sight of four or five Bedouin shepherd boys, early in the morning, calling to their flock; nor how, when this happened, the large flock split into groups to gather in front of their own shepherd. Each shepherd knew which sheep would follow them – and each sheep knew which was their shepherd. This is the background behind the various images and parables about sheep and shepherds in the Gospels.

12 The sheep, the gate and the good shepherd (John 10.1–18)

In John's own inimitable style, this passage explores the image of sheep and does so by roaming widely around the topic, looking at not just Jesus as shepherd, and then later 'the good shepherd', but also reflecting on his role as the gate of the sheepfold. There are three distinct sections to this passage (1–6; 7–10; 11–18), which we will explore in turn.

John 10.1–18

[1]'I say to you, and this is really true, that the one who does not come in to the sheepfold through the gate but climbs in by another way, that person is a thief and a bandit. [2]But the one coming through the gate is the shepherd of the sheep. [3]The gatekeeper opens to this one and the sheep hear his voice. He calls his own sheep by name and he leads them out. [4]Whenever he has brought out all of his own, he goes ahead of them and the sheep follow him because they know his voice. [5]They will not follow a stranger but they will run away from them, because they do not know the voice of the stranger.' [6]Jesus told them this parable but they did not know what he was talking about.

[7]Again, Jesus said to them, 'I say to you, and this is really true, that I am the gate of the sheep. [8]All those who came before me were thieves and bandits but the sheep did not listen to them. [9]I am the gate, anyone who enters through me will be saved and that person will go in and go out and will find pasture. [10]The thief only comes to steal and slaughter and destroy, but I come so that they might have life and they might have it extraordinarily.

[11]I am the noble shepherd. The noble shepherd lays down his life for his sheep. [12]The employee, who is not the shepherd and the sheep don't belong to them, sees the wolf coming and leaves the sheep and runs away – and the wolf grabs them and scatters them – [13]because they are an employee and they do not care about the sheep. [14]I am the noble shepherd and I know mine and mine own know me. [15]Just as the Father knows me and I know the Father and I lay down my life for the sheep. [16]But I have sheep who are not from this sheepfold. I must bring them as well, they know my voice and they will become one flock with one shepherd. [17]My Father loves me for this reason, because I lay down my life, so that I can take it up again. [18]No one takes it from me, I lay it down all my myself. I have authority to give it up and authority to take it up again. This is the command I received from my Father.'

Interesting words ...

- vv. 1 and 7: one of the characteristic features of Jesus' teaching in John's Gospel (especially in the 'I am' sayings) is the opening 'amen, amen'. We are used to using 'amen' to close a prayer, to indicate our agreement. The word is Hebrew in origin and means 'true' or 'it is so'.

The doubling of a word like this in Hebrew emphasizes the point. So 'amen, amen' means 'this is really true'.

- v. 1: the word for 'fold' is the normal word *aulē*, which refers to any kind of courtyard. It is literally the courtyard of the sheep. Likewise, the word for 'gate' is *thura*, which means 'door' or sometimes 'shutter'; that is, an opening that can be shut.

- vv. 1 and 8: 'thieves and bandits' – Jesus uses this description twice in this passage. Strictly speaking, the word 'thief' means someone who steals or cheats, whereas a 'bandit' was more of an outlaw with political motivation. This doesn't seem to be the usage here and was probably a catch-all phrase for people you can't trust.

- v. 6: the word 'parable' here is the Johannine word *paroimia* (see below and the Introduction, p. xviii and p. 61, for a little more on this).

- v. 10: the word translated 'extraordinarily' is the word *perissos*, which has a range of meaning from 'abundant' to 'remarkable' or 'extraordinary'. It can refer to quantity but also to quality.

- vv. 11 and 14: see box below, p. 63, for more on the word 'noble'/'good'.

The one who enters by the gate

The language Jesus uses in 10.1–5 suggests that the sheepfold he has in mind has multiple flocks within it. A hired hand (the Greek *thurōros* means 'doorkeeper' or 'porter') would have been paid to watch the sheepfold overnight and to prevent anyone other than the shepherds themselves from entering; as a result, the only other way in would have been to climb over the wall of the sheep pen. This kind of sheepfold might well have been found on the outskirts of a town or village and could have housed all the sheep from the place, with a hired gatekeeper to keep them safe at night.

The passage in context

There has been much discussion, and little agreement, among scholars about whether John 10.1–18 is in its original context or not. The current context, however, is interesting whether or not it was original. The last verse of chapter 9 has Jesus in conversation with the Pharisees. As a result, in its current context the implication of the passage is that those who climb over the wall into the sheep pen are those with whom Jesus is conversing – the Pharisees.

It is hard to communicate quite how derogatory Jesus was being in his description of those who do not enter the sheep pen by the gate. The leaders of God's people were often described as shepherds of the flock and, even in places like Ezekiel 34.1–8, where they were roundly chastised for being bad shepherds – taking care of themselves and not the flock they were meant to be looking after – they were called shepherds: *bad* shepherds, but still shepherds. Here they are described as 'thieves' (*kleptēs*) and 'robbers' or 'bandits' (*lēstes*), the difference being that the former just took things, whereas the latter took things with violence, were sometimes politically motivated in their actions, and either way were 'outlaws' – those outside of normal society. Jesus himself was crucified between two bandits on the cross. To suggest that the Pharisees were beyond the pale (literally) was profoundly rude.

God as shepherd and Israel as the sheep

The background to this image is the regular usage in the Old Testament of the language of shepherds taking care of sheep. Israel is often described as being 'sheep without a shepherd' (see Numbers 27.15–20; Jeremiah 23.1–4; Ezekiel 34.1–8; Zechariah 10.2). Conversely, good leaders are seen to be shepherds of the flock, the greatest of all of these being David, who was taken from being an actual shepherd to be king of all God's people.

This is an image that has flowed onwards into a lot of language about leadership in the Church today, and for good reason. It is a powerful image and is woven throughout much of the Bible. Nevertheless, the imagery should be used with care. It is all too easy to move from comparing leadership to being like a shepherd who takes care of the sheep, to treating people as though they are actually sheep who cannot think for themselves and must be commanded to do everything. Images can shatter if they are pressed too far, and this one should be treated with the utmost sensitivity - it is no fun to be herded around without being allowed to think for yourself, no matter how powerful the original image was.

The rest of the passage rests entirely on methods of Middle Eastern sheep farming that are still employed today. In the Western world sheep are herded from the back, with the shepherd standing behind the flock guiding them to their destination. In the Middle East, sheep are led from the front: a shepherd goes ahead of them calling, and they follow the shepherd's voice. Indeed in a multiple-flock sheep pen, which this one may well be, the custom would be for each of the shepherds to stand outside it and call. The sheep would come to their own shepherd, guided by the shepherd's voice.

Shepherds

It is worth noting that the role of shepherd normally fell to the youngest boy in a family (see, for example, the story of the young David, 1 Samuel 17.12–16). While a Western context might suggest a different model with older, more mature shepherds, shepherds were (and in the Middle East still are) young boys whose job it is to lead sheep to find pasture, often through dangerous territory. This task can be done with multiple shepherds together leading their various flocks, but often, especially at times of the year when food is scarce, it requires them to range across the wilderness alone in search of patches of grass or shrubs. It is worth pausing to adjust our mental image when we think about shepherds – ensuring that at least some of the time we imagine teenagers and not fully grown adults.

The calling of the sheep by the shepherd seems to be the practice indicated here but in an even more extreme form. Here the sheep don't just recognize the voice of the shepherd, they are called by name and they follow because they recognize the voice of the one calling them. It is unlikely that this was a common practice at the time of Jesus – there is very little evidence of any animals being named in this period; instead, it is more likely that John has picked up the common practice of the shepherd calling sheep and here taken it one step further, informed by the importance in John's Gospel of greeting disciples by name. Names are significant on more than one occasion in John, but nowhere more so than in John 20.16, when the distraught Mary Magdalene is called by name by the person she initially believes to be a gardener but in an instant recognizes as Jesus. Here we are surely intended to recall the passage about sheep being called by name and to make a connection.

John 10.1–6, therefore, focuses on relationship and recognition and in doing so offers a rich reflection on the nature of leadership. Leadership does not exist where it is claimed by the leader. It does not exist by right simply because it has always existed. Leadership, as with sheep and their Middle Eastern shepherds, exists where the depth of relationship evokes recognition and trust. It cannot be enforced or coerced; it cannot be claimed or controlled. Leadership only occurs where there is love and trust already in place – and there is no better illustration of such a relationship than that of Jesus and those who love him. Jesus calls us by name and, recognizing his voice deep within us, we follow him. It is the story of faith, the story of each and every Christian, even if the particular imagery of Middle Eastern shepherding is somewhat alien today.

Figure of speech

The Greek word translated 'parable' here is the word *paroimia* (see Introduction, p. xviii above). It is John's equivalent of *parabolē* and here, at least, it appears to have a similar meaning to the word used throughout Matthew, Mark and Luke.

It may be reassuring for us to note that Jesus' original audience also struggled to understand a *paroimia* just as we do. Unlike the chief priests and scribes after the telling of the parable of the tenants, the Pharisees did not understand that Jesus was telling this against them (even though it appears most likely that he was). This was probably because they were so accustomed to thinking of themselves as shepherds that the suggestion that they were thieves and bandits was too great a leap for them to take in.

One image or more than one?

One of the odd features of the image John uses here is that no sooner has he established it than he changes it. From verse 7 onwards, Jesus becomes the gate rather than the shepherd. Sometimes this shift in imagery is explained by the custom of, in some sheep pens, the shepherd acting as the gate. In this explanation the sheep pen is in the wild and is roughly made of stones or thorny bushes nearby.

A gap is left in the pen and the shepherd lies down across this gap in order to protect the sheep.

This explanation works until you read backwards in the text and observe the gatekeeper of verse 3, who specifically lets the shepherd into the pen through the gate and keeps the thieves and bandits out. It is also worth noting that in contrast to verses 1–6, from verse 7 onwards the suggestion of multiple flocks in the same pen has also disappeared. Try as we might, it is not possible to make both images sit alongside each other seamlessly.

John 10 seems to be functioning with at least two different sheepfolds – one with a gate and gatekeeper, and one without. It may even be that an entirely different *kind* of sheepfold is in mind. The second, unlike the first kind, doesn't have a gatekeeper – or a gate at all; instead, the shepherd lies down in the gap to be the 'gate'. Indeed, it is entirely possible to propose two different contexts in which each image works. The first would be in a village or town, where the pen would house all the sheep owned by the people who live there, who together hire a gatekeeper to watch over the sheep during the night. The second would be far out in the hills or wilderness, where the shepherd has travelled to find grass for the flock. In that case only one flock would be present (though more than one would also be possible) and a more makeshift pen and gate necessary. This kind of sheepfold would have been made from stones or shrubs out on the hillside (or an old one made by a previous shepherd found) as a temporary shelter for the sheep as they ranged far and wide looking for food.

If this is true, then John 10.1–18 has three different narrative images in it, which have been joined together due to the overlap of subject matter (an overlap that includes not only the presence of gates but of thieves and bandits too), but we shouldn't try too hard to read this passage as one seamless whole. After all, each narrative image makes a slightly different point: 1–6, as we have already observed, is about true leadership; 7–10 is about the entry point to new life; and 11–18 is about the shepherd laying down his life for the sheep. There are incredible overlaps, but each is very slightly different. They do, though, seem to make better sense read alongside each other – but not necessarily as a single narrative with a single image driving it.

The gate

Another feature that emerges when reading this passage is the recognition that the image of Jesus as the gate is allusive and suggestive and defies too tight an interpretation. If we press it too hard we end up having to ask where salvation is to be found – in the sheep pen itself or outside of it? Furthermore, do the sheep enter and leave salvation as they go in and out? Clearly, the image is more fluid than that. It is the gate, not where the sheep were coming from nor where they were going to, that is important. Passing through the gate is what is significant.

In fact the point of the narrative is very much *not* to keep the sheep penned up. The sheep pen provides safety from marauders and predators but not nourishment – nourishment is to be found outside it. Jesus came that all might have life and have it abundantly or extraordinarily: the sheep in Jesus' care do not have to choose between safety and nourishment because they can have both. Those who choose to pass through Jesus, the gate, are choosing a life of freedom, choice and abundance. They will be safe when they need safety and will be nourished when they need nourishment. A life in Christ is not a half-lived life, cowering in a place of safety lest harm should befall us. It is a life of plenty, of spaciousness and of liberty.

The good shepherd

'Good'

The word (*kalos*) often translated 'good' here – good shepherd – is a much bigger word than the English suggests. There is a word that means just 'good' (*agathos*) but *kalos* has more of a meaning of 'beautiful', 'noble', 'honourable' or 'ideal'. It is a stretchy word that cannot be fully captured in English, and so we have to make do with 'good'.

In some ways the word 'noble' renders better what is meant here. In Greek philosophy, dying nobly involved dying voluntarily and for the sake of others. This is clearly what is in mind here – the noble shepherd dies voluntarily on behalf of the sheep. Yet the word 'noble' is a difficult one in modern English, and Jesus as the noble shepherd just doesn't have the right ring to it.

The use of the word 'noble' for the shepherd illustrates the way the meaning of a parable can affect the narrative details it contains. Actually, a shepherd who died for the sheep would be of dubious value, because then the sheep would be alone and unprotected in the wild. A shepherd might, as a last resort, be prepared to die to save the flock but such a course of action would fall into the category of absolutely desperate measures.

This is one of those occasions when there is no doubt at all about what the *paroimia* refers to. The subject to which it points so overshadows the image to which it is attached that the original begins to break down. What drives the narrative is the meaning, not the original story. While it might be profoundly unhelpful – even disastrous – for a shepherd to die for the sheep, Jesus' death for his followers was quite the opposite. Indeed his death was the very definition of noble. Everyone reading verses 11–18 knows that the real subject is Jesus' death, not the putative death of a shepherd for the sheep, and that the 'real meaning' is driving the narration of the story.

'I have other sheep'

One of the most discussed elements of this narrative is the meaning of the phrase in the NRSV 'I have other sheep that do not belong to this fold' (10.16). One option is that it refers to those who do not belong to the fold of the Jewish people (Gentiles, in other words), though others take it to mean that there are those who follow Jesus who are not Christian.

The most obvious and likely meaning is the first option (especially if Jesus is still speaking to the Pharisees as he was at the start of this chapter), since the growth of Christianity into a religion that was separate from Judaism, and independently recognizable as such, was long and slow and far post-dated even the final form of John's Gospel, let alone Jesus' original words. As a result, he is very unlikely to have meant that he has other sheep who weren't Christian because no one was, technically, 'Christian' at the time of Jesus. It is much more likely that he was telling the Pharisees that he had sheep (followers) who were not Jewish.

At the time of Jesus, this 'flock' of non-Jewish followers was tiny, though it grew rapidly after Jesus' death.

As often happens in John, this whole passage has become a meditation on sheep and shepherds, looping in calling and leadership, safety and nourishment, and nobility and laying down one's life on the way. The variety of sheepfolds and shepherd images found in John 10.1–18 suggests that they did not all begin life in the same context but have been stitched together later after reflection. This chapter uses the springboard of sheep and shepherds to enable a rich reflection on a wide range of subjects. We engage with them best if we can allow the image to shift and change in our mind's eye as we go, possibly even moving from one kind of sheepfold to another halfway through, and also if we recognize that by the end of the passage it is the theology that drives the image and not the other way around.

To think about ...

Why does the imagery of shepherds and sheep still survive so vibrantly in a world that is, for many people, more urban than rural? What is it about the imagery that tugs at us so powerfully?

---

13 The lost sheep (Matthew 18.10–14; Luke 15.1–7)

The parable of the lost sheep is very well loved as a parable. What many people don't notice, however, is that the version they love comes from Luke's Gospel. The version in Matthew's Gospel – though similar in many ways – means something significantly different. For this reason I have included both versions below.

Matthew 18.10–14

[10]*See that you do not despise one of these little ones, for I say to you that their angels in the heavens continually see the face of my father in the heavens.* [12]*What do you think? If someone were to have a hundred sheep and one of them were led astray, surely he would leave the ninety-nine on the mountain and travel, looking*

for the one that had been led astray? [13]*And if they found it, I say to you – and this is true – that they rejoice over it more than over the ninety-nine who had not been led astray.* [14]*In the same way it is not the will of your Father in heaven that one of these little ones is lost.*

Luke 15.1–7

[1]*Now all the tax collectors and sinners were coming near to hear him.* [2]*And the Pharisees and scribes muttered among themselves saying: 'This person welcomes sinners and eats with them.'*

[3]*He said this parable to them:* [4]*'Which of you having a hundred sheep and losing one of them does not leave the ninety-nine in the wilderness and go after the lost one until they find it?* [5]*And, finding it, places it on his shoulders, rejoicing,* [6]*and coming into the house gathers friends and neighbours saying to them: "Rejoice with me because I have found the sheep that was lost."* [7]*I say to you that in the same way there will be more joy in heaven over one sinner that repents than over ninety-nine righteous people who have no need of repentance.'*

Interesting words ...

- In Luke, the word for the sheep getting lost – *apollumi* – means just 'lost' but in Matthew the word, from the verb *planaō*, has more of the sense of being led astray or deceived. For more on the significance of this, see pp. 68–9 below.
- Matthew's shepherd leaves the sheep 'on the mountain', whereas Luke's leaves them 'in the wilderness'.

On losing one and leaving the ninety-nine

Many of the parables, drawn from everyday life in the Gospels, make sense. They would have elicited a nod of agreement: yes, of course, that is how you would separate fish from a dragnet; yes, we can see how annoyed you would be if your fig tree had no figs on it; yes, indeed leaving weeds to grow with wheat until harvest does make sense. But this parable is very different. Indeed, it is easy to imagine the looks of puzzlement, if not outrage, at the suggestion that a shepherd would justify leaving ninety-nine sheep to look for one. It just makes no sense. A shepherd who leaves ninety-nine sheep alone to search for one sheep risks ending up with no sheep at all. In order for it to make any sense we need to step back a little and look at it again.

The passages in context

The first feature to notice about this parable is that it sits in a different place in both Matthew and Luke. In Matthew's Gospel it occurs in chapter 18 in a run of teachings to the disciples, which all focus in one way or another on the Church: 18.6-9 talks of what will happen to anyone who puts a stumbling block 'before one of these little ones'; then we have the parable of the lost sheep ending with the verse (not found in Luke): 'So it is not the will of your Father in heaven that one of these little ones should be lost' (see below, p. 69, for a discussion of who the 'little ones' were). Immediately following this parable Jesus moved on to what to do if a member of the Church sins against you (18.15-20); followed by the command to forgive a member of the Church seventy times seven. The context for this parable in Matthew's Gospel is the Church and how to relate to others in the Church.

The context in Luke is entirely different. Luke 15 contains three parables about losing and finding - the lost sheep (15.1-7); the lost coin (15.8-10); and the lost son - normally known as the prodigal son (15.11-32). All of these parables are told in the context of Jesus' dispute with the Pharisees and scribes about his eating with tax collectors and sinners; as a result, in Luke the parable is set in the context of sinners' repentance more than in the context of the Church.

Most Galileans would never have had a hundred sheep. Subsistence farmers would have had no more than a handful. If we think about the shepherd imagery introduced in John's Gospel that we explored above, it is clear that it is predicated on having a small flock all of which would know their shepherd and the shepherd's own voice. With a flock of this size it would have been easy to notice when one went missing. Someone with a hundred sheep would find it harder to notice when one went astray. Such a person would have to have been wealthy and could quite possibly have afforded one or more hired hands to look after the sheep. In this case leaving the ninety-nine would have been a less risky endeavour. In fact the original audience might have rolled their eyes at the hapless, wealthy owner. Imagine having so many sheep that you didn't notice one going astray before it was too late?

Having said that, it is possible that what Jesus is conveying here is the desperation of the owner. Which one of us, having done something stupid (like losing a sheep), hasn't compounded our mistake by doing something even more stupid (like leaving the rest of the sheep to go looking for it)? Of course, if we read the owner of the sheep as God, compounding stupidity with stupidity is a less likely option for interpretation, and you may prefer to go for the wealthy owner with hired hands to care for the remaining sheep. But another way to read this parable is as a profoundly human story of a sheep owner who makes a terrible mistake, and on realizing the mistake throws caution to the wind in his attempt to fix it. If a hapless owner of sheep, who has so many sheep he didn't notice when one wandered off, searches desperately for the one that is lost – how much more would God search for one he cared for deeply?

The point of the parable is the level of care and investment the shepherd was prepared to pour into a single sheep from the flock. Whether we are to read God as the shepherd or not, there is no doubt that the point here is that each individual matters. In our world this is something we claim to believe (even if we don't always act as though we do), but in Jesus' world, where individuality was almost unknown because corporate identity was such a strong phenomenon, this would have been a radical message indeed. Hearing the assurance that each individual sheep was so valuable that they were worth risking the whole flock for would have been surprising in the extreme.

Matthew's lost sheep

In the context of Matthew's Gospel, the shepherd who searches for the missing sheep is less likely to be God. As we noted above, the context of Matthew's parable sets it firmly within that of the Church. This context is highlighted by Matthew's word for the sheep getting lost. In contrast to Luke, where the word (*apollumi*) simply means 'lost', in Matthew the sheep is 'led astray' or 'deceived' (*planaō*). Thus in Luke the sheep just wandered off, whereas in Matthew it was led astray or deceived by someone. This changes the narrative significantly: in Matthew this is a story of malicious intent in which the one sheep is lured away deliberately by someone outside of the fold. If we then read the story with its first line in Matthew's Gospel in place, then despising the little ones (18.10) means treating individual members of the Church with little concern, not caring if they are led astray (because each of them has an angel in heaven who will notice and bring it to God's attention even if you don't). All in all, then, in Matthew's Gospel the parable of the lost sheep focuses on what a shepherd (that is, leader of a community) should do if they become aware that one of their sheep has been led astray – they should leave the others in the flock and search and search until they find it. They should not declare the loss of anyone unimportant because the angels in heaven would never forget, even if human leaders do.

'Little ones'

The title 'little ones' is strongly characteristic of Matthew's Gospel. It occurs in 10.42, 18.6, here in 18.10 and 14, and is probably used again in a different form in the parable of the sheep and the goats, where Jesus talks about 'the least of the members of my family'. It almost certainly refers to Jesus' disciples – both then and now – and may well be picking up his invitation to become like children in order to enter the kingdom of heaven (18.3–4). Those who have accepted this invitation would be 'little ones'.

While with many of the parables it is hard to discern how much comes from Jesus and how much from a later context, this is one of those occasions when the layers are much easier to discern. This parable was almost certainly said by Jesus (hence its use by Luke, even if in a different context) but it had begun to be interpreted, by the time Matthew wrote his Gospel, in terms of how to act in the Church (as there wasn't 'a Church' as such during the time of Jesus, it is unlikely he told it with exactly this emphasis during his lifetime). This is a fascinating insight into the growth of a parable in the early Church, from the lips of Jesus into something that helped them to know how to act in the context in which they found themselves.

Luke's lost sheep

In contrast to Matthew's lost sheep, which appears to be someone who is led astray from the Church, Luke's lost sheep appears to be the tax collectors and sinners who dined with Jesus, to the horror of the Pharisees and scribes. As with so many of Luke's parables, the setting of the parable gives it an additional emphasis that the parable alone might not have had. The setting of the conversation between Jesus and the Pharisees focuses initial attention on celebration. Although we are accustomed to reading the parable as being about 'the lost' and 'the found', Luke's context points us towards the celebration that takes place when the sheep, and subsequently the coin and the son, are found.

Tax collectors and sinners

One of the striking features of the Gospels is the often repeated phrase 'tax collectors and sinners'. It appears to assume there was a job description for 'sinners' just as there was for 'tax collectors'. The fact that they appear together so often implies that they both found themselves in the same situation and were seen in the same kind of light. The question is what that light was.

For many years, scholars assumed that tax collectors were hated because the Roman Empire engaged in tax farming. Tax farming was something the Romans inherited from Greek city-states and which allowed tax collectors (called in Latin *publicani*, hence the reference to publicans in the King James Version of the Bible) to buy the right to collect taxes from the Empire. They would pay for this right in advance and then recoup their money (plus extras) in any way they saw fit. However, by the time of Jesus this practice had largely been outlawed and instead taxes were collected by people paid by the Romans to do so. Tax collectors, therefore, would have been hated not so much because they were corrupt – though some probably were – but because they collaborated with the Roman Empire. As a result, they would have been ostracized from society.

The joining of sinners with tax collectors suggests that sinners found themselves in a very similar position to tax collectors – excluded and ostracized from normal relationships. This still leaves the question of why they found themselves in this kind of position. The term 'sinner' probably implies that they broke the law so often – or had committed a sin for which there was no forgiveness – that they were cast out of society. The phrase implies outsiders and misfits – those who were shunned from society for a range of reasons and left to find company with others who were similarly shunned.

Jesus' reply to the Pharisees and scribes turns his 'dining' with sinners into a full-blown celebration. The Pharisees complained that he ate with them; Jesus responded that he wasn't *just* eating with them. This was a party mirroring a similar celebration in heaven. The Pharisees, though, had more to worry about than the fact that Jesus was dining with tax collectors and sinners. What he was doing was far more significant than that – he was throwing a welcome-home party so that they might never be outsiders again. In Luke this parable becomes far, far more than people being lost and found again; it is about human value, about welcome and about the importance of authentic celebration.

Being lost and found, however, remains an important theme, and Luke's presentation of the three 'lost and found' parables next to one another in chapter 15 provides the context for a rich reflection on losing and finding. Each 'item' (the sheep, the coin and the son) were lost in a different way: the sheep wandered off; the coin just got lost somehow by accident; and the son made a deliberate choice to become lost (though he didn't know he was doing that at the time). While the sheep and the coin were found in the same way (by someone looking for them diligently), the son found himself (see the discussion on the lost son below, pp. 18–26). All this focuses our attention back on the celebration once more – people are lost in different ways and are found in different ways, but the celebration in heaven at their return is the one constant factor.

To think about ...

How good are we at celebrating like Jesus did? What would our communities look like if we were better at it?

14 The sheep and the goats (Matthew 25.31–46)

Matthew 25.31–46

[31]*When the Son of Man comes in his glory and all the angels with him, then he will sit on his throne of glory,* [32]*and they will gather before him all the nations and separate them from one another, like a shepherd separates the sheep from the goats.* [33]*He will make the sheep stand on his right hand and the goats on his left hand.* [34]*Then the king will say to those on his right hand, 'Come, those who are blessed by my father, inherit the kingdom that has been being prepared for you from the foundation of the world.* [35]*For I was hungry and you gave me something to eat; I was thirsty and you gave me something to drink; I was a stranger and you welcomed me as a guest;* [36]*naked and you dressed me; sick and you looked after me; in prison and you came to me.'* [37]*Then the righteous will answer and say, 'Lord, when did we see you hungry and nourish you? Or thirsty and give you something to drink?* [38]*When did we see you a stranger and welcome you as a guest? Or naked and dressed you?* [39]*When did we see you ill or in prison and come to you?'* [40]*And in answer the King will say, 'I say to you – and this is true – whenever you did it to one of the least of these my brothers and sisters, you did it to me.'* [41]*Then he will say to those on the left: 'Get away from me, you who are cursed into eternal fire that has been being prepared for the devil and his angels.* [42]*For I was hungry and you did not give me anything to eat; I was thirsty and you did not give me anything to drink.* [43]*I was a stranger and you did not welcome me as a guest; naked and you did not dress me; weak and in prison and you did not take care of me.'* [44]*Then they will answer and say, 'Lord, when did we see you hungry or thirsty or a stranger or naked or weak or in prison and not serve you?'* [45]*Then he will answer them and say, 'I say to you – and this is true – whenever you did not do it to one of the least of these, you did not do it to me.'* [46]*Then they will go away into the eternal punishment, but the righteous into eternal life.*

Interesting words …

- vv. 35 and 37: the word for 'feed' changes in this parable. In verse 35 it is *esthiō* (which is a highly irregular verb, so in the aorist infinitive – as here – it is *fagein*); whereas in verse 37 it becomes *trephō*, which has a wide range of meanings from 'cause to grow', 'to breed' and even 'to cherish' or 'to foster'. It is a much richer word and implies an ongoing action, not a single act of feeding. All the other words are the same when they are repeated.

- v. 33: the usual word for 'left' (*aristeros*) is not used here; instead, *euōnumos* is used. The word literally means 'of good name' or 'prosperous' but was sometimes used instead of *aristeros* since 'left' had such a bad omen associated with it that they avoided using the word.
- v. 45: the word translated 'serve' is the verb *diakoneō*, which can mean 'serve' or 'minister'.

An unusual parable

The sheep and the goats is one of the most cited of all the parables and would, for many Christians, be the passage that motivates them into social action and care for the poor. Doing what we do as though we were doing it to Jesus is a fundamental part of Christian life and service. Yet there are a vast number of problems within this parable, which raises questions about how it should be best interpreted.

The first thing to notice is that this is a very unusual parable in a number of ways:

- It is really a simile (which is rare for parables). The Son of Man will separate people like a shepherd separates sheep from goats. There is no imaginative leap required; no wrestling to work out how these two images fit with each other.
- The actual parable is very short (from the second half of verse 32 to the end of verse 33).
- The rest of the passage is an explanation – described as though we were there and witnessing it – of why the Son of Man/king separated the people as he did.

As a result, there are no other parables in the Gospels quite like this one and we should bear this in mind as we read it.

The passage in context

The parable with accompanying interpretation appears in Matthew's Gospel after a string of parables that might best be gathered under the title of 'What you do while you wait for the end'. The parables of the reliable and wicked slaves (Matthew 24.45-51, see pp. 135-8), the ten young women (25.1-13, see pp. 177-82), and the three slaves (25.14-30, see pp. 153-62), all of which immediately precede this parable, focus on *how* we wait, both by working as requested and by being prepared for the arrival. This parable continues the theme by reflecting retrospectively on how the nations responded to 'the least of these' members of God's family (25.40).

The separation of sheep and goats

One of the major points of discussion among scholars is why the sheep and the goats might be separated in the first place. One theory, which was very popular for a long time, is that goats were more vulnerable to the cold and would be separated from the sheep so that they could have greater protection. The problem is that there is no evidence at all to support this theory; nothing to suggest that this ever happened in practice. Another possibility, especially given the fact that the Greek word normally translated 'goat' (*eriphos*) actually means young male kid, is that the young male goats were being separated for slaughter. Or it could be that the ewes were being separated for milking. The reality is that there is no agreement at all on why the two might have been separated. It is unlikely that they would have been separated regularly and certainly not on a nightly basis. When they were separated (for whatever reason this was), it would probably have been unusual and occasional.

Some also like to say that sheep and goats look very similar and could therefore only be separated one from another by their own shepherd. The problem with this is that the majority of sheep in the Middle East are white and the majority of goats brown, so distinguishing them would actually be quite easy. The background of the parable, though, reflects the common practice of farming sheep and goats together in Palestine. Mixed herds were, and still are, a common sight.

It is also worth noting that there are absolutely no negative con-notations about goats in Old Testament tradition. The original audience would not have been expecting goats to be condemned because they were goats; those condemned could just as easily have been the sheep. The negative marker is found not in the goats but in their being sent to the right (positive) and left (negative). A much, much later rabbinic tradition, the *Midrash on Psalms* 90.12, placed Gehenna to the left of God's throne and the Garden of Eden to its right.

'All the nations' and 'the least of these my brothers and sisters'

There are two particular phrases in this parable that have caused the greatest controversy in interpretation: the first is 'all the nations' and the second is 'the least of these my brothers and sisters'. Their interpretation can change the meaning of the entire parable.

In the past 300 or so years this parable has been interpreted in very different ways. Although today most people would see this passage as referring to the judgement of all people, and the criteria for people being separated to the right and left as whether they have shown care towards the poor and needy, this has not always been true. For much of Christian history the parable was seen as referring exclusively to the judgement of Christians and the 'least of these' as needy Christians. As a result, it was used to motivate Christians to care for other Christians (but not non-Christians or Jews). In the eighteenth century a different interpretation began to be expressed, which saw in this parable a judgement of 'nations' around the world for their treatment of missionaries who came to bring the gospel to them. By the twentieth century this passage was being interpreted in so many ways that Sherman W. Gray, writing in 1989, counted 32 different understandings that people had of it (see Sherman W. Gray, *The Least of My Brothers, Matthew 25:31–46: A History of Interpretation* (Society of Biblical Literature Dissertation Series 114; Atlanta, GA: Scholars, 1989). This indicates that it is not going to be easy to find an interpretation that suits everyone, but there are a couple of issues to note that might bring us a little more clarity:

- 'All the nations': The word used for 'nations' here is the Greek word *ethnē*. It has a range of meanings, from simply a group of people living together, through 'a nation' or 'a people', all the way to foreign or barbarous people – those who are not 'us' (depending on the context, this was used by Israel to refer to Gentile nations or by Rome to mean the 'provinces'). When used elsewhere in Matthew *ethnē* means both Israel and the other nations. This nudges us towards thinking that Jesus is talking to 'all the peoples' – that is, everyone everywhere, no matter where they come from.
- 'The least of these my brothers and sisters': the Greek literally says here 'one of the least of these my brothers'. The language of 'brothers' and of 'little ones' (see above on 'little ones', p. 69) is widely used throughout Matthew to refer to his followers, especially his disciples. In addition, passages such as Matthew 10.40–42 talk explicitly of people receiving Jesus when they receive the disciples. This identification of the 'least of these my brothers' with the disciples also fits with Jesus' re-constitution of families in the kingdom when he said, 'Here are my mother and my brothers! For whoever does the will of my Father in heaven is my brother and sister and mother' (Matthew 12.49).

These two observations suggest that this parable in Matthew was originally about the judgement of all peoples – no matter where they came from – based on how well they treated Christ's disciples, who represented Christ to them. As such, this parable would have been an encouragement to Matthew's earliest readers that, even if people treated them roughly now, there would come a moment when those people would be judged for their actions.

Using the parable today

This throws up much food for thought. If the original context of this well-loved parable suggests that it was intended to focus attention on how people across the world react to Christians, it asks us to reflect on whether we are right to read it differently and as referring to motivation to care for the poor, the sick and those in prison more generally. If pressed, I would say that while the popular interpretation is not what the parable originally meant, it is still valid. The abiding popularity of seeing this parable as motivation to care for those in need points to the fact that it sums up, in a convenient and vivid form, much of Jesus' teaching about serving and caring for others, particularly the poor and outcast. Even if it didn't quite mean this in Matthew's original form here, Jesus certainly said it elsewhere and the parable so perfectly sums up his teaching that it is no wonder we bring it to mind so easily.

What is more, the parable of the lost sheep, which we explored above, also reveals that parables conveyed different meanings in different contexts. Jesus may have told them more than once with different emphases. The parable of the lost sheep certainly had a different resonance in Matthew's and Luke's Gospels. This is one of those occasions when a parable has more than one life – a life in its original context and a life beyond that context. Here the adage we laid down in the Introduction – that what is true of one parable is not true of all of them – becomes most helpful. Some parables clearly have one, and only one, meaning; some have multiple meanings even in the Gospels themselves, and others still speak so powerfully beyond their own context that they shift and change in meaning as we read them. This is what makes parables so challenging but also so transformative. We cannot be lazy when we are reading them. Each parable requires us to ask ourselves how we relate to it, and the answer to that question shifts and changes, depending on what we are reading.

To think about ...

If Jesus' original message in this parable, in the context in which we find it here in Matthew, was not that we should care for the poor, the outcast and the sick, how much do *you* think that matters? Can we still read it like this?

Reflection

It is interesting to note that there are fewer parables about shepherds and sheep than you might imagine from the importance of the idea in Christian thought. It is worth being aware, though, that it is an image woven through much of the Bible – often in contexts that wouldn't be identified as parables. From King David to the prophets, from Jesus to the epistles, the imagery of sheep and shepherds returns time and time again. It remains popular today – even though many people exist in contexts that have no sheep whatsoever – largely because it communicates care, nurture and nourishment.

However, it is important not to fall into the trap of over-romanticizing sheep and their shepherds. The parables we have explored in this chapter reveal the harsher side to this way of life, with thieves who seek to steal flocks; wild animals who prowl around waiting to devour the sheep; and even the danger of sheep wandering off and getting lost. Shepherds, young boys though they often were, were tasked with the perilous job of leading their flocks into dangerous, wild terrain in search of what little food they might be able to find. For most of the time the life was a far cry from any gentle, rural idyll that we might call to mind.

In a way it is this that makes this imagery so powerful. As we weave our way through the terrors and threats of life in search of the nourishment we need to survive, sometimes the journey can feel extremely precarious – dangerous even – but in the midst of this we are reminded that we are not alone on the journey. The one whom we follow loves us with a love beyond words and can be trusted to lead us where we need to go.

PART 2

Houses and Their Occupants

At the time of Jesus, houses could vary as much as they do today, if not a little more. They ranged from small, badly lit dwellings that had little daylight even in the middle of the day, to large luxurious villas staffed by many servants and slaves. The parables told by Jesus imagined houses at both ends of the spectrum. He told stories about those who had very little at all, like the woman who had to light a lamp to find a single lost but valued coin in the gloom, to a master who left the equivalent of 48,000 denarii with his slaves when he went away on a trip. Jesus' parables encompassed everyday scenarios from all sorts of different people, and they invite us in to empathize with them, from the poorest to the wealthiest, from the most honest to the most suspect.

As with many of the parables, some are easy to comprehend while others leave us scratching our heads in bemusement; but all of them introduce us to the richly varied experiences of life in the first century, reminding us that then, as now, it is almost impossible to say 'This is what living in the first century was like'. It differed from person to person depending on where they lived and how much money they had – and, most importantly, what kind of house they lived in.

5

Everyday Objects

Introduction

The everyday objects that Jesus talked about in his parables are genuinely eclectic. From garments to receptacles, from foodstuff to lights, it feels as though Jesus picked up whatever was at hand in order to make the points he wanted to make. What is particularly interesting in what follows is to notice that he did not always make the same point from the same object – in the case of salt and light, his point shifts in the different Gospels. This challenges us to reflect on whether he used his parables regularly in different ways; whether the points they were making were remembered differently by those who heard them; or indeed whether both of these is the case.

15 A new patch on an old coat; new wine in an old wineskin (Matthew 9.16–17; Mark 2.21–22; Luke 5.36–37)

These parables are closer to similes than most others. Not much work needs doing to understand their point here: caution should be applied before assuming that what is new and what is old will fit easily together.

Mark 2.21–22

[21]No one sews a patch of unprocessed cloth on to old clothing. If they do, the cloth that fills the hole pulls away from it – the new from the old – and the tear gets worse. [22]And no one pours new wine into old wineskins. If they do, the wine bursts the wineskins

and the wine is ruined, as well as the wineskins. Instead one puts new wine into brand-new wineskins.

Interesting words ...

- v. 21: the word for the 'patch' changes. The first time it is used the word (*rakos*) means a 'strip of cloth'; the second time the word is *plērōma*, which means 'that which fills' or the 'fullness'.
- v. 22: the word for 'new' (*neon*) in 'new wine' means young or fresh, whereas the word for new wineskins (*kainos*) has more of the emphasis of 'newly made'.

On patches and wineskins

The experience described here is not one particularly familiar in a modern, Western context. The sewing of patches on to clothing is increasingly rare and, even if you do this, you wouldn't give a second thought to sewing new material on to old. Even more rare would be storing wine in a wineskin: today it comes in a bottle and the only controversy is whether that bottle comes with a cork or a screw top. But the scenarios described here were, as with many of the parables in this chapter, a familiar part of everyday life.

The parable in context

In all three Gospels these two short parables come immediately after the question to Jesus about why John's disciples and the Pharisees fast but Jesus' disciples do not. This seems to further focus their meaning – Jesus' point is that there is nothing wrong with fasting. In the right context at the right time, fasting is valuable but you cannot simply assume that because it was right in one context it will automatically be right in another. Trying to force an old practice into a new context without thought and care will inevitably end in disaster.

The reference to 'unprocessed cloth' is a particular one here. The kind of cloth referred to is material that has not yet been treated by a 'fuller'. The process of fulling was important in the ancient world (and indeed for centuries after that). A fuller would take a piece of woven cloth and beat it, with a club or with the hands and feet, using something like stale urine, which both cleansed and whitened the material. The process would also 'felt' the cloth and make it more waterproof. A piece of unfulled cloth would therefore be a very different substance from fulled cloth and the two would not fit together at all; fulled cloth would be tightly woven and quite inflexible; unfulled cloth would be loose textured and more fragile.

In contrast, a wineskin was made from leather. At first the leather was soft and supple and able to stretch as the wine fermented inside it, but once it had already stretched it became brittle and liable to burst, thereby making it unsuitable for fresh wine.

It is worth noting here that in the case of cloth the new cloth is the less stable and more problematic; in the case of the wineskin it is the old leather that causes the problem. In other words, these two parables are the opposite of each other. The point seems not – as is sometimes asserted – that the new is better than the old, but simply that the old and the new don't fit easily together. Attempting to force them to do so will result in damage to the old and the loss of the new, and vice versa.

There is much wisdom in this and it applies in a wide range of different contexts. The challenge of fitting old and new together remains today.

To think about ...

If it is so hard to fit the old with the new, what should we do when faced with such situations in everyday life?

16 Salt (Matthew 5.13; Mark 9.49–50; Luke 14.34–35)

Matthew, Mark and Luke all contain Jesus' saying about salt, but in each it has a slightly different emphasis:

- In Mark the salt saying has two independent elements (though they are apparently connected), and the disciples are instructed to have salt in themselves – a quality that will bring peace.
- In Matthew the disciples are described as salt in a way that links this saying to the one that follows it in Matthew 5.14–15 about being light in the world.
- In Luke the focus appears to be more on staying the course – salt that runs out of saltiness is no good.

(*Note*: Only Matthew's Gospel calls the substance the salt of the earth; in the other two it is just salt.)

Matthew 5.13

¹³*You are the salt of the earth but if salt becomes insipid by what can it be re-salted? It is good for nothing except being thrown out and trampled underfoot.*

Mark 9.49–50

⁴⁹*For everyone will be salted with fire.* ⁵⁰*Salt is good but if salt becomes un-salty by what can you season it? Have salt among yourselves and be at peace with one another.*

Luke 14.34–35

³⁴*Therefore salt is good. But if salt has become insipid, by what can it be seasoned?* ³⁵*It is suitable neither for the earth or for the pile of manure. They throw it out. Let the person with ears to hear, hear.*

Interesting words ...

- In Mark the Greek word for what happens to the salt is *analon*, which literally means 'without salt'.

- In Matthew and Luke, however, the verb used is *mōrainō*, connected to the noun *mōros*, meaning 'stupid' or 'foolish' – the literal translation would be 'if salt has become stupid'. Attempts to explain this observe that in Semitic languages the same root means both 'stupid' and 'become insipid', so the use of the verb here may reflect an original Aramaic saying that has been badly translated into Greek.
- Mark and Luke use the same word for 'seasoned' (*artuō*); whereas Matthew uses *alizō*, meaning 'to serve something with salt'.

The parable in context

The differences between the uses of this saying in the Gospels are highlighted by the three contexts in which they are to be found. In Matthew the context – in the Sermon on the Mount – of this saying before the saying about lamps makes it clear that here it is focused on the effect of being a true disciple. In Mark it is in the context of a passage about sin and the importance of removing eyes or hands that offend. In a similar way, in Luke the passage is found in the context of a discussion about counting the cost of discipleship. As a result, in both Mark and Luke the focus is more on the importance of sustaining the impact of discipleship.

What is salt for?

You might think that this would be an easy question to answer but the opposite is true. This saying has caused all sorts of difficulty in interpretation and there is almost no agreement among commentators about what Jesus was talking about here. There are a cluster of issues, each of which adds complexity rather than illumination:

- Sodium chloride is a stable element and does not change. As a result, salt cannot become less salty. The only option for understanding how salt might become less salty might be to recognize that salt was often gathered from the Dead Sea in lumps that also included other minerals. If it were subject to a downpour, then the salt would dissolve and leave the other minerals behind – which themselves would not be salty.

- There has also been extensive discussion of Matthew's reference to 'salt of the earth' and Luke's reference to salt not being fit for the soil or the manure heap. Some commentators observe that this reflects the use of salt to fertilize soil, though there is disagreement about how possible this is. Others solve the problem by proposing that the salt referred to here was potassium nitrate – or saltpetre – which would be used as fertilizer but isn't really 'salt' as such. As a result, the salt referred to here would be salt that gave nutrients to the soil or manure heaps on which it was placed.
- A final point worth observing is that the apparently unconnected saying in Mark 9.49 about everyone being salted with fire might be connected to the command in Leviticus 2.13 that talks about adding salt to the fire of sacrifice – and therefore be referring to suffering by Christians.

All in all there is considerable confusion both in the original Gospels as well as among subsequent commentators about what this parable meant or means. Matthew and Luke have used an odd word ('to be made stupid') for 'without salt' – possibly caused by a confusion about the original meaning of an Aramaic word for 'insipid' – and commentators can't even agree what the salt was for: some think it was used primarily for flavour; others for preservation; others as a cleansing agent; others for fertilization; and others still a combination of some of these. As a result, it is almost impossible to work out what Jesus meant, how it was originally heard, or even how we are to understand it today (or indeed which section of this book it should be in). Any attempts to make sense of this parable involve ignoring the cautions issued by one scholar or another.

At peace with one another

It is Mark's version of this parable that most clearly hints that there is a meaning to 'salt' to which, today, we have no access. The language used in all three of the Gospels hints to us that salt had a range of meanings at the time that we struggle to comprehend today. Mark's Gospel, however, has a specific reference that is worthy of reflection

– people who have 'salt among themselves' will be 'at peace with one another' (Mark 9.50). This suggests that being salt in the world involves wisdom, thoughtfulness and reconciliation. We no longer have access to why it means this, but the Mark reference does point in this direction. If this can be read across all three Gospels, then being 'the salt of the earth' involves being a force for wisdom that brings about reconciliation.

The best we can achieve in interpreting this parable is to recognize that whatever we are called to be as disciples (adders of flavour, preservers of what is right, people able to cleanse impurity or fertilizers of the world around), we should ensure that we do not lose this quality over time. We should remain as 'salty' through our lives as we were at the start. Mark adds to this with the hint that people who are 'salty' have the wisdom to live at peace with others. It isn't much of an insight into this parable, but it is better than nothing.

To think about ...

Whatever 'salty' means, how do we, as Christians, ensure that we do not lose our 'saltiness' over time?

17 A lamp on a lampstand (Matthew 5.14–16; Mark 4.21–25; Luke 8.16–18)

As with the parable of salt, the focus of the parable of the lamp is different in Matthew's Gospel from the focus in Mark and Luke. In Matthew the lamp is 'you' (that is, the disciples), who are to shine before others so they may see your good works and give glory to the Father. In Mark and Luke the shining of the lamp is more connected to the understanding of the parables. It is also striking to read Matthew's version of this parable alongside John's 'I am the light of the world' (see below). In Matthew, the light of the world is the disciples; in John, it is Jesus.

Matthew 5.14–16

[14]*You are the light of the world. A city placed on the top of a hill cannot be hidden.* [15]*No one lights a lamp and puts it under a large measuring pot, but on a lampstand, and it shines on all in the house.* [16]*In this way let your light shine before people so that they may see your noble deeds and give glory to your father in heaven.*

Mark 4.21–25

[21]*He said to them: 'A light isn't brought in to be put under a large measuring pot or under a bed, is it? Isn't it put on a lampstand?* [22]*For there is nothing hidden that isn't revealed and nothing is kept secret that doesn't come into the light.* [23]*Let the person with ears to hear, hear.'* [24]*And he said to them: 'See what you hear. You will be measured in the measure you measure out, and it will be added to you.* [25]*For it will be given to the one who has and from the one who does not have, even what they have will be taken away.'*

(*Note*: Luke's version of this is very similar to Mark's so is not included here.)

Interesting words ...

The language used in all three of the Gospels refers to everyday items from around almost any house.

- A lamp (in Greek, *luchnos*) was a clay lamp filled with oil that would have been lit and hung on a lampstand (*luchnia*) to allow its flickering light to reach as far into dark corners as possible.
- Matthew 5.14 and Mark 4.21: a *modios* is a measure for dry material (like wheat) of around 2 gallons in capacity. It would have been a large basket and most houses would have had something like it. Jesus' question (unlike that asked about leaving ninety-nine sheep to look for one that had become lost (see above, pp. 65–71)) would have elicited widespread agreement. It would be insane to light a lamp and hide it under a basket. In contrast, Luke says that you wouldn't put a light under a *skeuos* or jar. The sense, however, remains the same.
- Mark 4.21: one of the features of Greek that we struggle to replicate in English is the ability to ask a question with an expected answer. A sentence that begins with *mē* expects the answer 'no' and those beginning with *ou* or *ouk* expect the answer 'yes'. The Markan

version of the lamp on a lampstand is a perfect example of a question expecting the answer 'no' (you don't put it under a measuring pot, do you?), followed immediately by a question expecting the answer 'yes' (but you *do* put it on a lampstand, don't you?).

- Mark 4.24: Mark's slightly clunky phrase seems deliberate – *blepō* ('see') what you *akouō* ('hear').
- Mark 4.25: this verse is found in Matthew and Luke at the end of the parable of the three/ten slaves.

The parable in context

As we noted above, Matthew's version of the lamp/light parable follows on directly from his use of the salt parable; in contrast, Mark's and Luke's are embedded in chapters with other parables. In both it follows the explanation of the parable of the sower. As such, whereas in Matthew one might legitimately question how firmly parabolic this narrative is, in Mark and Luke it is much more clearly a parable.

'You are the light of the world'

Being the 'light of the world', as in Matthew 5.14, was a phrase used in a wide range of Jewish sources and referred variously to God, Adam, various rabbis, Israel, the Torah, the temple and Jerusalem. Of all of these, and given in the second half of Matthew 5.14, the closest reference seems to be to Jerusalem as the light of the world/ city on a hill. Passages such as Isaiah 2.2–4, which talk about Jerusalem being raised high so that all the nations might stream to it, indicate that this kind of language suggests being a beacon placed high on a hill, which declares God to all those around so that they are drawn to it.

This certainly seems to be the point of Matthew's use of the phrase here. The disciples – just like Jerusalem – are to be a beacon that speaks of God to all those around, so that all who see it might acknowledge and praise the Father. What is important, especially at this point in Matthew's Gospel, right in the middle of the Sermon on the Mount, is that it is the works of the disciples that will shine such a light as attracts all those around.

In certain ways this is strongly reminiscent of 1 Peter 2.12, which encourages the readers of the epistle to live such good lives among the Gentiles that they will give glory to God on the day of visitation. It is this theme of living recognizably transformed lives that seems to capture the point being made here.

Nothing is secret that won't be brought to light

The use of this parable in Mark and Luke is very different indeed. Falling as it does in the chapters about parables, it points to the fact that although parables appear to obfuscate meaning and keep outsiders on the outside (see discussion above, p. 90, about the purpose of parables), they are in fact only temporarily confusing. A lamp will shine – though neither Gospel indicates when this will happen – in the dark and reveal what is currently unclear. In fact it appears to be the opposite message of that suggested earlier in both Mark 4.12 and Luke 8.9.

The hint given in these chapters is that it is not the lamp that helps us understand the parables but the parables themselves that are the lamp to be hung on a lampstand. The parables are what sheds light into dark corners. It is the parables themselves that help reveal what we don't currently understand. As a result, Jesus said, it was vital for disciples to pay close attention to how they listen to the parables. The closeness of their listening would affect how much they understood.

Although this seems paradoxical, there is something significant in it that warrants further reflection. The parables both make it hard for people to understand and, at the same time, shine a light into the dark corners to reveal what is otherwise hidden. They demand that we wrestle with them, that we pay close attention to what they are pointing to; and as they bemuse us, so at the same time they shed light into corners we didn't even know were there. This is the challenge of the parables but it is also their glory – what causes us to scratch our heads in bemusement can also shine a light of illumination into dark corners.

One parable – two meanings

The use of the same imagery for two almost entirely different emphases reminds us one more time that some of Jesus' parables are slippery and shift meaning depending on the context in which they are found. It suggests that he used the same imagery on more than one occasion to bring out different emphases and make different points, and that his stories were heard differently by different audiences and people. This is something, though, that shouldn't worry us too much: as we journey onwards with the parables, we will begin to recognize the different types of parable that we encounter – those that are fixed and those that change; those that have only one possible meaning and those that have more than one; those that are simple similes and those that require more reflection. Most of all, it reminds us that Jesus widened and broadened the use of the parables so extensively that it became impossible to say one thing about them that works for them all.

To think about ...

(From Matthew): what does letting our light shine mean for the decisions we make about how we live our lives?

(From Mark and Luke): in what way do the parables shine light in the darkness?

---

18 'I am the light of the world' (John 8.12)

John 8.12

¹²*Again Jesus spoke to them, saying: 'I am the light of the world. The person following me won't ever walk in darkness but will have the light of life.'*

Interesting words ...

- In the previous parable, Jesus spoke of a lamp (*luchnos*); here – and indeed in Matthew 5.14 above – he uses the word 'light' (*phōs*). While it can refer to the light that comes from a lamp or torch it is a much bigger word that takes in concepts (such as illumination) and general ideas (such as moonlight, starlight, windows and eyes) – anything that might be seen to illumine a person.

A lamp to my feet

Whereas the background to Matthew's use of the 'light of the world' appears to be drawn from Jerusalem, John's usage seems to draw more closely on language from Psalms about both God (see, for example, Psalm 27.1: 'The LORD is my light and my salvation; whom shall I fear?') and Torah (see, for example, Psalm 119.105: 'Your word is a lamp to my feet and a light to my path'). Indeed, the imagery of Psalm 119 is hinted at here. Those who 'follow' Jesus would be on a path following behind him; if he is the 'light of the world' he would therefore be the lamp to their feet and the light to their path.

In other words, the phrase 'light of the world' used in Matthew (above) and in John's Gospel (8.12) have slightly different meanings. In Matthew the light acts more as a beacon attracting people by its light so that, drawn towards it, they give glory to God; in John the light acts more for illumination – enlightenment – to live by. The difference is subtle but it is present. Some commentators note that Jesus was speaking, here, during the feast of the Tabernacles. The Mishnah states that on the first night of this great feast four large lamps were lit in the temple's court of the women that cast light across the whole city for the course of the festival. Here Jesus claims not just to enlighten Jerusalem but the whole world, shedding light on the path of all those who follow him.

To think about ...

Is the image of Jesus illuminating your life a helpful one for you? If yes, what does he illuminate for you? If no, why not?

19 Yeast (Matthew 13.33)

There are very few parables that feature a woman as their central character (the other four that do are the parables of the lost coin; of the ten young women; of the persistent widow; and of the woman in labour from John's Gospel). While one might wish that more parables had women at their centre, it is worth noticing that those that do feature them do so naturally. The women are not singled out for unusual comment: women baking bread or looking for a lost coin are as commonplace as a man planting a field of wheat.

Matthew 13.33

[33]*He told them another parable: 'The kingdom of the heavens is like yeast, which a woman takes and hides in three large measures of wheat flour until the whole is risen.'*

Interesting words ...

- v. 33: the word for 'large measure' is a *saton*. A *saton* is one and a half times the quantity of a *modios* (the measure referred to in the parable about the light of the world; see above, p. 88). So three *sata* are about 38 litres' worth of flour.

It is probably also worth noting that yeast was not regarded as positive in the Bible. The house was scoured at Passover to remove any traces of leavened bread – that is, bread with yeast in it – left within it. Even more than this, Jesus warned the disciples against the yeast of the Pharisees and Sadducees (Matthew 16.5–12) and of the Pharisees and Herod (Mark 8.14–21). Jesus' usage in both passages suggests that yeast was regarded as negatively contagious – it quickly and easily spread to raise dough.

This is worth bearing in mind as we reflect on Jesus' teaching about the kingdom. It is easy to domesticate this, making the images he uses to describe the kingdom nice and homely. The use of yeast here should cause us to question this. Jesus seems to be saying that the kingdom has the same qualities as the contagion of yeast – it can grow as quickly and spread as widely.

The parable in context

It is interesting to notice that the parable of the yeast is found among those about the growing of wheat. This may well reflect an ancient view of yeast, making it much more like a seed than the unicellular fungus it is known to be today. Thus hiding yeast in flour would have been closer to sowing seed than anything else.

The impact of this becomes even stronger when you consider the quantities of flour involved here. As noted above, Jesus said that the woman hid yeast in some 38 litres of flour. This is no single loaf of bread – it would make bread for around 100 people and feed the whole village. The contagion of the kingdom is extravagant and far reaching. It might look as though it is being hidden but, once hidden, quietly and secretly it spreads to the whole.

In an odd way, then, this is a profoundly encouraging parable in a world in which it feels as though our best efforts are defeated time and time again; where the struggle to bring kingdom values and principles to what we do can feel at worst dispiritingly impossible and at best pure hard work. It is comforting to know that despite appearances the kingdom grows and grows like yeast in a dough, often unseen but always increasing. Not only that but, like a woman baking enough bread for a whole village, the kingdom might start tiny but you can be sure it won't stay that way.

To think about ...

Can you think of an occasion on which you have observed the kingdom spreading as quickly as yeast does?

---

20 What contaminates you (Matthew 15.10–20; Mark 7.14–23)

This is a passage that challenges our preconceived ideas about what a parable is. You would be forgiven for wondering why it has been included at all. Neither its subject matter nor its style bears much resemblance to the other parables in the Gospels. It is not particularly suggestive; it contains almost no imagery; and probably most importantly, its meaning is relatively clear. The reason why it is included in this book is because in verse 17 it is called a parable by the disciples; if this were not the case, it might not have made the cut.

The reason why it is termed a parable is probably because, although what Jesus says seems pretty direct, it leaves a few details undefined. Jesus could have been clearer and stated that what he meant by 'goes into a person' was food (which would then have meant that Mark did not need to point this out in verse 19).

Mark 7.14–23

¹⁴*And summoning the crowd once more, Jesus said to them: 'Listen all of you and take notice.* ¹⁵*There is nothing outside of a person that, going in, can contaminate them but the things that come out of a person are what contaminates them.'*

¹⁷*And when he entered the house, away from the crowd, his disciples asked him about the parable.* ¹⁸*And he said to them: 'Are you so very foolish? Surely you know that nothing from outside that goes into a person can contaminate them?* ¹⁹*Because it does not go into the heart but into the stomach and goes out into the toilet (declaring all foods clean).'* ²⁰*And he said, 'That which comes out from a person is what contaminates them.* ²¹*For evil conspiracies are inside, they come out from the heart of a person – sexual immorality, theft, murder,* ²²*adultery, greed, wickedness, trickery, living with no boundaries, lack of generosity, abusive speech, pride, thoughtlessness.* ²³*All these come out from inside a person and contaminate them.'*

(*Note:* Although verse 16 of this passage was present in manuscripts used in earlier translations, it is missing from those used by scholars today.)

Interesting words ...

- The Greek word for 'contaminate' (sometimes translated 'defile' or 'make impure') is *koinoō*, which can also mean 'make common'. 'Contaminate' doesn't quite work as a translation but it has a more modern resonance than 'defile'.
- vv. 21–22: in Mark, though not in Matthew, the first six vices (from sexual immorality to wickedness) are in the plural form and the second six (from trickery to thoughtlessness) in the singular. It isn't quite clear why this is. One theory is that the first six are specific acts, which are therefore repeatable, whereas the second six are part of a person's character.
- v. 22: many of the words in the list of vices are common and found in numerous of the other 'vice lists' in the New Testament. One that is unusual is translated above as 'lack of generosity' – literally 'evil eye' (*ophthalmos ponēros*) – which is an idiomatic expression for envy or lack of generosity. A more common word (*aselgeia*) is often translated as 'licentiousness' but refers to acting beyond society's boundaries generally, sexually as well as otherwise.

The traditions of the elders

The point of the parable is simple and refers us backwards in Mark to the beginning of chapter 7. That chapter consists of a conversation first between Jesus and the Pharisees, which later includes the crowd as well. The issue was Jesus' observation of some of the 'traditions of the elders'. This phrase probably refers to the Pharisaic belief that there were two bodies of law – the written law and the oral law. Both were believed to be traced back to Moses – one in writing (the Torah) and one through oral tradition. The traditions of the elders were thought to have been passed down from rabbi to rabbi and were eventually written down themselves, well after the time of Jesus (around AD 200), in the volume now called the Mishnah. The Pharisees' challenge to Jesus in this chapter, therefore, was to ask why he didn't observe oral law – a law that set out a range of requirements that supplemented the basic laws in the Torah and covered a lot of day-to-day issues such as food, cleansing and so on.

If you only encounter the Pharisees in the Gospels it is easy to get the wrong impression of them. They seem grumpy, argumentative, sometimes even unreasonable. The important feature to bear in mind, however, is that the Pharisaic movement was a popular and dynamic one in the first century. Worship in the temple was, for many people, a long way off and quite remote. Although most did go to the temple three times a year, the rest of the time there was little they could do to express their love of God. The Pharisees brought devotion into everyday life and, through the regulations they observed, sought to encourage people to worship God with the whole of their being in every part of their life.

The reason they came into conflict with Jesus so often was that they and Jesus each had their own vision for following God in everyday life – the problem was that these diverged significantly. The Pharisees' vision focused on laying down boundaries, maintaining purity and following laws; Jesus' vision was one of inclusion, love and generosity. They clashed because they gave wildly divergent answers to the same questions, not because the Pharisees were inherently bad.

In this instance the question was about purity regulations and food. The Pharisees were shocked that Jesus was not practising the rules that ensured proper purity – what you ate, how and with whom, was vital for the Pharisees. Jesus' point was simple: what makes you impure is not what you eat but what is going on in your heart. The Pharisees, Jesus said, had lost sight of what was really 'good' and 'bad' – what makes a difference is what you think, how you act, what decisions you make. As such, this parable is remarkably close to the parable of the tree with good and bad fruit (see discussion above, pp. 24–7).

It's tempting to dismiss the Pharisees as a nit-picking, holier than thou, duplicitous group of religious zealots loitering around in wheat fields waiting to catch out unsuspecting passers-by as they broke tiny details of the law. But to do so would be wrong. Their vision for life arose out of their genuine love of God and a desire to help those around them worship God with their whole heart, soul and strength. The problem came when their vision clashed with the vision that Jesus brought. The question that emerges for each one of us is: if Jesus turned up tomorrow, how likely is it that we might find ourselves reacting as the Pharisees did? Jesus' point here rings as powerfully true today as it did then: we so easily get caught up with external fripperies – like what we wear, what we sing, how we do things – but what really matters is what goes on inside us.

Perhaps that is why we focus so much on external, unimportant matters, because looking long and hard at what is really going on deep within us is often too uncomfortable to contemplate.

To think about ...

What external, less important matters do you find yourself focusing on? Are there any that you have a sneaking suspicion Jesus might view in the same way he viewed the Pharisaic food laws?

---

21 'I am the bread of life' (John 6.35, 48–51)

This is the first of Jesus' 'I am' sayings in John's Gospel. The sayings are an intriguing mix of material that, as in this one, sits very close to words used in other parables (such as 'I am the light of the world', 'the gate', 'the good shepherd' and the 'true vine') and material that appears to be much more abstract ('I am the resurrection and the life and the way, the truth and the life').

John 6.35

[35]*Jesus said to them, 'I am the bread of life. The person coming to me won't ever be hungry, the person believing in me will never be thirsty again.'*

John 6.48–51

[48]*'I am the bread of life.* [49]*Your ancestors ate manna in the desert and died.* [50]*This is the bread coming down from heaven so that anyone who eats it might not die.* [51]*I am the living bread that comes down from heaven; anyone who eats from this bread will live into the age [to come], and the bread which I will give for the life of the world is my flesh.'*

Interesting words ...

- vv. 35 and 48: the word for 'bread' here is *artos*. When used on its own it probably referred to finest-quality wheat-bread; in John 6.9 (the feeding of the five thousand that precedes this statement) the small boy had five barley loaves (*artos krithinos*) and two fish. Barley bread was basic bread made with low-quality grain – tough and hard to digest. The contrast between the two is key. The crowd pursued Jesus in the hope of more barley bread – he declared himself to be the finest-quality bread of life.
- v. 48: the Hebrew word *manna* means simply 'what now?' and was what God's people said when they saw the 'manna' on the ground.
- v. 51: 'the age' – when John talks about eternal life he often calls it just 'living into the age'; it is slightly different from the idea of living for ever but this is often the easiest way to translate it. What it means is living into the time of the new heaven and the new earth when the dead will be raised.

Better than wisdom or manna

Some wonder whether the background to this particular saying is Ben Sirach (also known as Ecclesiasticus) 24.21, in which wisdom declares: 'Those who eat of me will hunger for more, and those who drink of me will thirst for more.' One might want to argue that hungering and thirsting for more and more wisdom is a very different thing from being satisfied in Jesus, so that the two are not really contrasting. But there is something quite reminiscent of St Augustine in this contrast: 'You have made us for yourself, O Lord, and our heart is restless until it finds its rest in you' (*Confessions*). A restless hungering and thirsting for wisdom might be good for us, but even better is finding our satisfaction and ultimate nourishment in Jesus.

The other Old Testament image that stands behind this saying is, of course, manna. The point of the manna was that it came each day for that day's need. It was not to be kept and would be renewed each day, with the exception of the Sabbath when two days' worth could be gathered. Unlike manna, the nourishment that Jesus offered lasted, and lasted. It does not go off. It does not disappear. It does not need replenishing day by day. Jesus provides long-term, fulsome nourishment, a nourishment that will carry us beyond this age and into the age to come.

To think about ...

If someone were to ask you to explain what Jesus' being the 'bread of life' means to you, how would you do it?

---

22 The lost coin (Luke 15.8–10)

This parable appears in a group of three: the one preceding it is the parable of the lost sheep and the one following it is the parable of the lost son(s), otherwise known as the prodigal son. It fits well with these others, forming an extended reflection on being lost and found again.

Luke 15.8–10

[8]*Or which woman having ten drachma, if she happens to lose one drachma, would not light a lamp and sweep the house and seek carefully until she finds it?* [9]*And once she finds it calls her friends and neighbours saying, rejoice with me because I have found the drachma that I lost.* [10]*In the same way I say to you there is joy before the angels of God when one sinner repents.*

Interesting words ...

- Although the question mark feels easier to insert after the end of verse 8 as above, some commentators think it should really be put at the end of verse 9, making the whole two verses a rhetorical question.
- v. 8: a drachma was a Greek silver coin worth the equivalent of the Roman denarius (the pay for about a day's labour for a man – a woman would have received less).
- v. 9: the friends and neighbours summoned by the woman to the celebration were all female – we know this because the ending is feminine plural. If there had been any men among them, the ending would have been masculine plural.

How valuable was a drachma?

One of the questions about the background of this parable is the significance, or otherwise, of the drachma. The sheep in the preceding parable is an everyday example, so this story could be similar. Luke may have used the word 'drachma' (rather than 'denarius') so that his largely Greek-speaking audience would understand the – small – value of the coin involved. An alternative is that the ten coins were special and were an unusual collection of Greek coinage not used every day, which therefore led to the loss of one of them being more significant. It is impossible to discern from the current form of the parable whether this was an everyday coin or a special one.

It was, for a while, fashionable to imagine that the coins were from a bridal headdress from which hung ten coins. This would therefore lend the coin sentimental as well as economic value. Scholars are now agreed that this is highly unlikely. There is no evidence, in this period, of women wearing such headdresses at all. This tradition comes from a later custom and would not have taken place during the time of Jesus. This does not mean, however, that the coin was unimportant. The key point seems to be that while we might not consider a drachma of great value, it was very important to her and therefore worth searching for. It might be that the choice of an everyday coin is exactly the point – it doesn't look much to us but to her it was of great value. Likewise, those who don't appear to us to be of great value are to God of supreme importance. Value is relative – just because something or someone looks unimportant does not mean that they are.

Is the woman God?

One of the questions that emerges from reading this parable is: who are we to understand the woman to be? Many people see the shepherd of the parable of the lost sheep as God (see pp. 65–71 above) and also the father of the prodigal son as God (see pp. 118–26 below). If this is the case then it also makes sense to see the woman as God.

Much as I would like to cast this woman as God, my own view is that none of them 'are' God. They illustrate a scenario featuring what would have been an everyday human situation at the time of Jesus – the loss of an animal, the loss of an object and the fracture of family relationships. The parables ask us to reflect, if in this everyday scenario this is what happens, how much more is it the case when God seeks us? For more on this, see the discussion of the prodigal son below (pp. 118–26).

On celebration and searching

There are two strands that come out of this parable. The first, just as in the parable of the lost sheep, is the importance of celebration (in this case an all-female celebration). The focus, again, is on the value of that which was lost and the joy caused by its being found. Again this reminds us that Jesus' eating with tax collectors and sinners was, in his view, the equivalent of a grand party – a celebration reflecting the joy in heaven experienced by the finding of those who had been lost.

The second strand focuses on the care the woman takes in searching for the lost coin. It is worth noting that Galilean houses in this period were built with very little natural light (some were even carved into caves in the side of mountains) to help regulate heat. Lighting a lamp would have allowed the woman to see into corners of the house that would normally remain in darkness even in the middle of the day. What communicates the value of the coin to us is the care the woman took in searching for it. As with the lost sheep, the overwhelming message of the parable is of the value to Jesus of the tax collectors and sinners and the extent of the celebration he had when they were 'found'.

To think about ...

Think about something that you have searched frantically for and the joy you felt when you found it. Imagine what our churches would be like if that joy was expressed more often.

Reflection

The everyday objects chosen by Jesus in this chapter were about as ordinary as they could be, ranging from clothes with holes in them to bread; from lights and food measures to small cheap coins. It is tempting when we think about God and God's kingdom to choose more significant items – fine churches or cathedrals or elaborate artwork or icons – but Jesus used whatever lay easily to hand. Nothing was too ordinary or cheap. One of the themes that comes through so strongly from his parables is his treasuring of the ordinary and everyday.

One of the key features of Jesus' teaching is that things did not need to be treated differently for them to be holy; they did not need to be elaborate or expensive for them to convey the kingdom; they did not need to be kept in a special place for them to communicate the things of God. In exactly the same way, people were equally valued no matter how society viewed or treated them. Right at the heart of Jesus' message was the belief that everyone – no matter who they were, where they had come from or what they had done – was valued simply because they were valuable. Nothing and no one was ever too ordinary for God.

6

Buildings and Their Owners

Introduction

One of the fascinating features that emerges from gathering parables of a similar theme together is noticing which themes are found in which Gospel. It is interesting to note that none of the parables in this chapter are from Mark, which has none about buildings and their owners. Mark's emphasis is more fully on agriculture and what grows than on buildings and what happens in them.

23 Two builders (Matthew 7.24–27; Luke 6.46–49)

Although this parable is most commonly known as the wise and foolish builders, this value judgement is only made in Matthew. In Luke neither word is used; readers are left to draw conclusions for themselves about the relative wisdom or stupidity of the action.

Matthew 7.24–27

[24]*Everyone who hears my words and does them will be like a wise man who built his house on the rock.* [25]*The rain fell, the river rose, and the wind blew and beat on that house, but it did not fall because its foundations were on rock.* [26]*Everyone who hears my words and does not do them will be like a stupid man who builds his house on sandy ground.* [27]*The rain fell, the river rose, and the wind blew and struck against the house – and it fell. The calamity was colossal.*

Luke 6.46–49

[46]*Why do you call me Lord, Lord, and not do what I say?* [47]*Everyone who comes to me and hears my words and does them, I will show you what this person is like.* [48]*This person is like someone building a house, who digs and goes down deep and places a foundation on rock. When a flood came, the river burst against that house but it was not able to shake it because it was built so well.* [49]*The one who hears and does not act is like a person building a house on the earth without a foundation. When the river burst against it, it collapsed right away and the ruin of that house was colossal.*

Interesting words ...

In Matthew 7:

- v. 24: the comparison verb *homoioō*, 'to be like' or 'to compare', occurs here in the future passive so needs a translation more like 'will be like' or 'will be compared to'. In Luke the comparison is more straightforward: 'is like'.
- v. 24: the word 'man' (*anēr*) is used here and not, as in most parables, *anthrōpos* ('person').
- vv. 24 and 26: the word for wise is *phronimos*, not the more usual *sophia*. In this instance the emphasis is more on being prudent or practically astute (a modern word for this might be 'canny') than on thinking wise thoughts; the word for 'stupid' is *mōros* and has the sense of dull or sluggish. There are no comparable words for 'wise' and 'stupid' in Luke's Gospel.
- vv. 25–26: the verb used to describe the wind beating against the house changes – the first time it is *prospiptō* and the second time *proskoptō*. It is not entirely clear why the word changes as the meaning is quite close. In Luke the storm described is less dynamic – it is just a flood that comes, no rain or wind as well.

In Matthew and Luke:

- 7.27 and 6.49: the same word (*mega*) is used at the end of each parable for the size of the disaster. It can mean 'great', 'vast', 'enormous' or, as I've used it 'colossal'.

The passage in context

Luke's version of this parable combines Jesus' condemnation of those who say 'Lord, Lord' but don't do the will of their Father in heaven with the parable itself, whereas in Matthew's Gospel this passage – although the parable still follows the saying (Matthew 7.21–23) – stands as an apparently separate unit. Those who say 'Lord, Lord' in Matthew are sent away without acknowledgement, whereas in Luke they are likened to someone who does not build foundations for their house. The end result may be similar but the context is different. In Matthew such a person is turned away on the day of judgement; in Luke the house (which we assume is their life) falls apart.

It is also worth noting that in both Gospels this parable concludes the Sermon on the Mount (Matthew)/Sermon on the Plain (Luke) – as a result, it has considerable impact since it is referring to how Jesus' teaching on the Mount and Plain respectively is to be received – that is, not just listened to but acted on as well.

Some striking differences

One of the most noticeable elements of this parable is that the best-known version of it comes from Matthew, not from Luke. In Matthew the two kinds of person are described as 'canny' or 'wise' and 'dull' or 'stupid'; in Luke they have no adjectival description at all. In Matthew the wisdom or stupidity of the people involved lies in the choosing of a good location (rock not sandy ground); in Luke the key is not the location but the preparation for building, involving the proper building of foundations and digging down to find solid rock. A final difference is that, in Matthew, the storm that strikes the house comes from all directions – rain, flood and wind; whereas in Luke the storm is just a river that burst its banks. All these differences are minor but they affect the parable as a whole.

> ### Understanding Judean terrain
>
> Matthew's version of the parable fits well with Judean terrain: the issue with land in this largely desert territory is that, in the hot summer months, sandy ground bakes hard and looks very similar to rock. Only a canny person knows - and remembers - what was actually rock and what was baked earth. The crucial difference of course is that, when storms come, sandy ground is easily washed away whereas rock is not.

Acting on Jesus' words

Despite all the differences, the fundamental point of the parable remains the same in both Gospels – and it is a very interesting point. The reason why we should act on Jesus' words, and not just listen to them, is because doing so will provide the strength and stability to weather life's storms (or floods). Jesus' teachings are not just important because they come from him and should shape the lives of all those who follow him, they are important because living by them will improve our quality of life; they will provide us with foundations in the storms of life. Living by Jesus' words is not just something we *should* do; they make our lives better too.

> ### To think about ...
>
> Do you agree that living by Jesus' teachings changes the quality and security of your life?

24 A house swept clean (Matthew 12.43–45; Luke 11.24–26)

This is a passage that occupies the grey edges in the definition of parables. While some think it is a parable, due to the application at the end to 'this evil generation' (making it a little like the 'children in the marketplace'); others think it is not and that it is instead a more general statement about evil spirits. This variety of opinion is even reflected in the Gospels themselves, since Matthew has the applicatory sentence but Luke does not. This suggests that Matthew might see it as a parable but Luke views it as literal advice against an evil spirit returning. In my opinion, the additional factor that pushes this closer to being a parable is the hypothetical phrasing ('Whenever the unclean spirit ...'); this is found in a good number of parables and suggests this passage might be seen as one too.

Matthew 12.43–45

[43] *Whenever the unclean spirit has gone out from a person, it wanders to and fro through waterless places seeking rest, and it does not find it.* [44] *Then it says, 'I will return to my house, the one I came from.' And when it comes, it finds it unoccupied, swept and made neat.* [45] *Then it travels and brings along with it seven other spirits more evil than itself and, entering, it lives there and the last state of that person is worse than the first. So it is with this evil generation.*

Interesting words ...

- v. 43: the word for 'rest' (*anapausis*) can refer both to any rest or to the repose of death. It is possible the repose of death is meant here – the spirit has no rest and doesn't know what else to do.

A parable or not?

This parable – if it is one – is important for our ongoing reflections on the parables and how we relate to them. It is easy to assume that Jesus functioned with a kind of style-book for parables so that it was obvious to all those listening which of his teachings were parables and which were not. We have already observed parables that were understood differently in different Gospels – possibly because they were told more than once in different contexts. This passage introduces a further complexity – a teaching of Jesus that seems to have been understood literally by Luke but as a parable by Matthew.

A clean, empty house

If, in Matthew, this is to be understood as a parable, the question is what sense we might make of it. The challenge we face is that this parable is spoken into a context, very different from our own, in which belief in demons and exorcism was vibrant and active. At the time of Jesus there were a large number of exorcists who travelled the country, casting out evil spirits from people. As a result, while for us this is an odd parable, at the time of Jesus this would have been as everyday a scenario as sowing wheat or herding sheep. It is quite possible, likely even, that an apparent healing would have been followed by an apparent return of the demon, so this whole setting would have been all too familiar to Jesus' audience.

Wandering to and fro in waterless places

The poetic turn of phrase suggested by 'waterless places' might indicate that Sheol is being suggested here. Sheol – in Greek, Hades – was the place of the shades, where all the dead went, in some models of resurrection, to await resurrection at the end of time. If understood like this, the story tells of a demon that cannot find its ultimate resting place and, unsettled, returns to the human realm to make its home there.

Jesus' message here seems to be that the generation of people who are currently following him have cast off the old – the old way of being, the old enslavement to external practices and so on – but all they have done is emptied the house and made it a clean and attractive dwelling. It is only by accepting Jesus' teaching and living it out that this evil generation will be able permanently to cast off the old and live without fear of a future that is worse than the past.

This is certainly one of those occasions when the 'everyday' scenario that Jesus is painting is so alien to people today that it is hard for us to begin to comprehend what he was talking about. In order to translate this parable into a modern context we would need to adopt an entirely different framework, one that made sense to us today. One option would be something that spoke of bad habits that can only be replaced by adopting the new and better habits that Jesus speaks of. Simply stopping old 'bad' habits risks having them return sevenfold. It is only when we inhabit wholeheartedly the kingdom vision that Jesus offers that we can be confident the old won't creep back in.

To think about ...

What 'bad habits' do you find hard to cast off that threaten to return at any moment just as bad as before – if not worse.

---

25 Treasures new and old (Matthew 13.51–53)

This is another passage that may or may not be a parable. The question is whether 'these parables' of verse 53 includes verse 52 as well as the rest of the parables in chapter 13. It is likely that this passage *is* intended to be included under the title 'parables' because it contains a 'likening' of something (here a scribe who has become a disciple) to something else (an owner of a house).

Matthew 13.51–53

[51]*'Have you understood all these things?' They said to him 'Yes'.*
[52]*But he said to them, 'Because of this, every scribe who has become a disciple in the kingdom of the heavens is like someone who is like an owner of a house who throws out from the treasure store both new things and old things.'* [53]*When Jesus had finished these parables he went away from there.*

Interesting words ...

- v. 52: the NRSV translated the word *mathēteuō* as 'who has been trained for ...'. This is an accurate translation but loses an element of emphasis. The verb *mathēteuō* – connected to the noun *mathētēs*, 'disciple' – has the resonance of being a disciple that is lost with the word 'train'. It also implies that the training is complete whereas 'has become a disciple' does not.
- v. 52: the choice of words for what the scribe does with the treasure

in the treasure store is an odd one. It is normally translated 'brings out', but the word is *ekballō*, which literally means 'throw out'. If the word really is being used here in the sense of 'throw out', it raises the question of what they will do with the treasure when they throw it out. Is it for display, as we commonly assume, or for disposal?

It is possible that, as Jesus suggests to the rich young ruler, the scribe who has become a disciple is getting rid of all their treasure no matter how new or old. Given the use of the same verb in Matthew 12.35, however, it is likely that 'bring out' is what is meant here, though the other translation is worth dwelling on – even if only for a short time.

- v. 52: the word translated 'treasure store' refers to a place in which treasure of any kind can be stored. Depending on the wealth of the person involved, it could mean a strong room or a strong box, a grain store or a casket.

Scribes

One of the interesting features of this brief passage is that those who have become disciples in the kingdom of the heavens are called 'scribes', not disciples. Although they often appear with different groups in the Gospels (such as Pharisees, Sadducees and chief priests), 'scribes' was probably a generic term for those who were able to read (and write) but in this context those who could also read and understand the Scriptures. Scribes were, in short, people who had been educated. It is fascinating to see Jesus, here, describing those who had become disciples in the kingdom of the heavens as 'scribes' – that is, those trusted by others to interpret the Scriptures.

Given the fact that this question is asked in the context of whether the disciples have understood what Jesus has said, it seems likely that he is referring to a future scenario in which they, and other disciples of the kingdom of the heavens, will be approached for help in the interpretation of Scripture. When they do, Jesus says, they will bring out what is new (Jesus' teaching) and what is old (the Scriptures) – the parables, complex though they may be, are to be used as a treasure store to help in interpreting the world around us.

To think about ...

If someone were to come to you for help in interpreting Scripture, which 'new' and 'old' treasure would you bring out to help them?

---

26 A narrow gate/door (Matthew 7.13–14; Luke 13.22–30)

This is another occasion when a short story in one Gospel (this time Matthew) is told more as a parable in another (this time Luke). Again we see the grey area between what is 'just' an image and what is a parable. Here the difference is not so much in the comparison made as in the narrative world evoked. Whereas in Matthew's Gospel there is a simple image about entering through the narrow gate rather than the wide one, in Luke's account we have characters as well as a conversation that leads to a conclusion. This more extensive narrative world suggests that Luke's account falls into the category of parable, even if hesitantly. Luke's parable lies halfway between the passage quoted from Matthew and the parable of the ten young women (see below, pp. 177–82). It combines the complexity of entering through the narrow door/gate with the urgency of being ready to do so at the right time.

Matthew 7.13–14

¹³*Enter through the narrow gate, because the gate is wide and the road spacious that leads to destruction, and many enter through it.* ¹⁴*But the gate is narrow and the road constricted that leads to life, and there are few who find it.*

Luke 13.22–30

²²*And he travelled through towns and villages, teaching as he made his way to Jerusalem.* ²³*Someone said to him 'Lord, is it a few people who will be saved?' He said to them,* ²⁴*'Struggle to enter through the narrow door because many will seek to enter and they*

won't be strong enough. [25]*Once the houseowner has got up and shut the door, and you begin to stand outside and to knock at the door saying, "Lord, open the door", he will answer and say to you "I do not know where you are from".* [26]*Then you will begin to say "We ate and drank in your presence, and you taught in our wide streets".* [27]*And he will say to you, "I don't know where you are from, go away from me, all you doers of injustice."* [28]*There will be weeping and gnashing of teeth when you see Abraham and Isaac and Jacob and all the prophets in the kingdom of God but you yourselves thrown outside.* [29]*They will come from east and west and from north and south and they will recline at table in the kingdom of God.* [30]*And look, those who are last will be first and those who are first, last.'*

Interesting words ...

- In Matthew, the portal that is narrow is a gate (*pulē*, verse 13) whereas in Luke it is a door (*thura*, verse 24) with a houseowner who owns it.
- Luke v. 24: the words translated 'be strong enough' is the verb *ischuō*, which can mean be able but has the quality of strength or power. It is 'able to' in the sense of being strong enough to do it.
- v. 26: it is interesting that what is said to the houseowner is not that we ate and drank 'with you' but 'in your presence'. The implication is one of greater distance. They ate in his house but, if it were a banquet, this might imply that they were not personally known to the houseowner.
- v. 26: the plea of those outside is that the houseowner taught in their wide streets; the same word is used in Matthew for the wide gate. This is no irrelevant detail. Most ancient cities had very narrow streets, which only widened out near the market (or the city gate) where business was conducted and teaching delivered.
- v. 27: although often translated as 'evildoers' the word used is 'doers of *adikia*' – that is, 'unrighteousness' or 'injustice'.
- v. 28: given the point about *ekballō* made in the previous parable, it is worth noting that it is used again here, and clearly means 'thrown out'.
- v. 29: the verb used for reclining at table is *anaklinō*, which means 'to lean' or 'lie down'; it is the word used for the posture adopted when eating in the ancient world.

Who is the parable about?

While there are some parables in which it is difficult to identify who the main characters should be understood to be, this is one of those that makes it very clear who the houseowner is. The key moment is when those outside the door say 'you taught in our wide streets'. Apart from that phrase this could have been an anonymous parable about a hypothetical houseowner and guests who sought entrance to a feast. This phrase, however, makes it clear that the houseowner is to be understood as Jesus, and the connection with him claimed is that he taught in their vicinity.

I don't know where you are from

The response that denies knowing the origins of a person reveals a cultural understanding about 'knowing' in the Middle East. Knowing where a person is from – including who their family are and how that family relates to your own – is a key element in 'knowing' someone. Jesus states on more than one occasion that following him involves new familial relationships in which those who follow him are his mother and brother and sisters. This may be implied here – those who have entered by the admittedly narrow and difficult door would now be in the newly constituted family of the kingdom, and therefore well known by Jesus.

What is interesting about the conversation between Jesus and those left outside is that, contrary to what the scribes and Pharisees clearly thought, when they say the sinners and tax collectors were eating with Jesus, simply eating in Jesus' presence does not signal a connection with Jesus. More action is required than this. Actually following Jesus, something that he acknowledges is difficult to do, can't be put off. Once it is too late it will really be too late and nothing will change the 'houseowner's' mind.

> ### To think about ...
>
> What is our equivalent of 'but we ate in your presence and you taught in our streets'? If Jesus were refusing entrance to people today, what might they say in their defence?

27 Houseowners and burglars (Matthew 24.43–44; Luke 12.39–40)

This parable is, to some extent, reminiscent of the passing comment by Jesus (so 'passing' that it doesn't quite qualify as a parable) that it is only possible to enter a strong person's house and plunder their property if first you tie them up (Matthew 12.29). Here a second possibility is offered for a thief entering: if the houseowner is asleep and not watching out. The two different contexts reveal the two different themes explored here. In Matthew 12.29 the discussion is about whether Jesus casts out demons by the power of Beelzebub, whereas here the theme is much more about watching, waiting and being alert, and so a different scenario is proposed.

Matthew 24.43–44

[43]*But know this, if the houseowner knew in what watch of the night the thief was coming, he would be watchful and not allow his house to be broken into.* [44]*Therefore be ready because the Son of Man is coming at an hour you don't imagine.*

Interesting words ...

- v. 43: 'watch of the night' refers to the practice of splitting the night into three-hour blocks so that someone could always be watching and guarding property.
- v. 43: the word for 'broken into' is *diorussō*, which means to 'dig through'.

Houses and their structure

The language used in this parable imagines houses very different from the ones we live in today. The verb used, normally translated as 'broken into', actually means to 'dig through'. At that time this would have made perfect sense: houses were made largely from mud bricks, so with the right effort it would be entirely possible to dig through a wall in order to break into a house as a way of avoiding the more closely watched door.

The passage in context

The theme of this parable is very similar to a range of others throughout the Gospels - that of being ready and not leaving it too late. In Matthew's Gospel this parable begins a string all on the same theme: the slave left in charge who doesn't know when his master will return (24.45–51); the bridesmaids who don't know when the bridegroom will come (25.1–13); and the 'so-called' parable of the talents (25.14–30). This parable begins the theme in its most general terms - that of readiness - and it is deepened and widened in the three that follow.

Keeping watch

The only real similarity between this parable and Matthew 12.29 is that they are both about breaking into a house. The point of them is very different. Matthew 12.29 is about controlling an otherwise dangerous houseowner; this one is about ensuring you don't make yourself easy prey by sleeping when the burglars arrive. Matthew 12.29 is about whether Jesus casts out demons by the power of Beelzebul; Matthew 24.43–44 is about how to wait well. This short parable fits very well into the parables that follow it, which all focus on how to live while waiting – the answer is by being alert, being prepared and living as required.

To think about ...

How do you think the attitude of watchfulness that Jesus commends here might translate into how we live our lives day by day?

Reflection

It is interesting to observe that there are far more parables about household relationships (see the two chapters that follow) than there are about the houses themselves. Indeed, there are no parables at all about houses in Mark's Gospel. If the parables were set in the twenty-first century (and in the West), there might be many more about houses and rooms in houses, boundaries between houses and gardens, not to mention all the stuff we keep in our houses. Today we seem to care very much more about houses, rooms and boundaries than the people of Jesus' day.

This reveals a society that, as a rule, owned so little by way of material goods that their fear of losing it was lower than ours. This, of course, is not entirely true. The sadness of the rich young ruler at the thought of giving away all he had reveals that there were people who feared the loss of what they owned, but it does not seem to be as lively or as widespread a concern as it would be today. This is one of Jesus' key messages – you are ruled by what you value: 'where your treasure is, there your heart will be also' (Matthew 6.21 and Luke 12.34). It was a hard-hitting message in Jesus' day, but I suspect it would be even harder hitting if he were teaching it today.

7

Families

Introduction

One of the great values of exploring the parables thematically is that it allows us to notice what is not there as well as what is. Among the more surprising gaps in the parables is the number about families (two) compared to the number about slaves and servants (eight). We often miss this simple fact because one of those two parables about families is that commonly called the parable of the prodigal son, and it is so abidingly popular – and read so often – that it feels as though there are more parables about families than there actually are.

It is interesting to ask the question of why there are so few. One unsettling explanation – though there are others – might be that much of Jesus' teaching was about the dismantling of the family unit (for example, 'For whoever does the will of my Father in heaven is my brother and sister and mother', Matthew 12.50) and its re-formation in the kingdom of God. It is possible that Jesus' attempt to reshape our understanding of family led him to avoid many parables about family units themselves.

28 The lost son(s) (Luke 15.11–32)

One of the key questions for interpreting this parable is what it is really about, which is most easily focused around the question of what we should call it. The traditional English name for it is, of course, the parable of the prodigal son, and that title focuses our attention on what the son has done wrong, since the word 'prodigal' means to spend money or resources recklessly. This seems to be an odd emphasis to make, though of course this did happen.

The text makes clear that the son wasted his money, but surely it is not the point of the story. The point is not what went wrong but the restoration and celebration that followed. The parable might be better called 'A father's love' or 'On celebrating a longed-for return'. In this book I have opted for 'The lost son(s)' to draw attention to its context in Luke 15, which also contains the lost sheep and the lost coin, though this admittedly omits the parable's own emphasis on celebration. 'Celebration at the return of a lost son' is a little cumbersome as a title. The reason I have put (s) in the title is because the parable ends with the suggestion that while one son was now back at home, the other – the elder son – was alienated; where one son was found, the other was lost.

Luke 15.11–32

[11]And he said: 'A certain person had two sons [12]and the younger one said to the father, "Father, give to me the share of the property that falls to me" and so he distributed to them his livelihood. [13]After a few days the younger son gathered everything he had and journeyed to a distant country, and there he squandered his wealth, living wastefully. [14]When he had spent everything, a mighty famine took place in that country and he faced collapse. [15]And travelling, he hired himself to one of the citizens of that country, who sent him to his fields to tend pigs. [16]And he longed to fill his stomach with the carob pods but no one gave him anything. [17]And he came to himself and said: "How many of my father's day labourers have more than enough bread? But I am perishing from hunger. [18]I will get up, go to my father and say to him: 'Father, I have sinned against heaven and before you, [19]I am no longer worthy to be called your son, treat me like one of your day labourers.'" [20]And getting up he came to his own father. But when he was still a long way distant, his father saw him and was moved with compassion, he ran and fell on his neck and kissed him. [21]The son said to him: "Father, I have sinned against heaven and before you, I am no longer worthy to be called your son." [22]The father said to his slaves: "Quickly, bring out a long robe – the best one – and dress him, and then put a ring on his finger and sandals on his feet, [23]and bring the fattened calf, kill it and we will feast and party. [24]For this son of mine was dead and is alive again, he was lost and is found." And they began to party.

²⁵*The elder son was in the field, and as he came near to the house, he heard singing and dancing.* ²⁶*And calling one of the young servants, he asked what might be happening.* ²⁷*He said to him, "Your brother has come, and your father has killed the fatted calf, because he has got back in one piece."* ²⁸*He became angry and did not want to go in, but his father came out and pleaded with him.* ²⁹*But he answered his father: "Look. For so many years I have slaved for you and I have never ignored your commands; and you have never given to me even a young goat so that I might party with my friends.* ³⁰*But when this son of yours, who has consumed your livelihood with prostitutes came, you killed the fatted calf for him."* ³¹*He said to him, "Child, you are always with me and everything of mine is yours.* ³²*But we had to party and rejoice, because this brother of yours was dead and lives; and was lost and is found."'*

Interesting words ...

- v. 12: both words for wealth or property have a depth to them that is hard to capture in English. The word used when the younger son asked for his share is *ousia*, which is connected to the verb 'to be' and means 'substance' and hence 'your property'. The second word is *bios* or 'life', so it is that which is your livelihood. The change in words communicates the cost to the father of the son's request – he asked for what he saw and wanted, the property; for the father it was his livelihood.
- v. 14: the usual translations of the word for what happened to the son in the famine don't quite capture how desperate he was. The verb *ustereō* literally means to 'come after' or 'later', but therefore more metaphorically means to fall behind and hence to be wanting or failing. The implication is that he comes close to death.
- v. 16: the word *keration* means 'little horn' and is used in the plural to refer to carob pods. The fruit of the tree was considered fit only for animals in this period and would have been eaten by none but the most desperate of humans.
- v. 17: the word for 'day labourers' indicates those at the lowest level of society who were hired day by day (see above, the parable of the workers in the vineyard, pp. 45–50).
- v. 20: the word for 'moved with compassion' (*sphlanizomai*) refers to a movement in the bowels, hence a deep feeling of empathy for another.
- v. 23: the word to describe the celebration that is called for (*euphainō*) is different from the one in the parables of the lost sheep and lost coin,

which both use *sunchairō* instead, or 'rejoice with'. *Euphainō* has more of a sense of 'make merry'.

- v. 27: the word used by the young servant for the state of the son who has returned is *hugiainō* – 'sound' or 'healthy'; a modern idiom for this might be 'in one piece' or, as the NRSV has it, 'safe and sound'.
- v. 31: when the father speaks to the elder son here he calls him 'child' (*technon*). This does just mean 'child', but when used of a grown son would have been a term of affection.

Interpreting the parable

This is probably one of the best loved of all the parables. It is also one of those that is fixed in people's minds as having a 'proper' interpretation that cannot be challenged. In a similar way to the parable of the sheep and the goats, this parable is seen to encapsulate something essential about Jesus' teaching. In this instance, God is the father and we are the younger son, who sins and goes away from the father's love; but God waits for us, looking out for our return, and welcomes us back with love and open arms when we do return. In more recent years, Henri Nouwen's beautiful book *The Return of the Prodigal Son* (London: Darton, Longman & Todd, 1994), which reflects on Rembrandt's famous painting of the prodigal son, has laid an extra layer of evocative commentary on top of this already well-loved interpretation. There are, however, a few issues we need to explore before returning to the question of the best way to interpret this parable.

The passage in context

As noted above (pp. 65–71 and pp. 100–6), this parable forms a triplet in Jesus' teaching on being lost and found. In the context of chapter 15 of Luke, the focus of the parable is more on the importance of celebration when what has been lost is found than on the process of either losing or finding. The celebration in this parable goes up a notch from that described in the others. In the lost sheep and the lost coin, friends and neighbours are invited to rejoice with the shepherd and woman respectively; here, the father throws a party that is so loud the elder brother hears it while returning from the fields. In case we are minded to forget the importance of the celebration to the narrative, the description of the party is so extravagant that it shouldn't escape our attention (though, fascinatingly, in many commentaries it does).

An unwise father

One of the disputes about interpreting this parable centres around the question of whether the father is God. The fundamental issue with declaring this is that the parable reveals not only tensions in the family's relationships but some ill-advised actions by the father. The first concerns the inheritance. In Jewish law, the first son was entitled to a double share of the property. So the younger son could reasonably expect one-third of his father's estate upon his death. To ask for his inheritance early would be considered unkind today, but at the time of Jesus it was *appalling* since it implies that the person asking wishes the father to be already dead. In an honour/shame culture in which shame is to be avoided at all costs, it is scandalous to encounter a son who implies that he wishes his father dead. One might think that such a scenario is so dreadful that it was unthinkable, but this does not seem to be the case, since Sirach (33.20–22) counsels against giving in to such a request:

To son or wife, to brother or friend,
do not give power over yourself, as long as you live;
and do not give your property to another,
in case you change your mind and must ask for it.
While you are still alive and have breath in you,
do not let anyone take your place.
For it is better that your children should ask from you
than that you should look to the hand of your children.

This suggests that such requests happened from time to time, to an extent that they needed to be advised against. Sirach's advice is supported in rabbinic literature, which regards those who transfer their property to their children during their lifetime as pitiable and not deserving of any help when they beg for it. The reason given for this attitude is that if you give an inheritance to children early, they may squander it and cause subsequent ill-will within the family. The parable of the lost son(s) almost feels like a story written to illustrate this advice – with the younger son squandering all the money and shattering the relationship not just between the two brothers but between the father and elder son too. Those who see the father as God argue that the father acted out of love for the younger son; those who don't see the father as God question whether the father's action was in fact loving – suggesting that it might be better seen as indulgent.

Another problem raised by the story is that in Jewish inheritance law, property cannot be split partially (in this case, the younger son would have been given his share but the elder son not). Indeed, in Luke 15.31 the father makes clear that the elder son now owns the rest of the inheritance. As a result, the father has thrown the welcome-home party with the elder son's property *and* did not even invite him to it (the elder son apparently didn't know what was going on and had to ask a servant). Such actions seem ill-judged and thoughtless, and not the kind of behaviour one would want to associate with God.

This raises the – I recognize unpopular – possibility that the father is not actually God but that a comparison has been set up that we have observed elsewhere. If this flawed, unwise father, who nevertheless loves his son immensely, behaved like this, how much more would God react with love to those of us who are lost and then return home again? While this is my view about what is going on in this parable, it won't be shared by everyone. The question of whether the father 'is' God or not is one that you will need to reflect and arrive at a view on for yourself. Commentators remain split on the subject.

On why the younger son was hungry

One of the interesting features of this well-loved parable is how easy it is to load our own perspectives on to the narrative. Mark Allan Powell, in his book *What Do They Hear?* (Nashville, TN: Abingdon Press, 2007), observed that people from different cultures and backgrounds 'heard' different things in the story. He read the parable with people from the USA, from Russia and from Tanzania.

When the American group heard the story, they associated the younger son's hunger with it being his own fault – he'd squandered the money and got what he deserved. When the Russian group heard the same story, they associated the son's hunger with the famine in the land – he fell victim to outside unforeseen circumstances. When the group from Tanzania heard the story, they attributed his hunger to the fact that no one in the new land helped him (see Luke 15.16).

What is fascinating about this is that all three are in the text – the squandering, the famine and the lack of help can all be seen clearly in the story, but people in one culture focused more on one strand than another. This reminds us of the importance not only of reading what is actually there as far as we can with fresh eyes but also of reading with people from different cultures and backgrounds, who will see and hear in the text elements that will often pass us by.

He came to himself

One of my own favourite moments in the story is when the prodigal son 'is found'. Luke's language here states that 'he came to himself and said'. This, to my mind, presents an important strand in a reflection on losing and finding. There are times in life when we are lost and we really need someone (as happened with the shepherd and the woman) to seek and seek and find us, but there are other times when it is us and us alone who can help ourselves. The son had gone off by himself and needed to come back by himself. He had to get to that moment of realization that his woes were all his own doing, but that he could undo them himself too.

On honour and shame ... and running

The society of the era underpinning this parable was so profoundly shaped by the honour/shame culture that we can make no sense of it without recognizing this. The prevailing culture was driven by a strong sense of the importance of honour. All actions and interactions were shaped by the question of whether they brought honour or not. This strand makes more sense of the outrage felt by the scribes and Pharisees at Jesus eating with tax collectors and sinners. This was an action that could only bring shame on him, and in such a culture would have been incomprehensible. The way this story is shaped reveals that the parable of the lost son adds an additional strand to the themes of celebration, and of lost and found, that have been established so far in the chapter. Throughout this story, honour and shame are challenged and subverted. Honour is willingly given up and shame transformed into honour through the power of love and forgiveness.

One of the key features of honour in a culture such as this is that it should be shown upwards – to those older or more powerful than you. The story begins, therefore, with an episode of chilling shame. The younger son shames not only his elder brother but also his father by requesting that the inheritance be shared early. We have already observed that this request is tantamount to stating that he wished his father to be dead, but in addition the request makes clear that the younger son has no intention of honouring or caring for his father in old age as the law commanded.

The shame of the younger son only increases as the parable unfolds: he has no money; he is forced to look after pigs; he has nothing to eat; and, in the end, decided that to return home in shame was better than the situation in which he found himself. Kenneth Bailey, in his book the *Cross and the Prodigal* (London: IVP, 2005), argues that a son who had acted as the younger son had done would have been rejected by the village. They would, he proposes, have performed a ceremony called *kezazah*, breaking a large pot in front of him and announcing that he was cut off from his people. At this point his shame would have been complete. Bailey suggests that the reason the father ran to greet his son was to get to him before the rest of the community did, ensuring that he was not shamed by the village. While not everyone agrees with Bailey's reconstruction here, his suggestion casts interesting light on to the precarious nature of the son's return. Whether the father ran for this reason or simply because he was so pleased to see his son, the point is well made that the father sacrificed his own honour for the sake of his son. He ran – something an elder would never have done – to greet his son. His son's shame was transformed into honour by the father's willingness to sacrifice his own honour for him. Where there are those who will sacrifice their own honour for the sake of others, there can be no shame.

The elder son

The parable ends on an uncomfortable note. We will never know whether the elder son was ever reconciled with either his father or his younger brother. It is striking given the themes of honour and shame that have flowed through this parable that the elder son addresses his father rudely. He gives him no honorific title, and criticizes both him and his younger brother.

Prostitutes

It is interesting to note the accusation by the older brother that his younger brother (whom he can only bring himself to call 'this son of yours') spent his money on prostitutes. His is the only suggestion in the text that this happened and, according to the logic of the story, he has not yet encountered his younger brother so can only have been making wild assertions. He was shaming his younger brother with the worst construction of his actions, while knowing nothing about what he had actually done.

This stands in great contrast with the father, who was willing to bring shame upon himself in order to protect the younger son from it.

The parable leaves us with the suspicion that the elder son will not forgive either his brother or his father and so will end up as a 'lost son' himself from now on, his lostness defined by his refusal to celebrate his brother's return. The parable of the lost son(s) leaves us, then, with the suggestion that there is a fourth reason why people and things 'get lost': some wander off; some are mislaid; some run away; and others are so lost in their fury that they are unable to receive and respond to the offer of love that stands before them, begging them to come in.

To think about ...

How does shame work in our culture? If we were to sacrifice our honour to protect another from shame, what might that look like for us?

---

29 The two sons (Matthew 21.28–32)

This parable is commonly called the parable of the two sons but organizing parables thematically, as in this book, reveals that this is potentially confusing as there is another, far more famous, parable about two sons. Nevertheless, it is probably the easiest name for it.

Matthew 21.28–32

[28]*'What do you think? A certain person had two sons. He went to the first and said, "Child, go and work in the vineyard today."* [29]*He answered and said: "I don't want to." But later he changed his mind and went.* [30]*Going to the second one he said the same thing. And he answered, "I'm going, Lord" but he did not go.* [31]*Who out of the two did the will of the father?' They said, 'The first.' Jesus said to them, 'I say to you – and this is true – that tax collectors and prostitutes will go into the kingdom of God before you.* [32]*For John came to you in the way of righteousness and you did not believe him. But the tax collectors and prostitutes did believe him, but you saw and did not change your minds later and believe in him.'*

Interesting words ...

- v. 28: the father called his son 'child' (*technon*), the same affectionate title as used by the father for the elder son in the parable of the lost son(s) above.
- v. 32: the word 'prostitutes' (*pornē*) – also used by the elder son in the parable of the lost son(s) – is the word connected to that used for fornication (that is, any sexual act that takes place outside marriage). The word was often used of female slaves so does not automatically imply that they were paid. It is interesting to note here that tax collectors are normally cited alongside sinners – in this instance (and nowhere else) the sinners are identified with a particular kind of sin.

Honour and shame again

The parable provides a nuanced reflection on honour and shame, which, given its importance in the parable of the lost son(s), becomes even more interesting since Matthew doesn't have that parable and Luke doesn't have this one. The first son gives the father no honoured titles nor indeed any assurance that what he asked would be done. In other words, he showed no honour to the father by his words, but then did honour him by doing what he said. The second son addressed his father with honour ('Lord') and agreed to do what he was asked, but then did not honour his father with his actions. The underlying point of the parable, then, is that just showing honour but not living out that honour ultimately shames the recipient.

This parable, therefore, picks up themes that we have seen so far in parables like the parable of the two builders: it is what you do, not just what you say, that makes a difference.

Displacement parables

(For a longer note on displacement and supersessionism, see above, p. 44). This parable about the two sons is one of three 'displacement' parables in Matthew's Gospel (this one, the tenants in the vineyard, and the wedding banquet). Each one explores the theme in a slightly different way: in this parable tax collectors and prostitutes will enter the kingdom ahead of those with whom Jesus was speaking; in the tenants in the vineyard, the vineyard would be taken away from the tenants; and in the wedding banquet, others were invited instead of the guests who declined. The themes loop around one another but present in a slightly different way in each one. Despite the differences, however, the common theme is response – how the characters in each parable respectively respond to the father, the landowner, and the king.

Tax collectors and prostitutes

At first, the sudden mention of the tax collectors and prostitutes in this parable is surprising, and seems to take it in a different direction. On further reflection, though, it begins to look quite similar to the parable of the lost son(s). There, the scribes and Pharisees disputed Jesus' eating with tax collectors and sinners; here, Jesus states that they will enter the kingdom before the chief priests and elders.

There, Jesus showed why he would eat with them – because he was celebrating their inclusion in the kingdom; here, he was explaining why they would enter the kingdom ahead of the chief priests and elders – because they had heard and responded to Jesus, not used honorific words and done nothing. This parable, like so many others, is about hearing, responding and acting. It is not enough to say the right thing; we need to do the right thing too.

To think about ...

We would be fooling ourselves if we claimed we were better at responding and acting on Jesus' words than his original audience. Is there anything that, at the moment, makes you more like the second son than the first in your journey of faith?

Reflections

Many parables can be translated easily into modern life but none more so than the parable of the two sons. As the mother of teenagers, this parable becomes, in my mind, the parable of the wet towels. I say to one, 'Please will you pick up your wet towels after use?' The first one grumbles and groans but does eventually do so; the other one says, 'Yes, Mum, I will' – and leaves them festering on the floor! It is one parable I relate to in my everyday life more immediately than almost any other.

At the heart of the family parables is the theme of response. In the parable of the lost son(s), the 'bad' younger son returns to the embrace of his father, while the 'good' elder son, lost in a cloud of righteous anger, can do nothing other than pour out his rage and disappointment before a father who yearns to welcome him home. In the parable of the two sons, the first son is obnoxious but does respond, and the second son is agreeable but does nothing. Both parables challenge us to re-evaluate what we consider to be 'good' and 'bad' and then to reflect on ourselves in the light of this – how often are we a troubling combination of the elder son from the parable of the lost son(s) and the second son from the parable of the two sons?

8

Slaves and Their Masters

Introduction

The parables that feature masters and their slaves/servants provide some of the trickier material to be found in Jesus' teaching. This is partly because slavery, and what it meant in the Roman world, is now so alien to us that it is hard to imagine ourselves in that context in any meaningful way. It is also because these parables themselves are often confusing and disturbing. It is easy to shy away from them and to attempt to domesticate them so they trouble us less. This does not seem to me to be the right way forward; we should allow ourselves to be properly disturbed by them and then to ask where they have taken us and what that means. If on the first, second or third time of this we remain as bemused as ever, we should persevere and, perhaps, one day they will begin to make more sense.

30 Watchful slaves (1) (Mark 13.32–37)

Although Matthew and Luke both have passages that are very like this one, with its mention of keeping watch and not knowing the hour, Mark's is the only Gospel that includes this mini parable involving slaves whose master has gone away in quite this form. The parable begins with the word 'as' which, although it is simpler than the usual 'to be like', has the same effect. The focus of the parable is the doorkeeper. The sentence narrows our attention down to this role. A person goes on a trip. They leave the house in the care of slaves to whom authority and different jobs are given; the doorkeeper is assigned the task of vigilance. The tasks of the other slaves are not important here. The only one we need to care about is the doorkeeper: we are to be like the doorkeeper whose job it is to stay awake, to make sure the house is safe – and to welcome the traveller on their return.

Mark 13.32–37

[32]*But about that day or that hour no one knows except for the father – neither the angels in heaven nor the son.* [33]*See that you are vigilant because you don't know when the moment is.* [34]*Just as a person, on a trip away from home, leaves his house and gives authority to the slaves, and work to each one, and commands the doorkeeper to be watchful.* [35]*Therefore be watchful, for you don't know when the lord of the house will come: in the evening, or at midnight, or at cockcrow or at dawn,* [36]*in case he comes suddenly and finds you sleeping.* [37]*What I am saying to you I say to everyone, be watchful.*

Interesting words ...

- There are two distinct words in Greek used for slaves and servants. *Doulos*, which normally means 'slave', refers to someone who was the property of someone else; *diakonos* refers to a servant who would be paid for their work. There is a discussion among scholars about whether *doulos* can, on occasion, mean 'servant'. While this is possible, most of the time it does refer to those owned by someone else and, as a result, although in some English translations *doulos* is translated as 'servant', in this book a distinction is made so it is easier to see which word is which. (For more on this, see the box below.)
- vv. 34 and 37: the word for 'watchful' is *grēgoreō*, which means 'to be awake' or become 'fully awake' – and therefore able to be watchful.

On waiting

One of the challenges we face, 2,000 years on from Jesus, is laid out precisely in this parable. The implication of the way this parable is told is that the 'master' would be returning very soon. What do we do, all these years later, when we are still waiting?

On slaves and servants

Although this parable is brief in the extreme, it provides a useful vignette of an aspect of the life of a slave. It is easy to assume that there was a hierarchy of welfare when it comes to servants and slaves, with servants clearly above slaves in status and well-being. This was not necessarily the case and depended, on a case-by-case basis, on their master or mistress, their role, and their relationships within the household. The key difference between slaves and servants was that slaves were owned by someone else, whereas servants were free.

However, the Roman slavery system was very different from the transatlantic slave trade that was such a blight on the world in the sixteenth to nineteenth centuries. When countries were conquered by the Romans they would make a large number of the population into slaves, but many could expect to be freed again after working as a slave for a period of time. While there is no doubt that some owners were brutal and ruthless, there were many who were not. Indeed, because a slave was the property of their owner, it was worth the owner's while to feed them well and look after them. As a result, the slave of a kind master or mistress could be far better off than a poor servant who struggled to find work and to make ends meet.

Also, as here, slaves were often left in positions of responsibility, taking care of the property of their owner in their absence. As noted above, the number of parables in this chapter that concern slaves left in charge of their master's property are so many that it indicates that this was a very common scenario with familiar and recognizable associated problems.

One answer given by scholars such as N. T. Wright to the question of what Jesus was talking about here is that 'the end' was not the end of time but the fall of Jerusalem, which took place in AD 70. On this interpretation, Jesus saw the inevitability of the cataclysmic clash between the Jews and the Roman Empire, which reached its climax in AD 70 and resulted in the destruction of the temple and much of Jerusalem. Others are sure that this was not what was being referred to by Jesus, but that the traditional view of the return of the Son of Man (commonly known as the *Parousia*) was what Jesus had in mind. A third option, which is one I favour, is that Jesus' teaching does not refer to one episode at all. Instead, it refers to more than one event – the fall of Jerusalem, the final return and multiple other moments as well, each of which could be seen as one when the master came back, leading up to 'the moment' of the end of all things.

The attitude needed for each of these potential moments is the attitude we need for them all, and it is vigilance and vigilance only that allows us to be ready for them when they come.

To think about ...

Given the length of the wait, what does it mean for us to 'keep watch'?

---

31 Watchful slaves (2) (Luke 12.35–38)

This parable feels a bit like a combination of the Markan parables about a doorkeeper being given responsibility to watch for the absent houseowner to return (see above), and a slave who should be caring for the master's household while he was away (see below). Yet again it suggests that very similar parables existed in slightly different forms – and that these different forms might even be traced back to Jesus himself.

Luke 12.35–38

[35]*Have your loins girded and your lamps lit;* [36]*be like people waiting for their lord to return from the wedding feast, so that when he comes and knocks they open to him right away.* [37]*Blessed are those slaves whom the master finds watching when he comes. I say to you – and this is true – he will gird himself, get them to sit down, and will come and serve them.* [38]*And if he comes in the second or third watch and finds them like this, those ones will be blessed.*

Interesting words …

- vv. 35 and 37: the girding of loins was a command specifically to men – who would wear their tunics flowing and loose inside the house. But these long flowing garments were cumbersome and needed tying up to do anything, so they would tie them up (between the legs) with a belt to make it easier to walk or, indeed, do household tasks. The command to gird your loins, then, was a command to be ready to act at any moment. The mention of lighting lamps suggests that the girding of the loins is not in preparation for going out, but for doing household chores in the middle of the night.
- v. 36: the word for 'like' here is *homoios*, the same word that is often used to open parables but used here to describe what we should be like.
- For more on wedding feasts, see the parable of the ten young women below, pp. 177–82.

Where the kingdom pops up in a parable

Another interesting feature of this parable is that, like a number of others, it slips in and out of character as it is recounted. By this I mean that many parables are small narrative worlds complete in themselves, but occasionally the interpretation inserts itself into the story and changes it. The narrative world of a household of slaves whose job it was to wait up for their master until he returned late at night from a wedding feast would have been familiar in the time of Jesus. Such a scenario would have been normal and expected. What would not have been expected, however, is the suggestion that the master, on finding the slaves doing what he wanted them to be doing, would suggest that they all sit down to dinner while he waited on them. This would have been not just unexpected but almost impossible to conceive.

What Jesus has done here is take an everyday scenario and give it a kingdom twist, in which slaves are given a place at the table and waited on by their master. The kingdom has broken into the narrative world and taken up residence there, disrupting the usual patterns of behaviour in the process.

To think about ...

What difference does the kingdom breaking into this parable and subverting societal norms make? If the kingdom broke into our world, what societal norms might it disrupt?

32 Reliable and wicked slaves (Matthew 24.45–51; Luke 12.42–48)

This parable joins a few others that are overtly hypothetical. While all parables are hypothetical to some extent, there are a few that obviously suggest that these are made-up scenarios. In this parable, that becomes particularly clear in verse 48, when the grammar becomes conditional and postulates what a wicked slave might say to himself. Whereas we begin the parable imagining an actual slave, halfway through we realize that the whole situation is imagined. Given this, the gruesome ending to the parable is even more surprising and shocking: that in this hypothetical situation the hypothetical wicked slave would receive a very gory hypothetical fate.

Matthew 24.45–51

⁴⁵*Then who is the reliable and sensible slave whom the master has appointed over his household to give provisions at the right moment?* ⁴⁶*Blessed is that slave who, when the lord comes, is found doing this.* ⁴⁷*I say to you – and this is true – he will appoint him over everything that he owns.* ⁴⁸*But if that wicked slave were to say in his heart, 'My lord is taking his time'* ⁴⁹*and begins to beat the other slaves and eats and drinks with people who are drunk,* ⁵⁰*the lord of that slave will come on a day he doesn't expect and in an hour he does not know.* ⁵¹*And he will cut him into pieces and put him with the hypocrites. There, there will be weeping and gnashing of teeth.*

Interesting words ...

- v. 45: the two words that I have translated 'reliable' and 'sensible' are the Greek words *pistos* ('faithful' or 'trustworthy') and *phronimos* (wise in a practical or prudent way, as opposed to *sophos*, which means generally 'wise').
- v. 45: the word translated 'household' is *oiketeia*. *Oikos* means house, so *oiketeia* refers to whatever property is in the house, including slaves.
- v. 48: the usual translation of this verse is 'says to himself', whereas the Greek says, 'says in his heart'. This reflects the Hebrew mindset in which decisions take place in the heart.
- v. 48: 'taking his time' translates *chronizō*, which means to prolong, be delayed and so on.

The reliable and sensible slave versus the wicked one

The key role of steward of the household was well known in this period. The steward was responsible for the day-to-day running of the household, for the care of the slaves and servants who worked within it and for taking care of the master's possessions. This slave does not, at the beginning of this parable, appear to be in such a position. One might almost guess that his appointment was what we would today say was for a probationary period. But having demonstrated that he was worthy of such trust, he was then appointed to be permanently in charge of everything. The interesting feature of this scenario is the care expected from the slave. This is quite different from the job of the doorkeeper, whose role was to sit and look out for the returning master; here the slave was meant to work very hard caring for the other slaves – so much so, in fact, that he might not initially notice his master's return.

The passage in context

Both this parable and the previous one are found in what are commonly known by scholars as eschatological discourses (that is, discussions about the end times). Although this parable is set up differently from the one in Mark, the focus of them both is very similar. Slaves, left to take care of their master's belongings, are meant to live in full and active expectation of their master's return.

In Matthew this parable sits in a run of three parables that are all in various ways about watching and waiting. This is the first one, followed by the parables of the ten young women and of the three/ten slaves (normally known as the parable of the talents). Each combines the twofold theme of being alert and doing what you should do while you wait. None of these parables is about passive waiting – quite the opposite: the third slave, in fact, is reprimanded precisely for being passive and not taking care of the money he was given. This theme of active waiting, then, runs through this section on Matthew.

In Luke, this parable comes straight after the watchful slaves parables and continues that theme in a slightly different form.

The hypothetical wicked slave, however, did not notice his master's return for another reason: he was too busy partying. The point here is not so much about seeing the master coming in the distance as about doing what you should be doing so that, when the master returns, he will be pleased with what you have done.

A brutal end

As we noted above, the wicked slave's punishment was brutal in the extreme, transgressing normal Roman custom. Although a slave was the absolute property of their master and therefore could be killed at any moment if the master so wished, it would be rare and certainly not widely talked about. As a result, it is clear that this conclusion to the parable is meant to be shocking and unsettling, as it points to the rage felt by the master at the slave's irresponsibility. Yet again it raises the question of who we identify the characters in the parable to be. In the previous parable, Luke 12.35–38, Jesus and the kingdom inserted themselves so clearly that it seems fair to say the master was Jesus; here it is more difficult. The extremity of the rage is scandalous and hard to associate with Jesus himself.

An additional odd feature of this ending is the statement that the wicked slave would be put with the hypocrites (for more on hypocrites, see below, p. 216). According to our definitions the slave had not been particularly hypocritical, and this draws our attention to the fact that in Jesus' teaching (see also the repeated use of the word in Matthew 23), a hypocrite was someone who said one thing and did another. The implication is that he had accepted charge of the household from the master and then did not live up to his word.

The question that emerges from this parable is what the household is over which we have been given charge. Is it the people in the Church? In the world? The planet? The implication of the parable is that those of us who follow Jesus will, like the master's slave, be commissioned to a task of caring for the household in the absence of the master, and that we will be held to account for the job we have done.

To think about ...

What do you think we should understand 'the household' to be? How pleased will the householder be with us regarding how well we looked after it?

---

33 On doing what you should (Luke 17.7–10)

This passage stands in startling contrast to Luke 12.35–38 (see pp. 133–4 above), where the master did precisely what Jesus said no one would do here. As pointed out above, that was clearly a moment when the kingdom broke into what always happens, changing its ways and showing a different way of being. This parable is about the world as it is.

Luke 17.7–10

⁷*And who among you, with a slave who has been ploughing or looking after sheep, when he comes back from the field says to him, 'Come here right away and sit down at the table'?* ⁸*Wouldn't you rather say, 'Prepare what I will eat and gird your loins to serve me while I eat and drink?' And after this you can eat and drink'?* ⁹*Do you thank the slave for doing what was ordered?* ¹⁰*In the same way*

you, when you do everything ordered, say, 'We are just slaves, we have done what we should do.'

Interesting words ...

- v. 10: the word I have translated 'just' is an interesting one. It is *achreios*, which can have a negative meaning ('worthless', 'useless') but can also have a neutral meaning ('in a manner in keeping with one's character or station'). While it is normally translated in a negative sense, I would suggest it should be taken neutrally here – they just did what they should as slaves.

On the treatment of slaves

One of the features that comes through in this section about slaves and their masters is that there are a range of scenarios being set out and the audience is meant to understand what each one is without explanation. The previous parables in this chapter have all presupposed a context in which there are multiple slaves, each with different roles. Here there is clearly a single slave who does everything, from ploughing to taking care of sheep to preparing meals. The context is probably a farmer who has enough money for one slave but not more than one.

The passage in context

This passage appears in a section of apparently miscellaneous sayings of Jesus, which range from how to respond when stumbling in faith happens, to having faith the size of a mustard seed, to this parable about not getting praise for doing what you should be doing. If anything, it is a collection of sayings about everyday faith and how to live it.

There are numerous occasions in the parables where the 'every-day' life of Jesus' original audience feels a long way from ours, but probably nowhere quite so clearly as here. In Jesus' world what is described here would be entirely just: the slave is not ill-treated and is still allowed to eat, but is worked very hard. In our world we would consider such treatment unjust and uncaring (though, if we are honest, our society still treats people this badly: there are plenty of people who work in this kind of way simply to earn enough money to live on). However, it is helpful if you read Luke 12.35–38 against this passage. What is proposed here is just, but it is not the justice found in the kingdom.

On being thanked

The point of this parable is a startling but helpful one, and will come to the fore again when we look at the so-called 'good Samaritan' (below, pp. 223–9). At no point in that parable is the Samaritan called 'good'; this is because he was just doing what the law required someone to do. That is not being 'good' – it is simply doing what you should do. The same point is made here. God does not thank us for doing what we are commanded to do. If we do this, we are simply doing what we ought to do. This attracts no especial thanks – God does, however, love us with a love that goes beyond all deserving, but doesn't love us more for doing what we should.

To think about ...

People often experience the Church as a place where they are not really thanked for what they do. Is this what Jesus meant here? Or was it something else?

---

34 The compassionate king and the unmerciful slave (Matthew 18.21–35)

The slightly startling feature of this parable is that the key character is a king (although this is only mentioned once right at the start). This is probably to allow for the extravagant amounts of money mentioned as being owed by the slave. You would need a very wealthy master for that amount of money, even if, as is noted below, the amount owed was a ridiculous figure that could not realistically have been owed by anyone.

The fantastic number cited was probably given to match Jesus' seventy times seven or seventy times seven times – a number so great one would lose count of how many times forgiveness had taken place.

Matthew 18.21–35

²¹*Then Peter came to him and said, 'Lord, how many times will a brother or sister sin against me and I forgive them? Seven times?'* ²²*Jesus said to him, 'I say to you, not seven but seventy times seven.*

²³*'For this reason the kingdom of the heavens has become like a person, a king, who wanted to settle an account with his slaves.* ²⁴*He began the settlement, and he ordered brought to him a debtor who owed him ten thousand silver talents.* ²⁵*Since he didn't have the means to pay it back, the lord ordered that he be sold – him, his wife, his children and everything he owned – and used as repayment.* ²⁶*The slave fell down and bowed before him saying, "Be patient with me, and I will give everything back."* ²⁷*The lord of that slave was moved with compassion and set him free, and forgave the loan.* ²⁸*That slave went out and found one of his fellow slaves who owed him a hundred denarii, and seizing him, he choked him and said: "Repay whatever you owe."* ²⁹*The fellow slave fell down and begged him, saying, "Be patient with me, and I will give everything back."* ³⁰*He did not want to so he went away and threw him into prison, until he paid back what he owed.* ³¹*When his fellow slaves saw what had happened, they were extremely upset and they went and reported everything that had happened to their lord.* ³²*Then the lord summoned him and said to him, "You evil slave, I forgave you everything that you owed because you begged me.* ³³*Surely you*

should have had mercy on your fellow slave, as I had mercy on you?" ³⁴And the lord was angry with him and handed him over to torturers until the debt was paid. ³⁵This is what my heavenly father will do to you unless you forgive your brother or sister from your heart.'

Interesting words ...

- v. 21: Peter's question asks, literally, how many times he should forgive 'a brother'. In the context here (see below), which is largely about relationships within the Church, it is most likely that this means a member of the Church and therefore is best translated a brother or sister or, as the NRSV has it, member of the Church.
- v. 22: although the Greek says 'seventy times seven', early translations of the text took it as seventy times seven times, which may well be what was intended.
- v. 24: the word for debtor (*opheiletēs*) is used only here and in Matthew 6.12 (the Lord's Prayer); the connection is almost certainly deliberate – 'forgive us our debts, as we have forgiven our debtors'.
- v. 24: the word 'talent' originally meant a balance or scale. It then meant the thing that was weighed and referred to a specific weight – about 30 kilograms – and then referred to a sum of money. A silver talent was worth around 6,000 denarii (a day labourer's wage was around one denarius a day). To give some scale to the figures quoted here, when Herod the Great died in 4 BC and his kingdom was split between his sons, the annual tribute owed to the Romans that was apportioned between them all was 900 talents. The parable therefore is referring to a fantastical amount of money – today, Jesus might have said he owed him gazillions of coins.
- v. 26: the word 'bow' is the verb *proskuneō*, which means 'to make obeisance', 'to prostrate before' (normally in relation to kings) and, in certain cases, 'to worship'.
- v. 27: the word for 'moved with compassion' here (*splagnizomai*) refers to being moved in the bowels since it was believed that emotion was located in the bowels.

A wealthy slave?

Although the amount of money owed by the slave is unlikely, the rest of the details in this parable are not unreasonable. In the Roman world, slaves were allowed to accumulate money that might come to them in the course of their duties. If they earned enough they would then use this money to buy back their freedom. In the same way, a trusted and honoured slave would work on behalf of their master in business arrangements. The scenario here is that some kind of business deal has gone badly wrong and the slave is to be held liable for the loss. The parable of the three/ten slaves below (see pp. 153–62) posits a similar scenario in which talents are given to the slaves and those slaves are held accountable for the money they received.

The passage in context

Chapter 18 of Matthew reflects on various issues in church life: from who was greatest in the kingdom (1-5); to what would happen to those who put stumbling blocks before 'these little ones' (6-9); from sheep who get led astray and the need to go looking for them (10-14); to calling to account those who sin (15-20); to this parable about the need to forgive. Although some translations make Peter's question about how often to forgive a separate section, this seems wrong – the final verse ('This is what my heavenly father will do to you unless you forgive your brother or sister from your heart,' verse 35) seems to make it clear that this is all connected. We forgive much because we have been forgiven much. Indeed, the final verse ups the ante even more – it is not just the quantity of forgiveness but the quality of it that is important. We are not just expected to forgive superficially but to do so 'from the heart'.

It is also worth noting that this parable comes immediately after the section about holding people to account. This is important. In that seemingly harsh section, if someone would not listen they were to become to the community like Gentiles and tax collectors. This section is all about forgiveness and reminds us that Jesus spent his ministry caring for Gentiles and tax collectors. They might be cast out of the community but they were still to be forgiven and cared for.

The reaction of the king to the slave who could not pay would not have been thought unreasonable in the period. The slight glitch in the narrative is that if the slave were owned by the master, the slave's wife and children would have been too, so their sale would have been more to consolidate assets than to gain new money. The problem with the notional debt of around 60,000 denarii is that their sale would have done no more than scratch the surface of the debt. A slave would have had the value of between 500 and 2,000 denarii depending on age and skill, and so even the sale of his whole family could not have repaid the money owed.

The other slave

The debt owed by the other slave is intentionally paltry in comparison to the forgiven debt. Nevertheless, it was still quite a lot of money – a third of a year's earnings for a day labourer. The first slave, apparently, did not make any connection between his own forgiven debt and the debt of this other slave, or maybe he did. His being called to account reminded him of the debt so he went out to find the slave as a result. An unnecessary detail in the story is interesting. The fellow slaves of both slaves were so upset by the first slave's actions that they felt the need to protest about it. This small detail raises the question of whether there is more in this parable than just the key characters and the key point. Perhaps there is a side point of the importance of not just observing injustice but of doing something about it and ensuring that it does not continue.

Handed over to torturers

When the first slave is imprisoned by the angry king at the end of the parable, he was handed over to be tortured until he paid his debt. This seems to be a self-defeating action since torture would not enable him to raise money any quicker. The point is that it matches his own actions towards the second slave, whom he imprisoned. The torture would have been carried out by jailers and the implication is that it was as much to do with punishment as anything else.

On compassion

The turning point of this parable is compassion. The slave just asked for an extension from the king; the king, moved by compassion, forgave the whole debt. There is no suggestion in the narrative that the first slave should have likewise been moved by compassion, simply that he should have made a connection between his own forgiveness and the forgiveness needed by the second slave. In modern parlance we might say that the expectation is of paying it forward. What he had received should have been paid forward to the other slave.

The word for 'debtors' draws a striking connection with the Lord's Prayer, which prays the opposite of this parable. If this parable has the principle of paying it forward, the Lord's Prayer has the far more uncomfortable principle of asking that we be forgiven as we forgive others – no more, no less. The implication there is that we cannot ask God to forgive us more than we forgive others. This parable is far easier to live with – God has forgiven us the equivalent of a treasure trove of debt. This forgiveness should stay firmly at the front of our minds as we decide whether to forgive others or not. We have been forgiven much and therefore need to forgive in precisely the same way.

Some of Jesus' most challenging teaching is about forgiveness. It was challenging at the time – since the expectation was that God forgave sin (though only unintentional sin) but human beings, within bounds, could exact revenge. Jesus' teaching turned the tables on this and made it clear that his followers were to forgive just as God did, only this time for all kinds of sin both deliberate and unintentional. Today we like to put all sorts of caveats around this – that people should be repentant, that they should deserve forgiveness – but the reality is that these caveats are not present in the teaching of Jesus. Jesus declares that we should just forgive and carry on doing so until we have forgotten how often we have done it. It is not that we just let people off – they are to be held to account for what they have done (see the passage before this one, Matthew 18.15–20, and the fellow slaves in this parable) – but that we forgive them. Unfortunately, despite the number of times Jesus taught about the importance of forgiveness, he never mentioned *how* we do it – just that we should do it. Although I suspect the 'how' comes with the seventy times seven times, eventually we have intentionally laid down our anger so often that the forgiveness has taken root in our hearts.

To think about ...

How good are you at forgiveness?

---

35 The shrewd manager (Luke 16.1–12)

This has to be one of the trickiest and hardest to understand of all the parables. So hard, in fact, that there is almost no agreement at all about what it means or how we should interpret it (for an enumeration of the various different theories, see any of the mainstream commentaries on Luke). One of the key questions was whether the steward was dishonest or to be admired. The common title in translations for the parable – the dishonest manager – suggests a greater agreement than there is among scholars about the honesty of his actions. As a result, 'shrewd' seems a better title as it does not give a value judgement about them.

Luke 16.1–12

[1]*Then he said to his disciples, 'A certain person was wealthy. He had a manager. Charges were brought to him that he was squandering his belongings.* [2]*And summoning him he said to him, "What am I hearing about you? Give me a report of your management, because you cannot be a manager any more." * [3]*The manager said to himself, "What am I going to do? My lord is taking the management away from me. I'm not strong enough to dig. I'm ashamed to beg.* [4]*I know what I'll do, so that when I am removed from being manager people will welcome me into their homes." * [5]*So he called the debtors of the lord one by one and said to the first, "How much do you owe, my lord?" * [6]*He said, "One hundred measures of olive oil." He said to him, "Take your bill, and sit down quickly and write fifty." * [7]*Then he said to another, "How much do you owe?" He said, "A hundred measures of grain." He said to him, "Take your bill and write eighty." * [8]*And the lord approved of the unjust*

*manager because he acted shrewdly. Because the children of this age
are more shrewd among their generation than the children of light.*
⁹*I say to you make friends for yourselves from unjust riches so that,
when it runs out, they will welcome you into the eternal dwellings.*

¹⁰*'The one who is reliable with a little is reliable with a lot. Whoever is unjust with a little is unjust with a lot.* ¹¹*If then you have not
been reliable with unjust riches, who will trust you with true riches?*
¹²*And if you have not been reliable with what belongs to someone
else, who will give you your own?'*

(*Note*: This parable ends in Luke with the parable about serving two
masters, which will be explored in the Matthean version below, pp. 151–2.)

Interesting words …

- v. 1: until this passage, all those who served a master have been called
  'slaves'. The manager is not. His title (*oikonomos*) refers to someone
  who is the manager, administrator or steward of an estate. It would be
  possible to put a slave in this position but they could also have been an
  employee. Here the person is clearly an employee, as he fears losing his
  livelihood rather than being sold on to recoup debts as in the previous
  parable.

  It is important to recognize that being the manager of a wealthy
  person's estate was highly sought after and there is evidence of people
  selling themselves to a master as a slave in order to get the chance to be
  in this role.
- v. 1: the word for 'squander' (*disaskorpizō*) means to 'spread around',
  'disperse' or 'squander'.
- v. 5: the word for 'debtor' is slightly different from that used in the
  previous parable. This one, *chreopheiletēs*, is a relatively rare word in
  Greek.
- vv. 6–7: the words for 'measure' changes according to what is being
  measured – in verse 6 the measure is a *batos*; in verse 7 it is a *kor*,
  which was a dry measure. There is no absolute agreement on how
  much these measures contained. The range is somewhere between 21
  and 39 litres for a *batos*, and between 48 and 131 litres for a *kor* (both
  measures appear to have changed size at different times in history).
  Nevertheless, even at the more conservative estimate the quantities
  referred to here are huge.
- v. 8: the word for how the manager acted is the same one – *phronimos*
  – as was used of the reliable and sensible slave in the parable above
  (pp. 135–8). *Phronimos* means to act wisely in a practical way. The

word repeats in the second half of verse 8. In this context, 'sensibly' is not such a good translation and 'shrewdly' might be better.

- v. 10: again the word for 'reliable' (*pistos*) is the same one as is used above (pp. 135–8).

A bit of background

This is one of those parables in which the culture and expectations of Jesus' day are so far away from our own that it is very difficult for us to make any sense of it. A few bits of background are helpful:

- All the people involved in this parable are wealthy. The debts owed to the master are thought to represent the produce of around 150 olives trees and 100 acres of land respectively. In other words, the debtors are themselves wealthy – just a little less so than the master.
- The most likely explanation of the debt is that each of the debtors were tenant farmers who had agreed to farm the landowner's land and to pay back a proportion of the produce in rent. They must, then, be farming enormous plots if this is only a proportion of the produce farmed.
- The Middle Eastern principle of reciprocity lies behind this parable – generous deeds would be repaid by similar generosity so the manager was laying up 'credit' in goodwill for himself with the tenant farmers, a currency that is largely alien in our modern context.

One element about which there is very little agreement at all is whether the manager cancelled actual debt or his own commission on it. The explanation has been offered, and accepted by some, that the manager had put his own commission on top of the rent and that this was what he cancelled so that the owner did not lose out at all. Others object to this on numerous grounds. It is not mentioned anywhere in the text itself and the only time the manager is called 'unjust' directly is when he is praised by the master for his actions in discounting the debt. This indicates that it was his action in cancelling debt that made him unjust, not charging a commission that was then cancelled. In addition, although a 20 per cent levy on grain might be considered within normal bounds, a 50 per cent levy on olive really would be excessive. In any case, the only way the commission could be conceivable is if it were commission and not interest, since charging interest to fellow Jews was against the law.

The passage in context

The crucial element of context here is that this chapter is all about money and those who love it. This parable is followed by the parable about serving two masters (see below); then by a confrontation between Jesus and the Pharisees who loved money, which itself was followed by the parable of the rich man and Lazarus. The focus of the parable, then, in this context is the love of money and what this causes people to do.

Why was the manager approved of?

The crux of the whole parable is why the master approved of the manager when he had, apparently, lost him a lot of money. There are two clues that might lead us to some kind of answer. The first is in the actions of the manager. The manager is brought to the master's attention because he had been 'squandering' or 'spreading about' the master's property. It may be that his squandering was that he had been letting out the land for the production of olive oil or grain, but had not been diligent in collecting the rent. When he discounted the rent, it could be that what he was doing was making it profitable in a way it hadn't been profitable before – thereby actually getting the master some income for that year, which otherwise he would not have had.

If this scenario works then the manager had still over-stretched and would still be sacked, despite the approval of the master (you might call it grudging approval), but through quick thinking he had thought up a temporary fix *and* guaranteed himself a warm welcome at the houses of each of the tenant farmers concerned. If this works (and if I am honest I am only half persuaded by it, but it seems better than most other options), then the real key to understanding this parable lies in 16.13 ('No slave can serve two masters'), which also appears in Matthew and will be explored below (Matthew 6.24, see pp. 151–2). The manager served 'riches' and used the rules of 'riches' to dig himself out of trouble, but his master recognized this and approved of his down-to-earth practical wisdom.

What does verse 9 mean?

So far so good, but we then hit the hardest verse of all in this whole parable: 'I say to you make friends for yourselves from unjust riches so that, when it runs out, they will welcome you into the eternal dwellings.' This seems to throw in the air almost everything else Jesus has said elsewhere. We need to begin with the acknowledgement that it is impossible to make this verse palatable, but we do still need to wrestle with it.

The logic appears to read that the children of this age are shrewd (*phronimos*) – down-to-earth and practical – in order to get what they want in this age; in the same way, the children of light need to be as shrewd in order to receive a place in the age to come. Down-to-earth practical wisdom leads to shrewd action, but the rules are different: the manager in this parable used the rules of riches to get what he wanted; the children of light should use the rules of God/the kingdom when it comes to 'unjust riches' (some suggest 'worldly wealth' might be a better translation of this). The rules of God concern care for others, not just yourself. In some ways this verse is reminiscent of 12.33–34 ('Make purses for yourselves that do not wear out, an unfailing treasure in heaven, where no thief comes near and no moth destroys. For where your treasure is, there your heart will be also').

Furthermore, if we read this verse alongside the parable of the rich man and Lazarus this also pushes in this direction. The rich man used all his wealth to make friends in this age, but then he died and was left with nothing. If you use worldly wealth well now, but with God's rules – by caring for the poor and outcast – then, when this age runs out, you have an eternal dwelling ready for you. If you use it unjustly now, you will have friends in this age but nothing when it really matters. You can use money to make friends now or then – your choice.

This message is extended in verses 10–12. Use of money now is also a trial for how we will be in the future. If we use money

– which equates to very, very little – badly now, how will we be trusted with the real treasure of the kingdom of God? That's the best I can do with this most difficult and bemusing of parables. It is far from perfect – in fact there are holes all over the place – but this is where I throw up my hands in defeat and frustration, and leave you to reflect on it further.

> ### To think about ...
>
> What sense do you make of this parable?

36 Serving two masters (Matthew 6.24; Luke 16.13)

At the heart of this parable is the verb 'to be a slave'. While it might be possible to serve two masters, it is very difficult to be a slave to two masters. A master owns a slave in entirety so having two masters in this sense is close to impossible. That is the sense that Jesus is using here, uncomfortable though we might find it: a master owns a slave so completely that another master cannot own them in the same way.

Matthew 6.24

²⁴*No one is able to be a slave to two masters, for either they hate the one and love the other, or they cling to one and look down on the other. You are not able to serve God and riches.*

Interesting words ...

- The verb normally translated as 'serve' is *douleuō*, which is connected to the noun for 'slave'.
- The first couplet of words are the usual words for 'hate' (*miseō*) and 'love' (*agapaō*); the second two are more complex. The first (*antechō*) can either mean 'to cling' to or 'to stand against' or 'withstand'. Given that the second word (*kataphroneō*) clearly means 'to look down on' or 'despise', it seems most likely that *antechō* should be taken positively here.

• The word 'riches' translates *mammon*. It is a Hebrew word that is not used in the Old Testament, but does appear in texts from Qumran and in the Mishnah. As Kenneth Bailey points out in *Poet and Peasant* (see p. xxvii for full details), it has the same root as 'Amen' and could have the resonance of 'that in which one places trust'.

The personification of riches

Riches are not normally personified in the Old Testament but Jesus gets close to doing so in this passage. It may be unusual but it does work in this context. Jesus is referring here to the way a love of money takes over the soul and takes ownership to the extent that there is no room left for any other allegiance. In his day, the best illustration of this kind of experience is that of a master and a slave. It is hard to think of an illustration that works as well in our modern world – the closest I can get to is, you can't give your heart in its entirety to two people, but even that doesn't quite work.

> ### The passage in context
>
> As noted above, in Luke's Gospel this parable serves as the final verse of the parable of the shrewd manager, and in one interpretation as the key to understanding the whole parable. In Matthew, the context is very different. The saying is in a string of sayings in the Sermon on the Mount on a wide range of subjects, from fasting to treasure, from the eye being a lamp to the body, to serving two masters.

As with many other of Jesus' sayings about money (not to mention the many parables in which wealthy landowners appear without condemnation), it is not having money that is the problem. It is allowing money to take over that is Jesus' concern – allowing it to rule to the extent that it usurps our love of God and the demands of God's kingdom.

> **To think about ...**
>
> What is your relationship with money? How confident are you
> that it doesn't rule you?

37 The three/ten slaves (Matthew 25.14–30; Luke 19.11–27)

Although this parable is popularly known as the parable of the
talents, talents are only mentioned in Matthew's Gospel. In Luke the
currency mentioned is 'mina'. In addition, although Luke mentions
ten slaves at the start of the parable, only three have a 'speaking
part', so it seems best to call this the parable of the three slaves.

Matthew 25.14–30

^{14}*For it is like a person going on a journey away from home who
called his slaves and gave them his belongings.* ^{15}*To one he gave five
silver talents, to another two, and to another one, to each according
to their ability, and he went away.* ^{16}*The one who had received five
talents went and did business with them and gained another five.*
^{17}*In the same way the one with two gained another two.* ^{18}*But the
one receiving one went away, dug up the ground and buried the
silver belonging to his lord.* ^{19}*After a long time, the lord of those
slaves came and settled accounts with them.* ^{20}*And the one with
five silver talents came bringing another five silver talents and said,
'Lord, you gave me five silver talents but look, I gained another
five silver talents.'* ^{21}*The lord said to him, 'Excellent! Good and
reliable slave, you were reliable with a very little, I will put you in
charge of many things, come into the joy of your lord.'* ^{22}*Then the
one with two silver talents came and said, 'Lord, you gave me two
silver talents but look, I gained two more silver talents.'* ^{23}*The lord
said to him, 'Excellent! Good and reliable slave, you were reliable
with a very little, I will put you in charge of many things, come into
the joy of your lord.'* ^{24}*Then the one who had received one silver
talent came and said, 'Lord, knowing that you are a hard person,
reaping where you did not sow and gathering where you did not*

scatter, [25]I was afraid and went and hid your silver talent in the ground. Look! Have what is yours.' [26]The lord answered him and said to him, 'Evil and lazy slave, you knew that I reaped where I did not sow and I gathered where I did not scatter? [27]You should have deposited my silver with the money changers, and when I came I could have received back what was mine with interest. [28]Therefore take the one silver talent from him and give it to the one who has ten silver talents. [29]For to all those who have will be given more and they will have more than enough and from those who don't have anything, even what they do have will be taken away. [30]Throw this useless slave into the outer darkness, where there is weeping and gnashing of teeth.'

Luke 19.11–27

[11]They were listening to these things so he went on to tell them a parable because Jerusalem was near and they supposed that the kingdom of God was about to appear immediately. [12]Therefore he said, 'A certain well born person travelled to a faraway country to receive a kingdom for himself and then come back. [13]He called ten of his slaves and gave to them ten mina and said to them, "Trade until I come." [14]But his citizens hated him and sent a delegation after him saying, "We do not want this person to rule over us." [15]He received the kingdom and returned, and gave orders to summon the slaves to whom he gave the silver so that he might know what they had gained by trading. [16]The first one arrived and said, "The mina has earned ten more." [17]He said to him, "Excellent! Good slave, because you were reliable with a very little, have authority over ten cities." [18]And the second one came saying, "Your mina, Lord, made five mina." [19]And he said to him, "And you rule over five cities." [20]And the other one came and said, "Lord, behold your mina which I put away for safekeeping in a cloth. [21]I was afraid of you because you are a harsh person, you take what you did not deposit, and you reap what you did not sow." [22]He said to him, "I judge you out of your own mouth, evil slave, you know that I am a harsh man, taking what I did not deposit and reaping what I did not sow. [23]So why didn't you put my silver with the money changers? Then when I came I could have collected the interest?" [24]To those who were there he said, "Take the mina from him, and give it to the one who had ten." [25]And they said to him, "Lord, he has ten mina." [26]I say

to you that to all those who have, more will be given, but from those who don't have even what he has will be taken away. ²⁷*Nevertheless, these enemies of mine, those not wanting me to rule over them, bring them here and slaughter them in front of me.'*

Interesting words ...

In Matthew 25:

- This parable has often been misinterpreted due to a misunderstanding of the word 'talent', which here is a coin and not an innate gift. (For the value of the silver talent, see note p. 142 above.) The implication of Matthew's parable is that the eight talents he gave to his slaves were the whole of the man's property and would have been worth around 48,000 denarii. Those who doubled the amount, then, made a vast amount of money.
- v. 21: the word translated 'reliable' is the Greek word *pistos*, used a number of times in this chapter.
- v. 27: the word translated 'money changers' is *trapezitēs* – which is connected to the word for 'table', since money changers and bankers sat behind tables to do their business.

In Luke 19:

- v. 12: the word for the 'faraway country' is the same as the word used in Luke 15 for the country that the younger of the lost sons went to (*eis chōran machran*).
- v. 13: the coins given in Luke's version of the parable are *mna*, which were Greek coins; they are normally called 'mina' in English. One *mna* was worth 100 *drachma*. A drachma (Greek coin) was very roughly the equivalent of the denarius (Roman coin) so was worth much less than the silver talents given in Matthew's parable. Note also that all the slaves were given the same amount.

  It isn't clear why Luke chose to use the Greek coinage rather than the usual Roman coinage here.
- v. 13: the word for 'trade/doing business' in Matthew is different from that in Luke. In Matthew it is *ergazomai*, which has a similar sense to Luke's word but with a little more emphasis on working; but in Luke it is *pragmateuomai*, which means 'to busy oneself', 'to labour at something' or 'to do business'. In verse 15, 'what they had gained by trading' is another form of this verb, which this time is *diapragmateuomai*.
- v. 15: the word for 'kingdom' – *basileia* – can also refer to the office or the reign of a king or queen (hence the phrase 'kingdom of God'

could also be translated as 'the rule of God', which in some instances is a helpful insight into its meaning). Here it could mean he received the kingdom or the right to rule.

- v. 19: the lord's response to the second slave doesn't have enough words in it; literally it says 'and you become over five cities', and extra words need adding for sense.
- v. 21: in Matthew the third slave says that he knows the master is hard (*sklēros*), whereas in Luke he says he knows he is harsh (*austeros*).

One parable, two versions

As we have observed a number of times already with other parables, although both Matthew and Luke have the same parable, there are some quite significant differences between the two.

- Matthew talks of the slaves having five, two and one silver talent respectively which, even with one talent, was still a considerable amount of money – 30,000, 12,000 and 6,000 denarii. It is so much, in fact, that it raises a question about the master commenting on the slaves' reliability with 'very little'. The sum of 30,000 denarii was *not* very little; Luke talks of their having one mina each, which was much less money – around a third of a year's wages for a day labourer.
- Unlike in Luke, where the same amount of money is given to each slave, in Matthew the amount of money apportioned to each slave is in proportion to their ability.
- In Matthew the money was just given to the slaves, whereas in Luke it was given to them with the strict instruction that they should 'trade'. In Luke the master's expectations of the money are made much clearer than in Matthew, though the first thing the master asks on return is for the slaves to settle accounts. This implies that the expectation was the same in both versions.
- Matthew talks of three slaves; Luke of ten – but then only goes on to mention three.
- In Matthew the third slave hides the talent in the ground; in Luke he hides it in a cloth.
- Luke includes the odd additional story about the citizens not wanting the lord to be their king and, when the first two slaves are rewarded, they are given cities to take care of – not just

money. The implication of this is that the slaves are given a share in their Lord's kingdom.

While there are significant differences between Matthew's and Luke's versions of this parable, the basic parable is the same in both. A landowner went away and left his slaves with a sum of money; two of those slaves traded well with that money and were rewarded, while one hid it and was punished.

The passage in context

In Matthew's Gospel this parable is very much focused on the future and, in particular, on waiting carefully and diligently for the master's return, placed as it is in a run of three parables all focused around this theme. The first of these – the parable of the reliable and wicked slaves, 24.45–51 (explored above, pp. 135–8) – involves simply doing what we are asked to do while the master is away; the second – the parable of ten young women (25.1–13) – emphasizes the importance of being ready; but this one has an additional focus: that of making the most of our time while we wait.

In contrast, in Luke this parable comes immediately after the story of Zacchaeus, and is clearly linked to it by verse 11 beginning, 'They were listening to these things so he went on ...' The story of Zacchaeus ends with Jesus proclaiming that, 'Today salvation has come to this house.' The implication seems to be that today the master had returned to Zacchaeus' house and found how he had traded with what he had. This might provide us with a lens through which to understand this tricky parable. It also, as often in Luke, makes the return much nearer than in Matthew. (On this, see more below.)

Aggressive trading

Despite its popularity, this parable is, in some ways, uncomfortably like the parable of the shrewd manager. Here aggressive trading and taking huge risks are rewarded, whereas being cautious and careful not to lose money are not. Even without Luke's additions this is a curious and slightly troubling parable.

Neither version of the parable tells us how the two slaves, who in Matthew's Gospel doubled their money and in Luke's Gospel increased it by 1,000 or 500 times respectively, did this. The language used implies that they did it by buying and selling aggressively. The problem at the heart of the parable is that the only real way to make that kind of money is to act unethically, but this behaviour is what is rewarded by the master on his return.

An additional discomfort is that the third slave, the one who hid his money, was chastised for not investing his money with the money changers or bankers. The Old Testament law forbade lending money with interest to the poor (Exodus 22.25; Leviticus 25.35–37) or to a fellow Israelite (Deuteronomy 23.19–20). Money was lent with interest to outsiders or strangers, so perhaps this is what was in mind here. Furthermore, there were no 'banks' in this period, so those who did such activity would have been unregulated money changers who made money in whatever way they could. Taking your money to one of these people would have been far from safe and could have resulted in losing it altogether. It is odd, therefore, that the master preferred this course of action to hiding it away – even if that hiding wasn't completely safe either (see below).

Money hidden in the ground

In a world in which banking was extremely rare and disapproved of, a poor person would often seek to hide what money they had to keep it safe. Burying it in the ground was a common solution – though the problem of this is revealed by the parable of the hidden treasure (see below, pp. 199–200), which was effectively stolen by the person who happened upon it and bought the field. Burying treasure wasn't without risk.

This is another parable, like that of the shrewd manager, in which the moral of the parable and the morals of the kingdom don't appear to align easily.

Who was the master?

We also need to ask the question of whether the master should be seen as God or Jesus, as is commonly assumed. The problem is the description of the master by the third slave as 'hard' (Matthew 25.24) or 'harsh' (Luke 19.21), 'reaping where you did not sow and gathering where you did not scatter' (Matthew 25.24) and 'you take what you did not deposit, and you reap what you did not sow' (Luke 19.21). This is surely the very opposite of the character of God, who sows liberally and generously and does not always demand recompense for what rightly belongs to God. God gives and gives far more than we expect or deserve.

An additional question concerns the additional material in Luke about the king who went away to receive his kingship and was challenged by his subjects. While it is possible to read this story as referring to Jesus' kingship – that Jesus came to be king and his subjects objected and attempted to challenge his rule – the bit that makes less sense is Jesus' going to a land far away to receive his kingship, unless that is a reference to his ascension. The story makes much more sense if the king is understood to be Herod Archelaus (see the box below). If that is the case, this is not a story directly about Jesus or God but about a well-known situation at the time that is inserted into this parable, and challenges us to think again about what is going on.

On Herod Archelaus

The story of Herod Archelaus, as told by the Jewish historian Josephus, is uncannily like the story of the 'king' in this parable. After the death of Herod the Great, the kingdom was split between three of his sons, Herod Archelaus, Herod Antipas and Philip the Tetrarch. Archelaus received the territory of Judea but the people were unhappy about this. Just before his death Herod the Great had installed a golden eagle over the temple entrance. This was regarded as blasphemy (as it was an image) and was torn down. Those involved in this act (over 40 people) were rounded up and burnt alive.

After his father's death, Archelaus sought to quell the subsequent riots with violence and ended up killing over 3,000 people. He then sailed to Rome to receive his kingship and a delegation was sent from

---

Judea to protest against this. Despite Judean arguments to the contrary, he was granted kingship and on his return punished his enemies
for their challenge. He was eventually deposed by the Romans in AD 6
when his ruthlessness went too far.

Reading through the lens of Zacchaeus

At this point, the story of Zacchaeus (Luke 19.1–10) might help
us make a little more sense of what is going on. Zacchaeus was
a tax collector and rich (verse 2). Tax collectors were regarded
with great suspicion at the time of Jesus, not so much because they
were corrupt – though undoubtedly some were – but because they
collaborated with the Romans to collect Roman taxes. Although
Zacchaeus is widely understood to be corrupt there is nothing in
the text to suggest that he was. His proposal to recompense four-
fold anyone he had defrauded only works if he doesn't think he
has done this very much. Otherwise, having given half his money
away to the poor, he would have nothing left at all. What is interesting, though, is that Zacchaeus clearly did trade, as did the first
two slaves in the parable, to make himself rich, but when salvation
came to his house he changed and acted differently. The rules of the
kingdom were different and required him to act differently.

It is possible therefore – but only possible – that this parable
functions like the shrewd manager, as a parable of contrast between
the rules of this world and the rules of the kingdom. If, using the
rules of this world, a master goes away and expects his slaves to
work hard in his absence, how much more is it true of disciples?
The master of the disciples is not hard or harsh but loving and
generous, but still requires them to work hard using the rules of
the kingdom, giving away their money to the poor, recompensing
anyone they have treated badly, caring and loving as their master
would. This begs the question of what the trading rules of the kingdom are – and the lens of Zacchaeus suggests that the rules are
generosity and love.

Another interpretation, however, is that the king is Jesus and
after his death he ascended to heaven to receive his kingship. Those
who objected to his rule will be punished on his return at the end
of all times, but in the meantime we are called to work hard, trad-

ing with the master's property until his return. Since the master's property is love and compassion, the ultimate point of the parable – not waiting idly but working hard while we wait for the master's return – remains no matter which option you choose.

To those who have ...

One of the hardest sayings in this parable is the one that declares that more will be given to those who have, and from those who have nothing even what they do have will be taken away. It doesn't just appear here – it can also be found in Luke 8.18 and Mark 4.25. This suggests that this was a saying that Jesus said more than once.

The difficulty is that it reads as stating what the world is like now. This is certainly true of the rich and powerful in our world now as then. The question is: what is it that 'those who have' have? In Mark's Gospel the phrase refers to those who are able to understand and respond to the parables; in this parable it is those who are able to work hard while the master is away. In other words, 'those who have' are those who have the key to the kingdom – this may well be what Jesus meant here.

It is worth adding that Matthew's setting of the parable allows us to take a step back and not worry too much about the internal ethics of the parable. Just as we don't interrogate too closely how the reliable slave took care of the other slaves (24.45–51), nor exactly what the oil represents in the parable of the ten young women (25.1–13), perhaps we should not worry too much about the trading and what it entailed. The point in each is that those declared good were doing what they were asked to do in preparation for the master's return. That may simply be enough.

So is this not about talents?

We cannot leave this parable without asking the question about the well-loved 'sermon moral' of using our skills to the best of our ability in the service of the kingdom. I would regard this in a very similar way to the parable of the sheep and the goats. There is a reason that it became so popular and so often preached in this way, which is that it served as a vehicle for a sentiment that is absolutely consonant with the Christian message. Those who follow Jesus are called to use everything they have – to use their talents in all their glorious multiplicity – to further the kingdom or, as St Paul would put it, to build up the body of Christ. If this is not quite what the parable means in either Gospel, it doesn't detract from the importance of the message (though personally I would preach it from a different passage, such as 1 Corinthians 12).

To think about ...

What do you think this parable is about? What is its key message? Does it change in the different versions in Matthew and Luke?

Reflection

One of the striking features of these parables, when gathered together, is that our sympathy, in each one, lies naturally with the master. We are concerned that the slaves do as they are asked. We worry whether the shrewd manager has defrauded the master of his money or not. We understand that the master wants a good return for the property he left behind (though if I'm honest I've always had a sneaking sympathy for the third slave, who was frightened of the master and hid his money instead). It is interesting to notice that the way the parables are told evokes our sympathy for the rich and powerful, rather than those with nothing.

This is probably because the parables sit alongside the world as it is, rather than turning it on its head. They are meant to represent a recognizable view of the world to the people of Jesus' day, and this is one in which the rich and powerful are not shaken from their positions (yet). This is probably why I have a liking for the exceedingly tricky parables of the shrewd manager and the three/ ten slaves. If read in a certain way, subversion lies at their heart. If the world works like this, what might a world that works on the rules of the kingdom look like? If we are as shrewd as the manager or trade as aggressively as the first two slaves, but with the rules of the kingdom rather than the rules of this world, what might that produce? What new way of being might emerge? What might we learn about kingdom living that we never knew before? These very tricky parables feel as though they lie a little beyond our grasp, but in wrestling to understand them it is possible that a new vision of the pure gold of the kingdom might appear.

9

Weddings and Banquets

Introduction

Just like today, weddings at the time of Jesus carried significant cultural importance, even if they did not fall into the 'everyday' category. This is revealed in the details of weddings outlined in the parables in this chapter – they were occasions on which to see and be seen, and in which honour could be established or increased. There were strict protocols to be followed and expectations to be upheld. This was equally true of feasts in general, but weddings appear to have held a greater emotional resonance than other kinds.

38 Fasting with the bridegroom (Matthew 9.14–15; Mark 2.18–20; Luke 5.34–35)

This is the parable equivalent of the well-loved Ecclesiastes passage: 'For everything there is a season, and a time for every matter under heaven ...' (3.1–8), and likewise notes the importance of recognizing the season for each activity. While fasting was necessary and right for those mourning and waiting for God's intervention, for Jesus' disciples, who celebrated Jesus' presence with them, it would not have been right.

Mark 2.18–20

[18]*John's disciples and the Pharisees were fasting and they came and said to him, 'Why do the disciples of John and the disciples of the Pharisees fast but your disciples do not fast?'* [19]*And Jesus said to them, 'Surely the sons of the bridal chamber cannot fast while the*

bridegroom is with them? As long as the bridegroom is with them they are not able to fast. ²⁰*The days will come when the bridegroom is taken away from them, then they will fast on that day.'*

Interesting words ...

- v. 19: the Greek uses the Hebrew idiom 'the sons of the bridal chamber'. This could either mean wedding guests in general or the special friends of the bridegroom (in our context, an extended version of the best man and ushers).

The reference to fasting does not seem to have been to the fasting that took place each Yom Kippur (or day of Atonement), nor to the individual private fasting Jesus talks about in Matthew 6.16–18 and recommends that no one knows you are doing it. It probably refers to the practice of the Pharisees (and apparently also of John the Baptist's followers too, though there is no evidence of this outside of this passage) of fasting together on a regular basis on Mondays and Thursdays.

The passage in context

In each of the Gospels this parable precedes those about new cloth and new wineskins. Jesus' point here seems to be that you cannot force an old situation on to a new one, but times change. What might be right at one time will not be right at another. We need to use judgement about what fits where and when.

It is clear from this passage that Jesus was not discouraging the practice of all fasting, merely pointing out that this was not the time for his disciples to be doing it. The issue raised by this parable is not just about whether we should fast or not (the answer to that is we should at the right time), but about judging when the 'right time' is for any of our habitual practices. Simply doing them because 'that's what we do' is to be discouraged because there is a time and season for everything. The question we are left with is how we decide what that time is.

To think about ...

Are there any practices we observe that fall into the category of there being a time to do them and a time to abstain? How do you decide what they are?

---

39 The highest and lowest seats at the feast (Luke 14.7–14)

This is one of those passages that might cause us to query whether it was, in fact, a parable had not Jesus called it one. It reminds us that while many parables are told in third-person narrative – for example, 'A certain person did this ...' – they can also be told in the second person: 'When you do this ...'. If this parable had begun 'A certain person was invited to a wedding ...' it would much more resemble what we expect parables to look like. Its message is very similar to that of a number of other pieces of teaching by Jesus about greatness in the kingdom (see, for example, Matthew 20.20–28, Mark 10.35–45 and Luke 22.24–27).

Luke 14.7–14

[7]*He told a parable to those invited, when he noted they chose for themselves the place of honour. He said to them,* [8]*'When you are invited by someone to a wedding, do not recline in the place of honour, lest someone more honoured than you might have been invited.* [9]*So that when that person arrives, the one who asked both of you says to you, "Give this person your place", and then, with shame, you would begin to take the lowest place.* [10]*But when you are invited, go and recline in the lowest place so that when the one who invited you comes he might say, "Friend, move up higher." Then you will have glory before all those reclining with you.* [11]*For all those exalting themselves will be humbled, and those humbling themselves will be lifted up.'*

166

^{12}*He also said to the one who had invited him, 'When you give a midday or evening meal, don't invite your friends or your brothers or your relatives or your wealthy neighbours, lest you be invited in return and are repaid.* ^{13}*But when you give a banquet, invite the poor, those who have been injured, those who can't walk, those who can't see,* ^{14}*and you will be blessed because they cannot repay you, for you will be repaid at the resurrection of the righteous.'*

Interesting words ...

- v. 8: the word used is the usual one for 'wedding' (*gamos*) but it can also mean 'banquet' more generally.
- vv. 8ff.: 'recline' (*kataklinō*) refers to how people would 'sit' to eat. Following the Roman custom they would lie at the table with their head closest to the table and their feet furthest from it. This custom was so widespread that the word became used as a shorthand for 'eating at table'. In verse 10 the word for 'recline' changes to *anapiptō*, which means roughly the same as *kataklinō* but is not used quite so often.
- v. 10: the word for 'lowest' here is *eschatos*, or 'last place'.
- v. 10: the word for 'glory' (*doxa*) does also mean 'honour', but given its use elsewhere of 'God' it is good to notice its presence here.
- v. 12: 'friend' here is *philos*, loved one.
- v. 12: the words Jesus uses for the meals here are precise – the *ariston* was the noonday meal and *deipnon* the evening meal. Jesus is saying *any time* you invite someone to eat with you.
- v. 13: the word translated here 'those who have been injured' is *anapeiros*, often translated 'crippled', and refers to those who have been injured in an accident. 'Maimed' or 'injured' feels a better translation today.

Honour and shame again

This is another parable governed almost entirely by cultural expectations about honour and shame. Both parts of it – that addressed to the guests as well as that addressed to the host – highlight how important the offering and receiving of invitations to meals was for people's status at this time. There was a complex web of honour and shame involved in not only *who* was invited but *where* they sat at table. Strict seating protocols existed for this kind of gathering, in which the most honoured guest would recline to the right of the host, the next honoured guest to the left, with every other place having a gradation of honour down to the 'last' place. The implication of the parable is that people would seek a place of higher honour than they deserved in the hope that it would not be pointed out, and that they would gain a higher status among their peers than they would otherwise have had.

The passage in context

This parable is told by Jesus while he is with a leader of the Pharisees on the Sabbath. This would probably have been the Friday-night meal, when friends and family would have gathered together to mark the start of the Sabbath. The setting of the parable is not the meal itself but the journey to the meal and the moment before the meal began when people were taking their seats.

Luke continues this same theme in the passage that follows this one, in the parable of the wedding banquet/great dinner.

If the dining room was ordered according to a classic Roman style, as many of the finer houses in Galilee and Judea were in this period, then there would have been somewhere between nine and twenty guests (depending on the size of the room). It is also worth noting that the more important the guest, the later they would come to the meal; this means there would be a very real chance of someone more important than you arriving after you. It is interesting that the word 'shame' is actually used to describe the emotion felt by the person who was asked to move, the only seat available at this late stage being the 'last' one.

Turning the whole system on its head

Jesus' two-part parable – the first aimed at the guest and the second addressed to the host – turns the whole honour/shame construction on its head. The rules of the kingdom are such that they demand that we do not seek honour for ourselves nor do we seek recompense for the honour we show others. Jesus calls us to give generously to those who need it most and not to seek to 'look good'.

While it is easy to set up the honour/shame culture as alien to us and to feel smug that we aren't driven by the same rules today, it is important to reflect on the ways our society has its own form of honour/shame. For example, tabloid newspapers are fuelled strongly by a 'shame culture' in which people formerly honoured are vilified in public day after day. Or in a more domestic setting, how often do you hear said – when perhaps fixing to have dinner with someone – 'No, it's our turn to have you'? These same streams still run in our culture and it is important to identify them.

To think about ...

Where do you see an honour/shame culture functioning most powerfully in our society?

---

40 An invitation to a banquet (Matthew 22.1–14; Luke 14.15–24)

Although various superficial details are different in Matthew's and Luke's accounts (in one the host is a king and in the other just 'someone'; in Matthew the feast is a wedding banquet, whereas in Luke it is just a feast), it is clear that both are the same story in slightly different form, focused around the hypothetical scenario of people declining an invitation at the last moment.

Matthew 22.1–14

[1]*Jesus answered and spoke to them again in parables, saying:* [2]*'The kingdom of the heavens has become like a king, who gave a wedding for his son,* [3]*and he sent his slaves to call those invited to the wedding, and they did not want to come.* [4]*Again he sent other slaves saying, "Tell those invited: look, I have prepared my midday meal, my ox and my fat calves have been killed. Everything is ready. Come to the wedding feast."* [5]*But they were unconcerned and went away: one to their field; another to their business;* [6]*the rest grabbed*

the slaves, mistreated them and killed them. ⁷The king was furious and sent his soldiers to destroy those murderers and set their city on fire. ⁸Then he said to his slaves, "The wedding is ready but those invited are not worthy. ⁹Go to the roads out of town, and whoever you find, invite them to the wedding. ¹⁰Those slaves went out to the roads and gathered everyone that they found, the evil and the good, and the wedding was filled with those reclining at table."

¹¹*'When the king came in he looked at those reclining at table, and he saw someone who was not dressed in a wedding garment. ¹²He said to him, "Friend, how did you come in here without a wedding garment?" But he was flabbergasted. ¹³Then the king said to the servants, "Bind him hand and foot, and throw him into the outer darkness, where there will be wailing and gnashing of teeth. ¹⁴For many are called but few are chosen."'*

Luke 14.15–24

¹⁵*One of those reclining with him heard this and said to him, 'Blessed is anyone who will eat bread in the kingdom of God.' ¹⁶He said to him, 'A certain person gave a great feast, and he invited many people. ¹⁷And he sent his slave at the hour of the feast to say to those invited, "Come, it is ready now." ¹⁸But they all began, one after the other, to make excuses. The first one said to him, "I have bought a field and I need to go out to see it, I ask you consider me excused." ¹⁹Another one said, "I have bought five pairs of oxen and I must go out to assess them. I ask you, consider me excused." ²⁰And another said, "I have married a wife and because of this I cannot come." ²¹So the slave went back and reported these things to his lord. Then the master of the house was furious and said to his slave, "Go out quickly into the wide streets and the narrow alley ways of the city and bring in the poor, those who have been injured, those who can't see, and those who can't walk." ²²And the slave said, "Lord, what you ordered has happened and there is still room." ²³And the lord said to the slave, "Go out into the roads and hedge ways, and force them to come, so that my house might be full." ²⁴I say to you that not one of those men who were invited will taste my feast.'*

Interesting words ...

Matthew:

- v. 1: the word for 'wedding' – *gamos* – refers both to the ceremony and to the feast associated with it; in contrast, in Luke (14.16) the event is just described as a 'feast' or 'evening meal' (*deipnon*).
- v. 3: the Greek contains a play on words based on the double meaning of *kaleō*, which can either mean 'call' or 'invite'. So here the slaves go out to 'call the called'.
- v. 4: note that the word used for the timing of the wedding feast in Matthew is *ariston* or 'midday meal'.
- v. 9: the phrase 'roads out of town' translates *diexodos* ('exits') and *hodos* ('road' or 'way'). Cities, particularly walled cities, would have restricted routes in and out for safety. Those on such routes would be coming or going and so potentially free; in Luke 14.21 the words are 'wide streets' (*plateia*), which refers to the gathering areas of the city like the marketplaces and entrances (as opposed to the narrow streets (*rumē*) that would make up most of the residential parts of the city).
- v. 10: although the NRSV has the 'good and the bad', in Greek they are listed the other way round – 'the bad and the good'; the word for 'bad' is *ponēros*, which I have translated 'evil' elsewhere and have done so again here.
- v. 12: 'flabbergasted' translates the verb *phimoō*, which means 'struck silent' or 'muzzled'. The idea here is that he was too horrified to speak.
- v. 12: the word for 'friend' here is not *philos* as in the previous parable but *etairos*, which can also be translated 'comrade' or 'companion'. It is relational but not warm.
- v. 13: note that here the word *doulos* – 'slave' – that has been used so far in the parable changes to *diakonos* – 'servant'. It implies a different group from the earlier groups.

Luke:

- v. 15: on 'reclining', see note above, p. 113.
- v. 24: the word *anēr* is used – 'man' – not the usual *anthrōpos* ('person'). The gender-specific term is unsurprising here, as women would not have been invited to this kind of feast.

One parable, three versions

A number of Jesus' parables have the same basic form (in this case, a man organizes a feast, and the original invitees decline to come so he fills it with others instead), but with striking differences between the versions. In this instance, there are not two versions but three, the third being found in the non-canonical Gospel of Thomas 64, which is worth including alongside the other two. There the basic shape of the parable is the same but the excuses given are different and reflect a more urban lifestyle than the rural one indicated in Matthew and Luke. In the Gospel of Thomas the excuses given are that the person has money with merchants who are coming that evening to meet with him; that he has bought a house and needs to go on a certain day to see it; that his friend is about to get married and he needs to arrange the feast; and that he has bought a farm and needs to go and collect the rent. At the end of the parable in the Gospel of Thomas, Jesus declares that traders and merchants will not enter his feast.

The differences between Matthew's and Luke's accounts are that:

- In Matthew the 'lord' is a king, whereas in Luke he is just a houseowner; in Matthew the feast is a wedding but in Luke it is just an important dinner ('a great feast').
- Matthew's version is the most violent of all three, in which some of the invitees kill the slaves bringing the message about the feast, and the king sends his soldiers to destroy those who killed the slaves and burn their city, and evicts a wrongly dressed guest. As a result Matthew's parable has more of a political edge than Luke's (or indeed the one in the Gospel of Thomas).
- The excuses given in Matthew's Gospel are vaguer and more generic; those in Luke are peculiarly specific.

The passage in context

In Luke's Gospel this parable continues the conversation between Jesus and the dinner guests at a leader of the Pharisees' house about who should be invited to a meal. In the previous passage Jesus has told a parable about inviting those who cannot repay the honour. This parable turns to those who are invited but then decline the invitation.

In the theme of honour/shame that we have been exploring in this chapter, the actions of the guests are highly shaming to the one who invited them. The purpose of the feast was to proclaim the honour of the king/lord. Those hearing the parable for the first time would have agreed with him that he should be furious at his treatment.

In Matthew the context is different. This features as the third of three parables (the first was the two sons, the second the tenants in the vineyard). They all seem, here, to be addressed to the same people: the chief priests and Pharisees of 21.23. All three parables are about response, and the different ones shown by people in various situations.

God's great banquet?

One common interpretation of this parable is that it is referring to the messianic banquet – the idea that at the end of all times, once the resurrection of the dead has taken place, the faithful will feast with God in heaven. This idea was very popular in early Christian art, which often depicted the Eucharist as a messianic banquet. The problem, however, with seeing this banquet as the messianic banquet is the implication at the heart of the parable that God would only invite the poor, the injured, those who can't see or those who can't walk as an afterthought – as a Plan B once Plan A had unravelled and the invited guests had declined. This seems to stand against everything that Jesus stood for in his ministry, where he especially sought out those on the margins of society first. It issues a profound challenge to us to reflect on whether we really think the poor would ever be asked to the messianic banquet as a Plan B.

It is possible that we are not meant in this instance to think too much about the poor being God's Plan B and instead should focus on those who declined their invitation – that is, those like the Pharisees with whom Jesus was dining. If this is the case, then the point is more that they were given a chance to respond but they declined, not that Jesus turned to the poor, for example, as an alternative. If we take this option, then this parable – like that of the tenants in the vineyard – is a full-blown displacement parable, explaining that the chief priests and the Pharisees willingly gave up their seats at the feast, messianic or otherwise.

People who are injured or cannot walk or see

The reference to the people who were brought into the feast is important. Those who had what was regarded as any kind of impediment were not able to enter into the assembly (that is, the gathering of God's people for worship) or indeed to participate in the sacrifices. See, for example, this quote from Leviticus, which makes this clear:

> The LORD spoke to Moses, saying: [17]Speak to Aaron and say: No one of your offspring throughout their generations who has a blemish may approach to offer the food of his God. [18]For no one who has a blemish shall draw near, one who is blind or lame, or one who has a mutilated face or a limb too long, [19]or one who has a broken foot or a broken hand, [20]or a hunchback, or a dwarf, or a man with a blemish in his eyes or an itching disease or scabs or crushed testicles. (Leviticus 21.16–20)

In later texts this commandment was expanded to include whether they could fight in the war at the end of all times. So, for example, in the text found at Qumran called 'The War of the Sons of Light against the Sons of Darkness' (1QM 7.4–5) it declares that 'no lame, blind, paralysed person ... none of these will go out to war with them'. In other words, being injured or unable to walk automatically rendered someone unclean and unable to worship God. In great contrast, Jesus declared all such people invited to the feast and thoroughly welcome in the kingdom of God.

Who was the king?

A question is also raised about the identity of the king in Matthew's version of the parable, who is vicious and violent when his honour is shamed by the guests, and acts seemingly arbitrarily towards the wedding guest who was not wearing the right clothing. Again, as with other parables, where the character of the one we might say represented God seems at odds with God's own character, the comparison between this parable and God may be more indirect than direct. So the king/lord does not 'represent' God/Jesus but we are intended to extrapolate from a story about this world, governed by the world's values, what the divine response might be when his generous invitation is declined.

Some parallels from Judaism

Some of Jesus' parables have intriguing parallels in Jewish literature. This is one of them. In the Jerusalem Talmud (*Hagigah* 2.2, but also found in *Sanhedrin* 6.6) there is a story about a holy man and a tax collector. When they died no one mourned the death of the holy man, but the whole town mourned for the tax collector because on one occasion he had a banquet for the leaders of the town, who did not come, so he let the poor come so that the food did not go to waste. Another parable in the Babylonian Talmud (*Shabbat* 153a) featured a man who summoned his servants to a banquet but did not tell them what time it would be ready. The wise got dressed and sat by the door waiting to go in; while the foolish did their tasks, assuming they had plenty of time (this parable seems like a blend between this one and the one that follows it – the ten young women).

A violent mob and a vengeful king

One of the most difficult features of this parable can be found in Matthew's version, where the slaves who invite the guests to feast are murdered, the king sends soldiers to a far-off town to raze it to the ground in punishment and, what is more, throws one of the last-minute guests out of the feast for wearing the wrong clothes. What are we to make of this?

The first feature to notice is that the murder of the slaves suddenly makes this parable quite close to that of the tenants in the vineyard (though notice it is the slaves – not the son – who are killed). It is also reminiscent of a passage in the Jewish historian Josephus' *Antiquities of the Jews* that depicts an episode not found in either 2 Kings or 2 Chronicles (see Josephus *Antiquities* 9.263–269). In this story, following his extensive reforms of the temple, Hezekiah sent messengers to summon the Israelites for the Passover (since the practice had lapsed before his reforms), but the people mocked the messengers and then killed them. Hezekiah, however, did not wreak vengeance but went to the temple to sacrifice instead. This reinforces the extent to which the king's anger is disproportionate, even when compared to the response of an Old Testament king. Indeed, the Greek word used for burning their city was used in the Greek translation of the Old Testament (the Septuagint) when describing what the Babylonians did to Jerusalem at the time of the exile.

Throughout this book we have noted that different parables require different types of interpretation. Some have a clear one-to-one correlation between the parable and the lives of its hearers; others have no obvious correlations and require more lateral creative thinking before connections can be made. This parable appears to be a different kind again, in which the feast may or may not be the messianic banquet, the king/lord may or may not be God (in my view probably not), but the guests may well be the Jewish leaders with whom Jesus is conversing at this point in Matthew. Indeed, the story may be making a deliberate allusion to the episode in Josephus about the reign of Hezekiah (which may well have been in folk history even though it was not written down at this point) to draw closer attention to the way the leaders had over time rejected God's call to them.

In other words, just because we can make a one-to-one correlation between one group of characters in the parables and a particular group of people, it does not follow that all other details should match up too. It is possible that Jesus exaggerated certain aspects of the story disproportionately (such as the violence and the vengeance) in order to shed a greater light on the one correlation that is clear.

... and a person in the wrong clothes

The detail in the story that at first reading causes the greatest discomfort is also the detail that warns us away from a lazy supersessionism inspired by Matthew's displacement parables (on this see above, pp. 44 and 128). If we take this parable as an 'independent story' governed by its own narrative structure, then the harsh treatment of the last-minute guest, punished for wearing the wrong clothes, is so unjust that it is almost impossible to contemplate. But if we accept that, in some parables, the interpretation inserts itself into the story and changes it, then this little episode makes more sense. In this context, the feature of the person in the wrong clothes warns against the newcomers, assuming that because they are the newcomers, brought in to replace the unworthy guests, they automatically deserve a place at the table. The first guests dishonoured their host by deciding not to attend the feast; the second wave of guests were then invited but they still needed to honour the host (in this case by dressing appropriately). New invitees need not assume that they can act dishonourably or lazily just because they have replaced others. They can be cast out too. Displacement was not about being Jewish (that is, supersessionism); it was about response to Jesus – a response that does not appreciate the honour of the invitation offered will evoke the same reaction no matter who you are.

To think about ...

Do we appreciate enough the honour of our place at the table? In what ways might we be guilty of wearing the wrong garments to the feast?

---

41 The ten young women (Matthew 25.1–13)

On one level this parable is supremely straightforward – there were ten young women: five brought oil in their lamps, five didn't. The bridegroom was later than expected and by then those without oil had left to get some – but had been shut out of the feast by the time they returned. All very straightforward, with the clear implication that those listening – and, by extension, us – should have the equivalent of oil with us ready for the return whenever it happens. So far so good. The nub of the parable is for us to reflect on what functions as 'oil' in our lives so that we are ready. Perhaps this might be not putting off responding to Christ. Perhaps it is not waiting until tomorrow to change our attitudes or actions. It is an important question and well worth spending time with.

Matthew 25.1–13

¹*Then the kingdom of the heavens will be like ten young women who took their own lamps and went out to meet the bridegroom.*

²Five of them were stupid and five were sensible. ³The stupid ones took their lamps but did not take oil with them. ⁴But the sensible ones took oil in a container with their lamps. ⁵The bridegroom took his time and they all became drowsy and fell asleep. ⁶In the middle of the night there was a shout, 'Look! The Bridegroom. Come out to meet him.' ⁷Then all the young women woke up, and they arranged their lamps. ⁸The stupid ones said to the sensible ones, 'Give us a bit of your oil because our lamps have gone out.' ⁹The sensible ones answered and said, 'On no account, there will not be enough for us and for you. Instead go to the sellers and buy some for yourself.' ¹⁰They went away to buy some and the bridegroom came. Those who were ready went into the wedding with him and the door was shut. ¹¹The rest of the young women came later and said, 'Lord, Lord, open [the door] to us.' ¹²But he answered and said, 'I say to you – and this is true – I do not know you.' ¹³Be vigilant, therefore, because you do not know the day or the hour.

Interesting words …

- v. 1: the word that I've translated 'young women' has caused great controversy. The word often implies virginity (it certainly does in Matthew 1.23), but if it does here it does so only indirectly. A *parthenos* was a young, unmarried woman (maybe between the ages of 12 and 14, since marriage took place as young women entered puberty); in contrast, the bridegroom would probably have been between 18 and 20. In the case of a *parthenos*, virginity and her age are, therefore, assumed. The old English word 'maiden' might be the best translation as it implies the same things; the only problem is that we don't really use it today. Some prefer to use the word 'girl', but I have avoided it as it can have a derogatory edge to it.
- v. 2: the words for 'stupid' and 'sensible' are *mōros* ('stupid' or 'foolish') and *phronimos* ('wise' or 'sensible'). These are the same words used to describe other characters in the parables, such as slaves and house builders.
- v. 6: although 'middle of the night' is sometimes translated as 'midnight' it is unlikely that the time was that precise. The point is that it was very late and dark – more detail was not needed.
- v. 7: the word 'arrange' – *kosmeo* – or 'make to look nice' is related to our word for 'cosmetics'. Whether it means 'trim' or something else depends on whether you think they have torches or indoor lamps (see discussion below).

- v. 11: the Greek just says 'open to us', but we need to add 'the door' to make the sentence make sense.
- v. 13: although the verb *grēgoreō* can mean 'stay awake' as well as 'be vigilant' or 'keep watch', it is clear that it does not mean 'stay awake' in this context, since all ten young women fell asleep. Their sleeping was not problematic; all that was expected in this instance was being prepared when they woke up.

Weddings at the time of Jesus

The problem with this parable – if you go beyond the very superficial reading noted above – is that as soon as you begin to ask any level of question about its internal logic, it begins to break down. Nearly all scholars are agreed that we don't know enough about the context of how local weddings in Galilee or Judea took place in the first century AD. What little we do know tells us that betrothals would have taken place in the bride's father's house and would have involved both ceremony and celebration. The bride then stayed at her father's house until the wedding. This could have been an extended period of time – often while they waited for the bride to be old enough to get married (that is, to have started puberty at somewhere between 12 and 14).

'Bridesmaids'

The ten young women in this story would have been too young to be married so would probably be around 11 or 12 years old. It is very unhelpful to call them 'bridesmaids' as this conjures up a modern context of smart dresses, flowers and a range of ages. These would have been young women/girls and this seems important in the narrative – that *any* of them thought ahead to bring oil is, at this age, impressive.

At the wedding itself, probably what would have happened was that following a feast at the bride's father's house, the couple would be accompanied with torches and a procession to the bridegroom's house. The celebration that followed would have lasted anything up to seven days; the wedding feast alluded to in other parables was probably the opening feast on the first day. This raises the question of why the 'young women' were waiting for the bridegroom and were not, instead, at the bride's father's house. If they were not, it is unlikely that they were 'bridesmaids' in any form that we might recognize. Another option is that the term 'wedding' was being used loosely, and the young women were with the bride at the bride's father's house and were awaiting the arrival of the groom at the pre-wedding feast, rather than at the groom's house. If you choose this option you then have to explain why it was the groom and not the bride's father who refused entrance to the five who had to go and buy oil. It is probably also worth noting that the bride herself is not mentioned at all in this story; she is no more than an implicit character throughout.

The passage in context

This parable appears in a string (with the reliable and wicked slaves immediately before it, and the parable of the talents and the sheep and the goats after it) that all, in slightly different ways, reflect on how we wait. This one focuses on the strand of making the right preparations so that we are fully prepared.

Lamps/torches

One of the oddest features of this passage is the lamps that the young women have. The Greek word *lampas* refers to a generic source of light and could have meant either torches – which were sticks with oil-soaked cloth tied on to the end and that would have been used to light the path from the bride's father's house to the groom's – or indoor lamps, with a reservoir for oil into which a wick would have been inserted to burn.

- On one level the former – torches – makes more sense as they would then have gone out with the torches to meet the procession or the bridegroom and accompany them back. The problem is that torches only burn for around 15 minutes, so it is hard to imagine how they could have been lit but be 'going out' (Matthew

25.8) only when the groom arrived much later than expected.

- This detail – of the lamps going out – suggests they had indoor oil lamps but begs the question of why they had brought lamps at all. If they were indoor lamps, they would have spilled if you tried to carry them in a procession, and it is unlikely they would have needed to have kept them lit while in someone else's house because the householder would have had their own lamps.

Another odd feature is the suggestion that those without oil went out to buy more in the middle of the night when no shops would be open at all. The implication must be that in a local setting the sellers would have been persuaded to get up and help if that is what was needed.

As with a number of the parables, this parable has its own internal logic, which does not cohere with everyday life in the first century any more than it does with that in the twenty-first. We are invited into the world of the parable with the suggestion that we shouldn't press the details too far because if we do it begins to fall apart.

The selfishness of the sensible young women

One of the grating elements of the story is the selfishness of those who had oil and their refusal to help those who had none. As with a number of the other parables, it is probably important to recognize that this one does not depict the kingdom in its entirety but is instead a description of the world as it is. The reaction of the sensible young women is probably what would happen in such a scenario if it had really happened; all that is being recommended is being sensible and bringing oil, not the rest of the behaviour.

Again we see that this is a parable in which one element correlates with a lesson to be learnt, but other things do not fit so easily (and the more we press it to make sense the less it does). What is more, the parable is slightly unwieldy, the details hard to pin down – even within the narrative itself, let alone in a one-to-one correlation with reality. This is a single-point parable – be prepared. The rest is harder to tie down.

To think about ...

Is the oil in the parable something specific that we should make sure we are well stocked with, or a general recommendation for preparedness?

Reflection

People love to state that 'Society today is not like it used to be'. I can't decide whether it is encouraging or depressing that the reality appears to be that it is exactly like it used to be – exactly as it always was. People treat one another with as little respect and honour as they always have: elbowing each other out of the way to get the best spot; inviting people to dinner who will be 'useful' but no one else; saying that they will come to an event and then pulling out at the last moment; and refusing to share what they have when other people need it too.

It seems that society today *is* as it has always been. This should cause us to pause and reflect. If the traits of human nature that err towards greed run as deeply through our society as they have always done, then how should we respond? It seems to me that the parables of Jesus speak as vibrantly today as ever – we may not recline to eat, have oxen to care for or oil lamps to trim, but apart from that not much has changed, and Jesus' voice of challenge has as much to say today as it always did.

PART 3

Money: Having It and Lacking It

In a way, most of Jesus' parables are indirectly about money. Throughout this book we have met subsistence farmers struggling to get by; wealthy landowners with large vineyards; masters with their slaves who look after the property; shepherds with far more sheep than they can keep count of; a woman who searches desperately for a single coin; and wealthy kings who throw lavish banquets. Money populates the backdrop of so many parables but only a few are directly about it – either what it means to have it or not to have it. The next two chapters look at those parables that focus either on having money, or the effect of not having it, on the lives and actions of the key characters in the stories.

10

Money: Having It

Introduction

Although a good number of the key characters in parables are wealthy (whether they be wealthy landowners or kings) – and are not censured for being so – the wealthy characters in the parables in this chapter are all criticized by Jesus not just for their wealth but also for what they do with it. Each of the three parables sees wealth (and the selfish use of it) as having a direct impact either on entering the kingdom at all or on what will happen after death.

42 Bigger barns (Luke 12.13–21)

At first glance this parable seems harsh. A man who has too much grain for his existing barn builds a bigger barn to hold it all – and then is called an idiot by God. The key point of the parable, however, is that God's economics and human economics are not the same, and the man has, crucially, forgotten a whole category – God's accounting – in his evaluation of wealth.

Luke 12.13–21

¹³*Someone in the crowd said, 'Teacher, tell my brother to divide the inheritance with me.' ¹⁴He said to him, 'Friend, who made me judge or arbiter over you?' ¹⁵He said to them, 'See! Keep watch over all greediness, because someone's life does not thrive because of their possessions.' ¹⁶Then he told them a parable, saying: 'The land of a certain wealthy person was very productive. ¹⁷And he pondered to himself saying, "What shall I do? I do not have anywhere to gather the crops into." ¹⁸And he said, "I will do this. I will tear*

down my barns and builder bigger ones. And there I will gather in all the grain and my good things. ¹⁹I will say to my life, you have many good things stored up for many years, relax, eat, drink and celebrate." ²⁰But God said to him, "Idiot, this very night your life will be demanded from you. Those things you have prepared, whose will they be?" ²¹Thus it will be for those saving up for themselves but are not wealthy towards God.'

Interesting words ...

- v. 14: when Jesus addressed the person from the crowd he said *anthrōpe*, or 'person'. There is not an easy word in English to substitute here.
- v. 14: the word translated 'arbiter' is *meristēs*, which is connected to the word 'divide' – such a person would ensure the division was fair.
- v. 19: the word translated 'life' is *psuchē*, sometimes translated 'soul', but as 'soul' has very different meanings in Hebrew and Greek thinking, it is often wiser to avoid using the word 'soul' too much. *Psuchē* appears again in verse 20, where 'life' seems to be a better translation.
- v. 20: the word translated here as 'idiot' is *aphrōn*, which means 'without sense'.

A shared inheritance

The scenario briefly described at the start of this passage would have been a familiar one in Galilee and Judea. What appears to be the case is that a father has died and left the inheritance to his sons, and the elder of those sons is following the practice, common in this period, of insisting that the property stay together and that they farm it or look after it together (it is interesting to reflect on this in the light of the parable of the lost son(s), where the younger son not only got his money early, he also split the property). The younger son here also wants to split his property from his brother's and be independent.

Not splitting an inheritance

The first-century Jewish historian Josephus made mention of the Jewish practice of not splitting an inheritance in his account of the *Jewish War* 2.122:

> These men are despisers of riches, and so very communicative as raises our admiration. Nor is there any one to be found among them who hath more than another; for it is a law among them, that those who come to them must let what they have be common to the whole order - insomuch, that among them all there is no appearance of poverty or excess of riches, but every one's possessions are intermingled with every other's possessions: and so there is, as it were, one patrimony among all the brethren.

It appears that the custom, when someone wanted to split their inheritance against the will of the elder brother, was to ask a rabbi to arbitrate for them. The younger brother, here, treated Jesus as a rabbi who might make a judgement for him.

On having lots

The parable features a person who starts off being wealthy but who worries about his ability to store all that he has. One might wonder why he doesn't either just sell the crop immediately or build another barn adjoining the first, rather than tearing it down and building a new barn. The answer maybe twofold:

- At harvest time the market was saturated with others selling their crops, so the price would be lower. This man intended to keep his crops until there was less competition and the price would be higher.
- The land was of such a quality that, in future, it would produce bumper crops again, so the man did not want to waste this land by covering it with too many barns.

If this is true, then Jesus is portraying a shrewd businessman who was used to getting maximum returns for what he had. As a result,

Jesus shows him as an example of the greed he warned against in verse 15.

The passage in context

This parable can be found between two passages that contain instructions not to worry (Luke 12.4–12 and 22–34). This parable, therefore, illustrates these two commands. We should not worry because those things we normally worry about, like money, are not what is important in life.

Wealthy towards God

The end of the parable adds a clinching feature to this scenario. The wealthy man featured was clearly shrewd and had factored in everything he needed to ensure that his wealth would grow. He had simply forgotten to factor in one key element – wealth towards God. The word used for 'will be demanded from you' – *apaiteō* – can be used for the calling in of a loan. What the wealthy man had not accounted for is that his life was on loan from God and could be recalled at any time. During his life he had neither located his life in relation to God nor used his wealth to care for those around him; this, Jesus stated, was a massive miscalculation.

The question the end of the passage leaves us with is: what does 'being wealthy towards God' entail? The answer appears to be relatively simple and found in the summary of the law (love of God and love of neighbour), neither of which can be discerned in this man's life.

To think about ...

What do you think being wealthy towards God entails? What might the markers of this kind of wealth be?

---

43 Camels and eyes of needles (Matthew 19.24; Mark 10.24b–25; Luke 18.25)

This short parable is both vivid and challenging. It is worth reflecting on why, as will become clear below, so much effort has been spent attempting to make it less challenging.

Mark 10.24b–25

²⁴*Jesus said to them again, 'Children, how hard it is to enter the kingdom of God. ²⁵It is easier for a camel to pass through the eye of a needle than for a rich person to enter the kingdom of God.'*

Interesting words …

- v. 24: 'children' – *teknon* – is often used as a form of address from elders to their youngers. This is the only place in Mark where Jesus calls his disciples 'children'; he might have done so here because of their distress at what he was saying about wealth and the kingdom.
- v. 25: *trumalia* or 'hole' is the word normally translated 'eye' here; a *raphis* is a needle.

On impossibility

Although Jesus' saying here is brief, interpretation of it has not been. Two attempts in particular have been made to make this short parable less impossible.

- One suggestion is that Jesus didn't mean *camēlos* ('camel') but *camilos* ('rope') – still very difficult, but maybe slightly less impossible than passing a camel through the eye of a needle.
- Another suggestion is that the *camēlos* was the small gate in the larger double gate of a city wall. People on foot would pass through this small gate without the need to open the larger gate, but a camel train would require the larger one. Preachers since the nineteenth century have made much of this and of the need for the camel to take off its packs and go through this gate on

its knees. It's a great image and you can see why it became so popular – the problem is there is no evidence for it whatsoever. To quote Kenneth Bailey: 'There is not the slightest shred of evidence for this identification. This door has not in any language been called the needle's eye, and is not so called today' (K. E. Bailey, *Through Peasant Eyes*, Grand Rapids, MI: Eerdmans, 1980, p. 166).

The passage in context

In all three Gospels, the brief parable about the camel passing through the eye of a needle is found in the context of the conversation between Jesus and the rich young ruler who struggled with the thought of giving up his wealth in order to follow Jesus.

The key feature of both of these attempts is that interpreters were trying to make the scenario less impossible. The point is that it was impossible – there is a similar saying in the Talmud (*Babylonian Berakhot*, 55b), which likewise, when citing something impossible, talks about an elephant passing through the eye of a needle.

The challenge of this passage is not only what Jesus originally said – that it is impossible for a rich person to enter the kingdom of God – but the lengths that subsequent commentators have gone to argue that this is not what he really meant. If this doesn't pull us up short and force us to think again, very little will.

To think about ...

Why do we try so hard to make this parable less impossible than it is?

---

44 The rich man and Lazarus (Luke 16.19–31)

There are some who claim that this is not a parable but, in fact, a historical story about actual people. It is an idea that has been very popular among preachers for many years. The problem is that Luke presents it as a parable with his characteristic opening phrase 'a certain person ...' and locates it in a string of other parables – the lost sheep, the lost coin, the lost son(s), the shrewd manager, and then this one. Also, the end of the parable would be hard for someone to know as 'historical fact' and makes far more sense if told as a parable.

Luke 16.19–31

[19]*There was a certain person who was wealthy. He dressed in purple and linen and feasted magnificently every day.* [20]*A poor man – by the name of Lazarus – was thrown by his gate, covered in sores.* [21]*He craved to fill himself from what fell from the table of the rich man, and even dogs came and licked his ulcers.* [22]*The poor man died and was carried away by the angels to the lap of Abraham. The rich man died and was buried.*

[23]*And in Hades, where he was being tormented, he lifted up his eyes and saw Abraham far away, with Lazarus on his lap.* [24]*And he cried out, 'Father, Abraham, have mercy on me and send Lazarus to dip the tip of his finger into water and cool my tongue because I am suffering in these flames.'* [25]*Abraham said, 'Child, remember that you received your good things in your life and Lazarus, likewise, evil things, but now he is comforted while you are suffering.* [26]*And besides this, between us and you a great chasm has been set up so that those wanting to step over from here to you are not able, nor are they able to pass through from you to here.'* [27]*He said, 'I ask you therefore, father, to send him to the house of my father.* [28]*For I have five brothers, so that he might warn them solemnly so that they won't also come to this place of torment.'* [29]*Abraham said, 'They have Moses and the prophets, let them listen to them.'* [30]*But he said, 'No, father Abraham, but if someone were to go from the dead they would repent.'* [31]*He said to him, 'If they do not listen to Moses and the prophets, they will not be persuaded even if someone were to rise from the dead.'*

Interesting words ...

- v. 19: the word for 'purple' – *porphura* – can refer either to marine snails or the dye collected from them. Also known as Tyrian purple, it is thought that this purple dye was used by the Phoenicians as early as 1570 BC. It was particularly sought after in the ancient world because the dye became brighter with time rather than more faded. It was very expensive because it was difficult to make. The word *bussos* can refer either to flax or the material made from it. Purple and linen were a sign of extravagant living and were worn by kings and those who wanted to flaunt their wealth.
- v. 21: the food that fell from the table does not refer to food that 'fell off' but to the bread that people would use to wipe their greasy hands on (since they did not use napkins), which would then be thrown under the table.
- v. 22: *kolpos* refers normally to the front of a woman and can mean either her bosom or her lap, or the fold of material that falls in front of both. The implication of it is one of being embraced.
- v. 26: the two words normally translated 'cross over' are different – the first is *diabainō* and the second *diaperaō*. The first means to 'step over'; the second is to 'pass through'. There is not much significance in the differences and they might simply have been used for variety.
- v. 28: 'warn solemnly' translates *diamarturomai*, which is an intensive form of the phrase 'to bear witness'.

On blessing and cursing

At the time of Jesus this was a radical reversal parable. It was widely assumed that wealth signified someone who was blessed by God. The wealthier they were, the more blessed. Conversely, those who were poor and/or ill (they often went together) were cursed. An example of this view is the question asked of Jesus by the people enquiring about the man born blind (John 9.2). Add to this the importance of burial for a 'good death'. In Hebrew, burial was vital so that those around knew that this had been a good death. The rich man was buried and we are left to assume that Lazarus was not. It would therefore have come as a great surprise to Jesus' original audience to discover that, after death, the rich man was cursed and Lazarus was blessed.

The passage in context

This parable joins those that very clearly are spoken against a group of people – in this instance, the Pharisees who, Luke tells us, love money (16.14). They, then, are clearly meant to understand themselves as represented by the 'rich man' in the parable. There is no evidence that the Pharisees as a group were especially wealthy – unlike the Sadducees, who were largely drawn from the ruling families – and the emphasis is more on their love of money than on how much they had.

It is worth noting that this outcome is hinted at even at the start of the parable, where the rich man remains unnamed throughout and the poor man is called by his name – Lazarus. It is important to resist the common practice of calling this parable 'Dives and Lazarus'. Dives simply means 'rich man' in Latin, but its usage implies that the rich man is in fact named, whereas the whole point is that he is not. The name Lazarus, which is a shortened version of Eliezer and in Hebrew means 'God helps', was very common at the time of Jesus and there is no reason to connect this Lazarus with the one raised in John 11.

Links between this parable and the lost son(s)

There are a few intriguing links between these two parables. In both, Lazarus and the younger son respectively yearn to be filled with food and both have contact with impure animals (both Lazarus' sores, and the dogs that licked them, were 'impure' according to the purity laws). Some also suggest that there is a link between Abraham and the father. Beyond that, however, the main theme of each of these parables is quite different, other than the love and compassion shown to both the younger son and Lazarus.

Life after death

This parable presents an unusual model of life after death within the Bible. The usual model is the expectation that, after death, those who have died await judgement at the end time and then are raised. This model has the judgement made immediately upon death and the reward or punishment allotted straightaway. It is also interesting to note that rather than a popular Christian notion of the good going to heaven (above earth) and the evil going to hell (below earth), both Lazarus and the rich man are in the same place (Hades), with only a chasm between them – albeit a chasm that cannot be crossed. This does not automatically rule out the more usual biblical understanding of resurrection at the end times; the fates of Lazarus and the rich man may be temporary until the final judgement, when they will be made permanent.

One of the more frustrating features of the parable is that it does not make clear *why* the rich man is consigned to suffering, and Lazarus to the lap of Abraham. We might have wished that it was made clear that the rich man's punishment was due to his lavish and selfish use of wealth, or his lack of care for Lazarus, or his lack of wealth towards God, but none of this is identified. In the same way we are not told if Lazarus was especially righteous (despite the fact that he was impure because of his sores and the dogs licking him), or had acted generously in other ways. This is a radical reversal parable that calls to mind Mary's song (the Magnificat, Luke 1.46–55): the rich have been brought low and the poor raised up. The threads are left hanging and we need to reflect on them, allowing ourselves to feel the full discomfort that they suggest.

They will not listen 'even if someone were to rise from the dead'

Luke's Gospel is dotted with irony, as though we, the readers, are being ushered into a private joke that we can understand from our vantage point even though the original characters could not. The conversation between Abraham and the rich man is one of those occasions. We know that someone will rise from the dead and those who currently are not listening will not listen then either.

It is interesting to observe the point that Abraham asserts: that the rich man ought to have been able to work out what he needed to know from the law and the prophets.

The law and the prophets

The phrase 'the law and the prophets' is one that appears time and time again throughout the Gospels. It is probable that it is a specific phrase that denotes the first two of the three collections of books in the Hebrew Bible: the first five books of the Bible (Torah, law) and Joshua, Judges, 1 and 2 Samuel, 1 and 2 Kings, the three major and twelve minor prophets (the prophets). The regular lack of mention of the 'writings' (the third collection containing books such as the Psalms, Esther, Proverbs) is intriguing.

This may contribute to our thinking about what the rich man did wrong. The parable indicates that he showed neither love of God nor love of neighbour (in this case, the neighbour right outside his house), but it still challenges us to interrogate our own actions to ask where, come the great reversal, we might find ourselves.

To think about ...

What do we need to learn from the themes of reversal here?

Reflection

Anyone who has read the parables in this chapter and does not feel profoundly uncomfortable should probably go back and read them again. Conversations about money and how much we have are not ones, culturally, we like to engage in. The topic makes us defensive, and sometimes even aggressive. But it is hard to talk about Jesus' attitude to wealth and wealthy people without at least asking ourselves the question of whether we are like a camel trying to fit through the eye of a needle or like the rich man oblivious of what the future holds for him.

We can counter these parables with the other parables we have explored earlier in the book that depict wealthy people without criticism, but eventually we have to read and reflect deeply on the ones in this chapter. I have no easy answers for what we do with them other than to allow them to disturb and discomfort us, and then to ask ourselves whether we might want to live differently.

11

Money: Lacking It

Introduction

One of the surprising issues to note in Jesus' parables is that, while the critique of those who have wealth but keep it to themselves is as fierce as we might expect, there are far fewer parables that focus on poverty. Indeed, of the five parables in this chapter, two are about people discovering unexpected wealth and one is about a money-lender who cancels debt. Perhaps the daily grind of living with little or no money was so hard that inviting people to think creatively from such a perspective would have been difficult.

45 A moneylender who forgives debts (Luke 7.41–43)

One of the striking features of Jesus' parables is the number of times lending money with interest is mentioned as though it were a natural part of everyday life. The Old Testament forbade the lending of money with interest to fellow Jews, and the Talmud, a later collection of rabbinic sayings, states that the borrower as well as the lender break the commandment if they borrow or lend with interest. It was permissible to lend to non-Jews but there is nothing in this or the other parables to suggest that the characters were not Jewish. As a result, it is likely that these parables reveal the reality of everyday life – a reality that made lending and borrowing at interest necessary – rather than the ideal that prohibited it.

Luke 7.41–43

[41]'*There were two people who owed money to a moneylender. One owed five hundred denarii, the other fifty.* [42]*When they were unable to pay he let them both off. Therefore which of them loved him more?'* [43]*Simon answered, 'I assume it was the one forgiven more.' He said to him, 'You have judged correctly.'*

Interesting words ...

- v. 41: the word for 'owed money' is a noun describing the people (*chreopheiletēs*) – money owers or debtors. Literally the verse reads 'There were two debtors to a money lender.' The word only occurs twice in the New Testament, here and in the parable of the shrewd manager (Luke 16.1–12).
- v. 42: the verb *charizō* (translated here as 'let them off') is connected to the noun *charis*, 'grace', which means to act graciously towards another or to forgive.
- v. 43: in Simon's answer – that is, the assumption that the one who loved more was the one forgiven more – the word *hupolambanō* means 'to suppose', 'to accept' or 'to assume'. The tone implies that Simon is aware he has been caught in a trap, but must answer as Jesus wants.

The passage in context

This parable is directly embedded in the conversation between Jesus and Simon the Pharisee in Luke 7. Simon the Pharisee objected to Jesus allowing himself to be touched by a sinner. This parable is told by Jesus to Simon to illustrate why the woman will love more extravagantly than Simon and his friends will.

The response Jesus assumes from the debtors supposes that we are already reading the case of the woman's forgiven sins into the parable. Loving a moneylender because they forgave a debt seems an excessive response. You might expect the debtors to be over the moon with gratitude but not, necessarily, to express love. The love – and the woman's expression of it by anointing Jesus – reframes the whole episode. She acted not because she should, but out of a deep and profound love; Simon the Pharisee, we discover in verse 44, did not even do what he should. As with a few of the parables, the application of the parable drives the shaping of the narrative itself.

To think about ...

How much have you been forgiven?

---

46 Hidden treasure (Matthew 13.44)

The practice of hiding treasure is one that can be found in all societies that do not have a robust and trustworthy banking system. If there is nowhere to keep your money safe, then the best course of action is to hide it and hope that no one else finds it. This parable is given added frisson by the fact that, in Matthew's version of the parable of the talents (25.14–30), the slave buried his talent in the ground to keep it 'safe'. This parable reveals how risky that course of action was – someone might have found it and found a way to steal it. The scenario, cleverly painted in just one sentence, is of a person – the implication is that they were not well off since they needed to sell everything they had to buy the field – who finds someone else's buried treasure, re-hides it, and then rushes off to buy the field so that they could then own the treasure as well.

Matthew 13.44

[44]*The kingdom of the heavens is like treasure hidden in a field, which a person finds and hides. With great joy they go and sell everything that they have and buy that field.*

Interesting words ...

• v. 44: the word for the treasure being hidden in a field (*kruptō*) is the same as the one describing what the person who finds it does – that is, they hide it.

But is it moral?

The morality of this person's actions is, at best, dubious. We are left to assume from the parable that the owner was unaware of the treasure buried in their field. This means that it was probably the hard-earned cash of someone too poor to look after it in any other way; a wealthy person would have had a strong box guarded by slaves. Someone who had no other option but to bury it in someone else's field was clearly poor. This parable, then, depicts ruthlessness and therefore may well be seen as akin to Luke's parable of the shrewd manager (16.1–12), in which the manager was equally ruthless in attempting to achieve what he wanted.

To think about ...

Given the dubious morality of this parable, in what way is the kingdom like this?

---

47 The valuable pearl (Matthew 13.45–46)

This parable makes more sense when you know that pearls were of much greater value in the ancient world than they are now, and were held more precious than diamonds. A pearl merchant would have been someone on the lookout for the biggest margin between the buying price and the selling price. Though not quite as ruthless as in the previous parable, the implication is that the merchant sought a great profit on his purchase (hence his willingness to sell all he has), and therefore might not have paid as fair a price to the seller as he should have done.

Matthew 13.45–46

[45]*Again the kingdom of the heavens is like a person who is a merchant in search of fine pearls.* [46]*When he found a very valuable pearl, he went away, sold all he had and bought it.*

Interesting words ...

- v. 45: the word for 'fine' is *kalos*, which is used often in parables to refer to things that are not just good, but noble, precious and beautiful.

The passages in context

This parable and the one that precedes it – the hidden treasure – are in a run of three at the end of Matthew's long parables chapter (chapter 13). This one and the hidden treasure clearly go together, with their emphasis on the joy evoked when one finds something valuable. The third parable is the parable of the net, which fits better with the wheat and the weeds than these other two.

These two parables – like numerous others that we have explored in this book – are not exemplars of good behaviour. There is nothing in them to suggest that this is what Jesus thought would be the right way to act in everyday life. Instead, the point of both parables is that if we are prepared to act in that way for mere treasure or precious stones, then how might we react when faced with the most precious thing of all – the kingdom of the heavens? It is striking in both parables that their protagonists' enthusiasm caused them to sell all they had; this may be what is in mind here. If, as we observed in the previous chapter, those with wealth cannot enter the kingdom of God, then in our enthusiasm to enter the kingdom we should do what both characters in these parables did and sell all we own.

To think about ...

What would make you sell all you had?

201

48 A friend in need (Luke 11.5–8)

This is another honour/shame parable. The point of it is that to receive a guest without proper hospitality would bring shame not only on the person but on the whole household. The threat of this shame causes the person to go to his neighbour and act 'shamelessly' in front of them, since that would be less shaming than not feeding a visiting guest who had dropped in at midnight. It seems that a sudden visit at midnight is not unlikely since people often travelled by night to avoid the worst of the heat of the day.

Luke 11.5–8

5And he said to them, 'Who among you has a friend, and if you go to them at midnight and say to them: "Friend, lend me three loaves, 6because a friend of mine has arrived from the road, and I do not have anything to set before them." 7And he answers from inside, "Do not cause me any trouble. The door is already locked up and my children are with me in bed. I am not able to get up and give you anything." 8I tell you even if they will not get up because they are a friend; they will rouse themselves and give you whatever you need because of your shamelessness.'

Interesting words …

- v. 5: the grammar is a little clunky. The question is 'who among you …' but then changes to the third person; as a result it is easier to put it into the second person, 'you'.
- v. 5: in previous parables 'the middle of the night' has been somewhat vague – here the word *mesonuktion* does mean 'midnight'.
- v. 7: *kopos* can mean 'beating' or 'suffering', but can also mean 'fatigue' or 'trouble'.
- v. 8: the word for 'get up' changes from *anistēmi* in verse 7 and the first half of verse 8, to *egeirō* in the second half of verse 8, which has more of a sense of 'awaken' or 'arouse'.
- v. 8: the word for 'shamelessness' – *anaideia* – means lack of proper restraint; here, your willingness to behave improperly in order to honour your friend.

On bread

The slight anomaly of the parable is that bread was baked and consumed daily; the hypothetical scenario, then, is that the friend might not have consumed all their bread the day before. Three loaves is the usual amount of bread that a family might consume at an evening meal.

The passage in context

This parable is embedded in the centre of Jesus' teaching on prayer. The disciples asked Jesus to teach them to pray, to which Jesus responded with the Lord's Prayer (Luke 11.1–4); this parable follows and then the command to ask and it will be given (Luke 11.9–13). How then do we pray? As though our honour depended on it.

The question that arises is, in respect of the disciples' request that Jesus should teach them to pray, what does this parable tell us? The popular answer is that Jesus is advising persistence in prayer. This, however, may confuse this parable with the final one in this chapter – the persistent widow, also from Luke's Gospel. While persistence is certainly a theme, at the heart of the parable another theme may be even more important. The key element of the story is the willingness of the person asking for bread to embarrass themselves socially in order to get what they need. What they needed was far more important to them than looking good – so persistence is a theme, but it is persistence fuelled by knowing the importance of that for which you pray. If I were to give that a name, it would be 'wholeheartedness'.

To think about ...

What is so important to you that you would be willing to embarrass yourself publicly to make sure you get it?

---

49 The persistent widow (Luke 18.1–8)

In a few parables, we have noted already that one option for understanding them is 'if this happens with this ... how much more will God ...'? So far most of these kinds of parable have done this subtly, leaving us to wonder whether or not the key character is God; this parable, though, makes it very explicit. Here we meet a judge – probably located in a small town where he is the only source of justice. He is unjust and uncaring; he does not even fear God so there is little hope of his changing. In a single brushstroke the parable ensures that we know that the judge is thoroughly unfit for his job.

Luke 18.1–8

¹*Then he told them a parable that they must pray at all times and not lose heart.* ²*He said: 'There was a certain judge in a certain city who was neither in awe of God nor did he have regard for people.* ³*In that city there was a widow who kept coming to him saying, "Give me justice against my opponent."* ⁴*For a time he did not want to but after these things he said to himself, "Even though I do not fear God nor have any regard for people,* ⁵*because this widow is causing me trouble I will decide her case, so that she does not finally wear me down with her coming."'* ⁶*The Lord said, 'Listen to what the unjust judge says.* ⁷*Will not God give justice to his chosen ones who cry to him day and night? Will he be slow to help them?* ⁸*I say to you that he will give justice to them swiftly. Except, when the Son of Man comes, will he find faith on earth?'*

Interesting words ...

- v. 2: the word for 'have regard' (*entrepō*) means 'to turn about' or 'towards'. In terms of people, you would turn towards people to give them regard or respect.
- v. 2: 'people' translates *anthrōpos*, but the Greek noun is in the singular – he does not have regard for 'a person'.
- v. 3: the verb used of the widow going to the judge is in the imperfect which, in Greek, implies ongoing action, meaning that she went more than once or twice.
- v. 3: the verb for 'decide the case' is *ekdikeō* ('decide a case', 'avenge'

or 'punish'). It can mean 'give justice' in the sense to decide in someone's favour, or it can mean just decide it either way. The end of the parable makes it clear how it is being used here. The word for opponent is *antidikos* – that is, the person against you in a law case.

- v. 4: the Greek literally says 'after these things' but doesn't say what things – the best explanation is that it is the number of times.
- v. 5: 'wear me down' translates *hupōpiazō*. The verb comes from a boxing match and means to strike under the eye and therefore to give them a black eye. There seems little in the text to suggest that the judge feared that the widow would actually give him a black eye, so it is more likely that the verb is used metaphorically here to mean 'to bruise' or 'wear down'.

A remarkable character

Although the text does not say so explicitly, it hints that the judge also took bribes and that the widow's inability to get him to take any notice of her was because she had no money with which to bribe him. The Old Testament makes it clear that widows and orphans were the most vulnerable in society and therefore should be given the greatest care and protection. The contrast set up by this parable, then, is between the male judge who sat at the centre of power and the widow who sat outside power entirely. At the time of Jesus the justice system was male, and it was expected that suits would be brought to the courts by male relatives. The fact that the widow was forced to bring it showed that she was alone in the world. The judge had total power; the widow had none.

On justice and judges

Justice and impartiality were vital expectations of a judge in the Old Testament. See, for example, Jehoshaphat's speech to judges he had just appointed:

> Consider what you are doing, for you judge not on behalf of human beings but on the LORD's behalf; he is with you in giving judgement. Now, let the fear of the LORD be upon you; take care what you do, for there is no perversion of justice with the LORD our God, or partiality, or taking of bribes. (2 Chronicles 19.6–7)

Those in search of strong female characters in the New Testament often overlook the persistent widow, but we should not. The expectation of the judge, of the culture in which she lived and possibly also of us the readers, is that as a widow she would be a victim and, once refused help, would do what women were meant to do and give up gracefully. But this widow did not. She never gave up and returned again and again until the judge gave in and granted her justice. It is a remarkable portrayal of determination and worth noting that Jesus approved of it. Even today women like this are often regarded as bossy or shrill, but Jesus made no such judgements. He held up for admiration the conduct of a woman who stood up for herself and fought for justice, which suggests that we should too.

How much more will God ...

We noted above that this parable is set up as a parable of contrast. If an unjust, uncaring judge will eventually act in this way, how much more will a loving and gracious God act? The answer is, of course, infinitely more. There is another strand, however, which loops around this parable and is worth noticing. The parable begins as an exhortation to prayer; it then talks about getting justice; and it ends with Jesus asking if, when the Son of Man comes, he will find faith on earth. The three strands appear to be connected.

When we think about prayer we often think about praying for those things that we care about – our health, our loved ones, our worries – but this does not seem to be what Jesus has in mind here (though he does talk about this kind of prayer elsewhere). The prayer Jesus is talking about here is a fighting for justice and not giving up, and faithfulness is cast as never giving up. The God who is just, and cares for people so much that he can even number the hairs on everyone's head, wants us to cry to him for justice in the world – and never give up.

To think about ...

What should we fight for justice for with the determination of the persistent widow in this parable?

Reflection

The parables about lacking money or other things, like bread, are not really about poverty itself – and certainly not about getting riches when you have none. They are about the emotion one has when we find treasure or the determination we might feel to get what we need even if someone is reluctant to give it. Those two emotions – joy and resolve – are emotions of the kingdom and Jesus challenges us in different ways to ensure that they are a part of our response to the kingdom and all it offers: is the kingdom as precious to us as a treasure trove, and are we as excited about the kingdom as we would be about buried treasure or the most valuable jewel in the world? In the same way, are we prepared to put everything we have on the line and to do anything – sacrificing any status and respect we might have – to fight for justice? Earlier in the chapter I used the word 'wholeheartedness' to refer to the action of the neighbour who needed bread – it seems to be a word that resonates with all the parables in this chapter, and raises the question of how wholehearted we are in our response to the kingdom.

PART 4

Odds and Ends

There are a few parables that don't easily sit with any of the others. This is either because their subject matter is unusual (like John's woman in labour) or because they jump from topic to topic (like Matthew's and Luke's parables on judgement – having specks and planks in the eye and being led by a person who cannot see). They reveal the sheer variety of subject matter that Jesus covers in his teaching, from the games children play in a town centre to what a king might do when going into battle. No subject is too small or too large, too ordinary or too grand, to be included in Jesus' teaching.

12

Parables That Don't Fit Easily Elsewhere

50 A woman in labour (John 16.21–22, 25)

As with a few of the parables we have explored in this book, this passage is only here because Jesus himself called it a parable rather than because we might immediately assume it was one. This is one of those occasions in John when something is called a *paroimia* and therefore becomes a passage for this book.

John 16.21–22, 25

[21]*When a woman is giving birth, she is in pain, because her hour has come. But when she has borne a child she does not remember the distress on account of joy that she has brought a human being into the world.* [22]*And you, therefore, have pain now but I will see you again and your hearts will rejoice and no one will take your joy from you ...* [25]*I have said these things to you in parables.*

Interesting words ...

- v. 21: the verb used of a woman 'giving birth' is *tiktō*, which can be used of either men or women to refer to their bringing a child into the world.
- v. 21: the second verb – 'borne a child' – is *gennaō*, which can also be used both of men and women; it has more of a sense of 'produce'.
- v. 25: 'parables' here comes from the plural of *paroimia*; for more on the meaning of this word, see the Introduction, pp. xviii and xxiii.

On childbirth

Women who have given birth to children may regard this parable of Jesus slightly sceptically. It may be true of some but certainly not all experiences of childbirth. I would say that I did not forget the 'distress' of childbirth in the slightest, but would certainly agree that the joy of my children's births made the distress worth it. It is useful to note, however, that this is not true of all women and that, for some, the distress stays with them for years. If a woman had written this parable it might well have taken a slightly different form.

Nevertheless, the image is a powerful one. It draws heavily on Old Testament ideas of the pain of waiting suffered by God's people as they look for the promised joy (see, for example, Isaiah 21.3 or Micah 4.10). The potency of the image focuses our attention not only on the intensity of the suffering but also on the fact that it is temporary and will pass when the promised outcome appears.

To think about ...

Does all the pain we face in life fall into this category of 'the pain of waiting', or is it a specific kind of pain that Jesus has in mind?

---

51 Specks, planks and the blind (Matthew 7.1–5; Luke 6.37–42)

The striking feature of the string of sayings in Matthew 7.1–5 and Luke 6.37–42 is that they gain their clearest form in the saying about measurement. We will be measured (the implication is by God) using the measure that *we* use to measure other people. The background that seems to lie behind this is the vessel used to measure corn. If you choose a small, measly vessel with which to measure others, that will be the measure used when God judges you. It is a powerful and somewhat unsettling message and picks up something we pray regularly in the Lord's Prayer: 'forgive us our sins as we forgive those who sin against us'. We ask God to forgive us in the same kind of way that we forgive other people – that's enough to send a chill down anyone's spine.

Matthew 7.1–5

[1]*Don't judge so that you aren't judged.* [2]*For you will be judged with the judgement you use to judge, and you will be measured with the measure you measure out.* [3]*Why do you see the small dry stalk in the eye of your brother or sister but you do not notice the beam of wood in your own eye?* [4]*Or why do you say to your sister or brother, 'Let me take the small dry stalk out of your eye', when there's a beam of wood in your own eye.* [5]*Hypocrite! First take the beam of wood out of your own eye and then you will be able to see clearly enough to take the small dry stalk out of your brother's or sister's eye.*

Luke 6.37–42

[37]*Don't judge and you will not be judged; don't pronounce people guilty and you will not be found guilty. Forgive and you will be forgiven.* [38]*Give and it will be given to you. A fine measure, pressed down, shaken together and overflowing will be poured into your lap. For by the measure you measure out, you will be measured in return.*

[39]*He told them this parable, 'Surely a blind person can't guide a blind person? They'll both fall into a pit won't they?* [40]*A pupil is not above the teacher but everyone who is fully trained is like the teacher.* [41]*Why do you see the small dry stalk in the eye of your brother or sister, but you don't notice the beam of wood in your own eye?* [42]*How can you say to your brother or sister, "Brother, sister, allow me to take the small dry stalk out of your eye", while you do not see the beam of wood in your own eye. First take the beam of wood out of your own eye and then you will see clearly to take the small dry stalk out of your brother's or sister's eye.'*

Interesting words ...

Matthew 7:

- v. 3: the word here is 'brother'. Some translations opt for 'neighbour' or 'friend' but they lose the familial sense of the word. I have opted for 'brother or sister' but it does feel a little clunky.
- v. 3: the word often translated 'speck' refers to a small dry thing, like a dry stalk or dry twig. It is likely that in the threshing process it would not be uncommon to get a bit of the stalk from wheat in the eye and that is probably what is being referred to here. The contrast is important since a small dry twig is the smaller version of a large beam of wood.

Luke 6:

- v. 38: the word for 'being measured' (*antimetreō*) makes it clear that the measuring is reciprocal, much more so than Matthew's account, which simply put 'measure' into the passive.
- v. 40: the word translated 'pupil' here is a disciple – and it is being used in the classic sense of someone who learns from a teacher.

On disciples and their teachers

In the order that Luke lays out these sayings, they do not obviously fit together. On further reflection, however, an interesting connection emerges. Luke's version of the passage goes into greater detail than Matthew's about why we should not judge. Three reasons are given:

- First, because God will use the same measurement for judgement on us as we use on others.
- Second, because we do not know everything. We are the disciple and not the teacher, and if we judge, we would be like someone who can't see showing the way to someone else who can't see. We would be likely to fall into a deep, dark pit.
- Third, because in any case we have a huge beam of wood in our eye and can't see clearly enough to judge anyone else.

While Matthew's account has only two of these three reasons, Luke's has all three, each underpinning the opening command that we should not judge others lest we find ourselves judged too.

The passage in context

Luke's setting of this parable places it immediately after the command to 'Be merciful, just as your Father is merciful' (6.36). This gives added sense to the mish-mash of commands here – there is a reason to be merciful, not least because it is advantageous to those of us with beams of wood in our eyes and who therefore cannot see clearly.

The logic of Luke's Gospel suggests that, although it looks as though there are three different sayings here – the command about judgement; the parable about the blind leading the blind; and the parable about stalks and beams – they all combine to make one powerful point, which joins the teaching on judgement with the parable about stalks and beams. As a result, it makes sense to take the passage as one, even though verses 39–40 at first glance don't quite fit with the rest.

It is also interesting to notice that, in Luke's Gospel, this section is followed by the parable of the good and bad fruit. This adds a reflective complexity to what is said here – do not judge others and condemn them for things you don't quite understand, but do be wise and make sure you recognize that what they say and do reflects what is going on deep within them. Kingdom life involves both generosity and wisdom – not condemning others but being able to recognize what is really going on.

Jesus' teaching here is both profoundly sensible – for the reasons laid out here – but also very difficult. It is teaching we would do well to remind ourselves of daily. It is so very easy to slip into the trap of writing others off with a lack of generosity we would not want God to use with us; the trap of looking down on people even though we do not know everything about them that would allow us to evaluate them and their actions fairly; and the trap of criticizing them for something we do ourselves. Jesus' teaching here is spot on and very necessary – though we might wish he had given extra guidance about how to live it out in practice.

Hypocrites

Jesus uses the word 'hypocrite' on numerous occasions in the Gospels (Matthew 6.2, 5, 16; 7.5; 15.7; 22.18; 23.13, 15, 23, 25, 27, 29; 24.51; Mark 7.6; Luke 6.42; 12.56; 13.15), but it occurs far more often in Matthew than in Mark or Luke. It was a word that had a particular resonance in Greek thought. It came from Greek theatre and was the name given to actors (who often wore masks), and therefore were 'pretending' to be what they were not. Calling those in leadership or public office a 'hypocrite' was a profound slander, as it suggested that they were not who they claimed to be. In this passage, although it is important not to make too much of it, it is interesting to note that the word comes from *hypo* ('under') and *krinō* ('judge'). A hypocrite, therefore, was lacking in good judgement.

To think about ...

How good are you at not judging others?

---

52 Children in the town centre (Matthew 11.16–19; Luke 7.31–35)

This is an unusual parable in that it is one of the few that is explicitly making a comparison to 'this generation' – Jesus' own contemporaries – rather than to the kingdom itself.

Matthew 11.16–19

[16]*'But to what shall I liken this generation? It is like young children sitting in the town centre, who call out to one another,* [17]*saying "We played the pipe for you and you did not dance. We sang a sad song and you did not beat your breast." * [18]*For John came neither eating nor drinking, and they said he has a demon;* [19]*the Son of Man came eating and drinking and they said "Look, a gorger and a drunk, a*

friend of tax collectors and sinners." Wisdom is shown to be right by her deeds.'

Interesting words ...

- v. 16: 'compare' is the usual translation of *homoioō*, used to convey 'liken' or 'compare' in many parables.
- v. 16: 'town centre' or 'market square' is *agora* and refers to the place in a town or village where people would gather. The *agora* is where speeches were made and markets held.
- v. 17: 'We played the pipe' translates the verb *auleō*, which refers to the playing of an instrument made from a hollowed-out pipe or tube.
- v. 17: 'We sang a sad song' – this is also a verb, *thrēneō*, and most often refers to singing a lament or a dirge, though it can also mean 'bewail'.
- v. 17: the verb translated 'beat your breast' is very culturally bound and hard to put into modern English. *Koptō* means 'to beat' or 'to strike' and, at funerals, refers to the public mourning that took place when people beat their chests and wailed. We have little with which to compare it today.
- v. 19: the word used for 'shown to be right' is *dikaioō*; it can also be translated as 'to be justified'.

Differences between Matthew and Luke

These passages are very similar in Matthew and Luke, with just a few notable differences:

- Matthew talks of them 'beating their breasts', which was a custom well known in Galilee and Judea in this period for mourning; Luke instead refers to the more Hellenistic practice of 'weeping' (*klaiō*) at a funeral.
- At the end of the passage, wisdom is shown to be right in Matthew 'by her deeds' and in Luke by 'her children'.

The passage in context

In both Matthew and Luke this passage appears in the context of Jesus' comments on John the Baptist after John's disciples had come to visit him: Matthew 11.2-6 focuses on what John thought about Jesus and verses 7-15 show us what Jesus thought about John.

The game

The scenario imagined is a group of young children playing in an open space in the middle of their town or village. The game seems to be that some of the children played and sang and the others were meant to dance or mime their response. The two occasions evoked seem to be a wedding or other kind of celebration where dancing would take place, and a funeral where people would weep and wail and strike themselves with their fists. It is worth noting that men would have danced at weddings whereas women were the chief mourners at funerals. It is a fascinating, if fleeting, glimpse into the games that young children played together at the time of Jesus. The way Jesus spoke about this implies that this was a common game everyone would have recognized. One can imagine children saying 'Let's play weddings and funerals'.

What is more complex is how this parable relates to the context in which 'this generation' is so critical about both John and Jesus because of who they are and how they live. The best option seems to be that Jesus is to be seen as the one piping a celebratory dance and John the one singing a sad song, and 'this generation' are the ones refusing either to join in with the celebration or the lament. This would seem to fit with the surrounding context. If this is right, then the challenge to us is to be people who listen intently to the message of God brought to us – whether a message of joy or one of lament – and are prepared to respond to it wholeheartedly.

Wisdom is justified ...

The final phrase of this parable is somewhat surprising. The personification of wisdom is common in passages such as Proverbs 8.1–31, but it is rare to find this tradition quite so overtly in the

Gospels. Some see Jesus as wisdom (and passages such as John 1.1–18 certainly suggest this), but here this kind of connection does not seem likely given that the passage is about both Jesus and John. The slightly surprising inclusion of this phrase in a context that has not been discussing wisdom at all does suggest that in some form or other (Matthew's or Luke's accounts or both), this was a common saying at the time, which Jesus used to conclude his teaching.

In Proverbs 8.1–31 and allied passages, wisdom is portrayed as being alongside God, assisting in creation and calling people to live well with prudence and intelligence. Her children (Luke) would be all those who listen and respond to her voice; her deeds (Matthew) are likewise seen in those who have listened and responded. First among these are Jesus and John and all that they have said and done, but it also includes those who align themselves with them and their message – very much not 'this generation' who would neither dance nor mourn.

To think about ...

How good are we at listening to God's message and responding to it in either celebration or mourning?

---

53 On building a tower or going into battle (Luke 14.25–33)

These two parables do not even pretend to include examples from the lives of their hearers. Only the wealthiest people would have cause to build a tower to guard their vineyard, and only a king would weigh up the advisability of going into battle. Although many of the parables use examples from everyday living, not all do. These two illustrate that in some instances even Jesus' original hearers had to make an imaginative leap into a context of which they had no direct experience. Although some scholars do suggest that the tower builder/king are to be seen as God, their arguments are not particularly persuasive or widely accepted; these are parables in which we are not expected to locate ourselves in the narrative but to use the narrative to reflect further.

Luke 14.25–33

25 *Huge crowds were travelling with him and he turned to them and said,* 26 *'If anyone comes to me and does not hate their father and mother, wife and child, brother and sister, and even life itself, they will not be able to be my disciple.* 27 *Whoever does not carry their own cross and come after me is not able to be my disciple.* 28 *For who among you, wanting to build a tower, does not first sit down and calculate how much it would cost, to see if you have enough to complete it,* 29 *so that they don't get to the point where they have laid the foundations but don't have the power to finish it, and all those who see them begin to make fun of them,* 30 *saying, "This person is not able to build and does not have the power to complete it."* 31 *Or which king goes to another king to engage him in battle and does not sit down first to decide if he is able with ten thousand to oppose the one coming against him with twenty thousand.* 32 *If he cannot, while he is still far away, he sends an ambassador to ask for peace.* 33 *Therefore from among you everyone who does not give up all their property is not able to be my disciple.'*

Interesting words ...

- v. 26: there is a debate about the meaning of the word 'hate' (*miseō*). Although the Greek word does mean hate, the Semitic words and concepts suggest something more nuanced. 'Hate' is often said, in Hebrew usage, to have more of a sense of 'love less' rather than 'hate' as we understand it. This certainly seems to be how Matthew understood it; see 10.37, 'Whoever loves father or mother more than me is not worthy of me; and whoever loves son or daughter more than me is not worthy of me.' There is also the idea of 'turning one's back on' something, renouncing it.
- v. 27: the more usual term for 'disciples' means to 'follow' Jesus, but Luke does not use that here, choosing instead 'come after'. However, the sense is the same.
- v. 28: the word for 'tower' – *purgos* – refers either to a tower attached to the city walls to defend it from attack, or a movable tower used by an army to storm city walls. It can also refer to a tower built to guard property such as vineyards from theft.
- v. 29: the usual word for 'able' is *dunamai*. However, this isn't used here and instead it is *ischuō*, which is a stronger word that means 'to be strong enough' or 'to have the power to'.

- v. 32: the word for 'ambassador' – *presbeia* – means seniority or the right of an elder, and hence an ambassador. Only those considered wise with years were trusted with this kind of role.

Other similar passages

The Gospel of Thomas (98) has a passage with a similar theme, though expressed rather differently. It goes like this:

> The Kingdom of the Father is like a man who wanted to kill a powerful man. He drew the sword within his house and ran it through the wall, so that he might know he would be strong enough. Then he killed the powerful man.

All in all, we should be glad that this version – about an assassin who makes plans for murder – is not in the canonical Gospels.

It is worth observing, though, that the scenario of the king going into battle – or the equivalent – was discussed quite widely in the ancient world: 1 Kings 22.1–40 features the request from Jehoshaphat to Ahab to ensure it was wise to go into battle; a similar scenario can be found in the Dead Sea Scrolls, in the Temple Scroll 68.1–21, which gives advice on how many soldiers should be sent into battle. So although Jesus' audience would not have had direct experience of this kind of event, the discussion of it was relatively well known.

Honour and shame again

As with so many of Jesus' parables, the theme of honour and shame is vivid here. In our culture, beginning to build something and not finishing it would not be ideal, but at the same time not disastrous. In the tower parable, the thought of being mocked for being unable to complete the task clearly conjures feelings of absolute horror. In a similar way, the king who went into battle was concerned not just with defeat but with the shame that would come when the knowledge of that defeat became known.

The parable in context

It is interesting that these two parables in Luke 14.25–33 – with their linked discussion of discipleship – come straight after Luke's version of the parable of the great dinner (in Matthew, it is the wedding banquet). Matthew's parable ends with the unfortunate guest who was evicted for wearing the wrong clothes. It is possible that this passage in Luke functions in the same way. Even the newcomers were expected to respond to the invitation with honour; here Jesus makes it clear that there is a cost to discipleship. The message isn't quite the same, but there is an interesting overlap.

Luke 14.25–33 ends with a different command from the one with which it begins, but one that is no less uncomfortable. Just as disciples are instructed to renounce their families, they must also renounce their possessions/property. Following Jesus requires people to be 'all in', prepared to abandon all those things they might identify as vital in their lives. These certainly count as some of the hardest of Jesus' sayings, and ones that are the least observed. Indeed, the movement away from them can even be seen as early as in the book of Acts. This does not mean that we can ignore them or stop feeling uncomfortable about them. Even if we – as most of us do – opt to remain with our families and to keep some possessions, Jesus' teaching still holds: the decision to follow him will require everything from us, and we need to sit down and calculate our ability/willingness to offer him that. The calculation should include, however, the overwhelmingly generous and transformative love of Jesus in our lives. This adds a significant amount to the plus column.

To think about ...

Do you feel you are sufficiently 'all in' in following Jesus? Are you holding anything back?

---

54 The neighbourly Samaritan (Luke 10.25–37)

This is deservedly a well-loved parable. Its themes, though clearly embedded in the culture of Jesus' day, translate powerfully into our own lives and are as relevant today as ever.

Luke 10.25–37

25Look! A certain lawyer stood up to test Jesus, and said: 'Teacher, what should I do to inherit eternal life?' 26He said to him, 'What is written in the law? How do you interpret it?' 27He answered him, 'You shall love the Lord your God from the whole of your heart and in the whole of your life and in the whole of your strength and in the whole of your mind, and your neighbour as yourself.' 28He said to him, 'You have answered correctly. Do this and you will live.' 29But wanting to justify himself, he said to Jesus, 'And who is my neighbour?'

30Jesus replied and said, 'A certain man was going down from Jerusalem to Jericho and he fell among bandits, who stripped him and beat him and went away, leaving him half dead. 31By chance a certain priest was going down that road and, seeing him, passed by on the opposite side. 32Likewise a Levite came to the place and seeing him passed by on the opposite side. 33A certain Samaritan was travelling, he came and saw him and was moved with compassion. 34He went to him, bandaged his wounds and poured oil and wine on them. He put him on his animal and brought him to an inn and took care of him. 35On the next day he took two denarii and gave them to the innkeeper and said, "Take care of him and whatever else you spend I will give to you when I return." 36Which of these three seems to you to have been a neighbour to the one who fell among bandits?' 37He said, 'The one acting mercifully to him.' Jesus said to him, 'Go and do likewise.'

Interesting words ...

- v. 26: when Jesus asked the lawyer how he interpreted what was written he used the word *anaginōskō*. This could mean 'know well', 'to perceive', 'to recognize' or 'to read out loud'. So it could mean to read but probably means more than that – hence I chose 'interpret' – that is, making sense of what you read.

- v. 27: although the summary of the law is normally translated 'with' your whole heart and so on, the Greek word is *ek* – meaning 'out of' or 'from' – and feels slightly different from 'with'. The preposition then changes for 'life' and 'strength' to *en*, or 'in', which again seems important.
- v. 27: although *psuchē* is normally translated 'soul' here, it does not mean 'soul' in the way we often think of soul – that is, as something separate from our bodies. I argued in a previous book, *Body: Biblical Spirituality for the Whole Person* (SPCK, 2016), that 'life' or 'life-force' is a better translation, so I have used that here.
- v. 30: the word for 'bandits' (*lēstēs*) is significant. The other possible word, *kleptēs*, refers to someone who steals things. *Lēstēs* means more than that. Bandits or bands of robbers were sometimes politically motivated but they were always violent. In Jesus' time there were a good number of bandits operating – some seeking to overthrow the Romans in guerrilla-type attacks, others simply roaming the countryside in groups and using extreme violence to rob people. The mere mention of them would have struck fear into Jesus' listeners.
- v. 32: a Levite was a descendant of the tribe of Levi who offered assistance to priests in the temple. Their specific tasks were as temple musicians, as guards and as gatekeepers.
- v. 33: the word *splanchnizō* – 'to feel pity' or 'compassion' – is related to the noun *splanchnon* – 'the bowels'. The idea was that deep compassion was felt in the bowels rather than, as we would have it, in the heart. In the Gospels the word is only used to describe how Jesus felt (usually about the crowds) or about characters in parables – for example, it is used of the master of the unforgiving slave in Matthew 18.27, of the father's reaction to the return of the lost son in Luke 15.20, and here.
- v. 34: the word for 'animal', *ktēnos*, is the generic word for a domesticated animal.
- v. 35: although 'inn' is used in Luke's birth narrative in most English translations (Luke 2.7), the word used there is *kataluma* ('upper room' or 'guest room'), so 'inn' may not be the best translation; the word here really does mean 'inn' (*pandocheion* – literally 'all welcome').

Who is my neighbour?

Although the conversation between Jesus and the 'lawyer' is set up as a 'test', the two questions he asked here were relevant issues: 'the nature of eternal life' and 'who my neighbour is' were widely discussed in this period. The question of who counts as my neighbour can be traced all the way back to Leviticus 19.18. This established that God's people should love their neighbours as themselves, but later in that chapter it went on to say: 'The alien who resides with you shall be to you as the citizen among you; you shall love the alien as yourself, for you were aliens in the land of Egypt: I am the LORD your God' (19.34). 'Alien' meant someone who was not born in the land but who now lives there for whatever reason. This inevitably gave rise to extensive discussion about precisely who counted and who did not.

One of the key themes in the whole passage is 'doing'. In response to the lawyer's question and declaration of the summary of the law, Jesus said, 'Do this and you will live.' At the end of the parable he said, 'do likewise'. Since the rest of the conversation is about 'love', this is striking, focusing our attention on the interaction between love and action. It is insufficient to feel a gentle warm glow towards our neighbours – however we define them – if we then do not enact that love through action.

The passage in context

Jesus told the parable in response to a lawyer who was trying to test him (Luke doesn't tell us what kind of lawyer; the options are a Pharisee, a scribe or a priest – if the lawyer was a priest, that would make this parable even more hard-hitting). The test was the question about eternal life. Sadducees did not believe in life after death whereas Pharisees and a range of other Jews did. The real question, then, was which group will you align yourself with in your answer? As so often, Jesus deftly sidestepped the question with a question of his own.

His question was a clever one – to ask a lawyer how they interpret the law is immediately to put them at their ease and draw them into conversation. The lawyer responded with the summary of the law that was widely accepted in this period and cited not only by Jesus but other rabbis too. The summary was drawn from Deuteronomy 6.4–9 and Leviticus 19.18.

The logic of the parable slightly skews the original conversation, whose logic was 'love your neighbour'; the lawyer's question was 'but who is my neighbour?' The answer is the Samaritan. This therefore means he should love the Samaritan (the one who offered help to someone in need). The end of the parable suggests he should 'do likewise' – that is, offer help. Both are probably intended: being a neighbour involves not only giving *and* receiving help but also loving those who help us.

A good Samaritan?

The well-known rivalry between the Jews and the Samaritans in one way makes the popular title of this parable a helpful one, provided that we remember that in this period, for those who lived in Galilee and Judea there was no such thing as a 'good Samaritan'. In the Sermon on the Mount Jesus quoted what was apparently a well-known saying (though it isn't documented anywhere): 'You have heard that it was said: "You shall love your neighbour and hate your enemy"' (Matthew 5.43). Since the Samaritans were the epitome of 'enemy' there would be no framework in which 'loving your neighbour' would have included them. What Jesus was doing here was recalibrating the whole nature of 'neighbour' away from location and towards relationship.

There is very little agreement about the origins of the Samaritans. The Samaritans themselves trace their roots back to the tribes of Ephraim and Manasseh, and they trace the split between them and their Jewish neighbours as far back as the priest of Eli (1 Samuel 1—4), when the southern tribes split away from the rest. Within Judaism the split is traced back to the great influx of people from Assyria that occurred after the fall of Samaria in 722 BC and the period of the Babylonian exile. The key question is whether Samaritans derive their devotion from ancient Israelite practice (as the Samaritans maintain) or from new non-Israelite practices influenced by the Assyrians.

Samaritanism is a religion similar to – but also quite different from – Judaism. It survives today, though with only a very small number of followers. There are around 500 Samaritans today, living both in Nablus on the West Bank and Holon just south of Tel Aviv. Their worship is based on the Samaritan Torah (a text of the first five books of the Bible, which is the entirety of Samaritan Scripture). There are many small differences between the Samaritan Torah and the Torah read by Jews, but the key one is the commandment to build an altar on Mount Gerizim. Worship on Mount Gerizim, rather than in Jerusalem, was the major symbolic difference betweeen the two for many years.

There were three people: a priest, a Levite and a Samaritan

Various scholars note the 'rule of three' in the parables – that is, the common formulation of a story that involves three key characters (a father and two sons; three slaves given talents or mina and so on) – featuring again here. Certainly the rule is common in many stories (and jokes) through the centuries, as three is an easy number to remember. One of the key questions about the other two characters – the priest and the Levite – is why they did not stop to help the man. Many people's favourite explanation is that they were on the way to the temple and could not risk the possibility of touching a person who could have been dead. (The Levitical purity code states that a priest should not touch a dead person except for those in their own family; Leviticus 21.) The problem with this explanation is twofold.

- Luke makes it very clear that the priest was going *down* the road – that is, to Jericho and away from Jerusalem and the temple. While purity concerns may have been important if the priest were going to the temple, they would not have been pressing if going in the other direction.
- The law also made it clear that priests and Levites should care for the neighbour/stranger (see especially Leviticus 19.18 and 34). This would have involved checking whether the person on the road was dead or not. Levitical purity codes would not have released them from the responsibility to care for those around them.
- If the man had been dead, the law still required a priest to bury an abandoned corpse if he found one on the wayside.

So why did the priest and the Levite not stop? Part of the answer might be related to fear. The road from Jerusalem to Jericho was notoriously dangerous. There were plenty of places for bandits to hide on it and the bandits' treatment of the man has already revealed how brutal they were. The priest and the Levite could well have been frightened that they too would fall among bandits – the movement to the opposite side of the road hints at this. Most of the answer, however, is that we don't know because this is a parable. We don't know why the woman lost her coin; why the younger son wanted to take his money and go; why the third slave decided to hide his talent; or why the king evicted the person wearing the wrong clothes from the wedding banquet. Parables are not complete narratives and they leave many threads trailing; this is simply one of those trailing threads.

Priests and Jericho

Jerusalem is around 2,500 feet above sea level, and 18 miles from it is Jericho, which is around 825 feet *below* sea level. The road between them was notoriously dangerous and rocky despite the number of people who travelled up and down it.

According to the Babylonian Talmud, half of all priests lived in Jericho (while it doesn't mention Levites explicitly, it might have included them as well):

The Sages taught: There were twenty-four priestly watches in Eretz Yisrael, and twelve in Jericho. The Gemara expresses surprise at this statement: Twelve in Jericho? In that case there are too many of them, as this makes a total of thirty-six watches. Rather, the baraita should be read as follows: There were twenty-four in total, twelve of which were in Jericho. How so? When the time arrived for the members of a certain priestly watch to ascend, half the priestly watch would ascend from all over Eretz Yisrael to Jerusalem, and half the priestly watch would ascend from Jericho, in order to provide water and food to their brothers in Jerusalem from Jericho. (*B. Ta'anit* 27a)

Priestly watches were outlined in 1 Chronicles 24 – the idea was that they served a week at a time in the temple (with the exception of the major festivals when they all served at the same time), and so would serve roughly twice a year. What isn't clear from the Talmud – which appears to say two different things – is whether half of all priests lived in Jericho or just 12 of the 24 watches. Either way, it would not have been at all uncommon for a priest to be travelling from Jerusalem to Jericho.

On compassion

The point of the parable is not that we should blame the priest or the Levite for failing to stop, it is that we should notice and applaud the Samaritan *for* stopping. It was an act that demonstrated that his compassion was stronger than an entirely legitimate fear. This is what Jesus holds up as true neighbourly love in this parable. We noted in the interesting words above that the only characters in the Gospels to be moved by compassion other than Jesus are the master who forgives his slave of a debt and the father who welcomes his lost son home. In both of those parables, some argue, the master and father respectively are God. Whether this is true or not, the key point is that they acted as God would have done. Acting extravagantly out of love and compassion is a hallmark of divine action in the Bible, which makes it all the more remarkable that the one doing so in this parable is a much-hated Samaritan.

As the passage comes to an end we have no idea whether the lawyer will or will not 'go and do likewise'. The exchange ends and we hear no more about him – just as we never know whether the older son in the parable of the lost son(s) will go in to celebrate his younger brother's return. This reminds us that the real point is not what they did but what we would do in similar circumstances. Would we place compassion above our own fears and act in extravagant love as God would do, or pass by gripped by fear? The challenge is not an easy one – but then it isn't meant to be.

To think about ...

When might you be asked – or when have you been asked – to place compassion above your own fear?

55 The Pharisee and the tax collector (Luke 18.9–14)

The scenario that Jesus has in mind here is praying in the temple. In order to understand it we need to banish as far as we can 'going to church' from our minds. People who lived in Galilee or other far-flung parts of the region would only have gone to the temple three times a year for the major festivals (Passover, Pentecost and Tabernacles), or for a life event such as the arrival of a firstborn son. People who lived in Jerusalem and its environs might have gone more regularly to pray but not necessarily daily or weekly. There were daily morning and evening prayers but these do not seem to be implied here – the context seems to be private prayer.

Luke 18.9–14

⁹*But he said this parable to those who trusted in themselves that they were righteous and despised others.* ¹⁰*'Two people went up to the temple to pray: one was a Pharisee and the other a tax collector.* ¹¹*The Pharisee stood by himself and prayed these things: "God, I give thanks to you that I am not like other people – robbers, unrighteous people, adulterers or even like this tax collector.* ¹²*I fast twice a week; I donate a tenth of everything that I acquire."* ¹³*But the tax collector standing at a distance did not want even to raise his eyes to heaven but beat his chest saying, "God, be gracious to me, a sinner."* ¹⁴*I say to you, this man went down to his home justified rather than the other. Because all those exalting themselves will be humbled and all those who humble themselves will be exalted.'*

Interesting words …

- v. 9: 'others' – there is not an English word that quite does justice to *loipos*. It does mean 'others' but in particular means 'the rest'. The implication of the context is that it means the rest of the Jews, those whom the 'righteous' did not judge to be up to their standard.
- v. 11: the words in the Pharisee's list are *harpax* – someone who robs people; *adikos* – someone who is the opposite of righteous; and *moichos* – someone who has sex outside of marriage.
- v. 13: the beating of the chest was a common sign of grief and

mourning. Also, since the heart was seen as the place where decisions were made, it was thought to be where sin came from in the body.

The temple

The temple was a vast complex. Although the original structure – rebuilt after the return from exile – had followed the basic footprint of the first temple, Herod the Great undertook massive building works between about 20 and 10 BC. This included a huge plaza (approximately 480 by 300 metres) around the temple to accommodate increasing numbers of pilgrims to the temple site. When the parable says, then, that the tax collector stood at a distance, this would have been entirely possible. If the Pharisee went to the court of the men in the inner temple and the tax collector stayed in the court of the Gentiles in the plaza, outside of the court of the women, then he would have been at a considerable distance. The only issue is that the Pharisee indicated 'this tax collector', implying he could see him. It may be that this was introduced for artistic licence or that they were not standing quite that far apart.

Pharisees

This is another one of those passages in which Pharisees get a bad press in the Gospels. For the problems of this, see above, Part 2, pp. 96–8.

It is important to remember that it was not Pharisaism per se that gave rise to such behaviour but an assumption that following the law to the letter made someone righteous. Jesus is pointing out here that the Pharisee had missed a whole portion of the law by despising his neighbours and not loving them.

Praying and righteousness

It is worth noting that although the way the parable describes the Pharisee implies that the fact that he was standing reflected arrogance, both he and the tax collector stood to pray. This was a normal posture; although people knelt to pray in particular circumstances, such as times of grief (like Jesus in the Garden of Gethsemane), the more common posture for prayer was standing. Although Jesus condemns hypocrites in Matthew 6.5: 'And whenever you pray, do not be like the hypocrites; for they love to stand and pray in the synagogues and at the street corners, so that they may be seen by others.' It is not the standing that Jesus criticizes so much as doing it publicly. The same issue is being addressed here.

The Pharisee in the parable was pleased with himself because he fasted twice a week, which was more than the law required, and tithed – that is, gave 10 per cent of everything he acquired even if the tithe had already been paid by the seller. Jesus was not criticizing this kind of action – far from it, for elsewhere he spoke warmly of both fasting and giving generously – rather his criticism was of the Pharisee's smugness and disdain for others. In the same way, he was not praising the tax collector for what he had done – no value judgements were given by Jesus on how the tax collector had acted. The focus of the whole parable is on attitude in prayer, the contrast being between someone who knew they were 'good' and someone who knew they were not and came before God humbly. The whole point is that it is God who declares someone justified, not human beings, and here Jesus says this is done on the grounds of attitude towards God and towards other people, not according to sinful deeds that may or may not have been done.

This parable is a glorious, ironic trap into which it is all too easy to fall. In it Jesus condemns those who despise others and think themselves better than them – inviting us to fall headlong into the trap of rolling our eyes and tutting at the Pharisee for his arrogance and smugness. The whole point is not that he is a Pharisee but that his attitude to others – condemning them and looking down on them while knowing nothing about them – is a seductive snare. If we are unaware that we have done this, then we are as bad as the Pharisee we are looking down on.

To think about ...

It is so very easy to be like the Pharisee in this parable, looking down on someone else for the way they have behaved. When was the last time you did it?

Reflection

These 'Odds and Ends' – parables that don't fit easily with other themes in this book – remind us of the breadth of the subject matter Jesus dealt with. The parables as a whole contain a dizzying array of themes and life settings. Some have a rural context; others an urban one. Some ask us to feel empathy with someone who is poor and struggling to get by; at other times, we are meant to feel empathy with rich landowners who had multiple slaves. Some parables imagine everyday scenarios like sowing wheat or losing a coin; others evoke things that none of Jesus' hearers would ever have had to do – such as planning to go into battle. Some of the characters are attractive and easy to relate to; others are morally dubious and worrying. In some of Jesus' parables it is easy to make a correlation between the characters of the parable and ourselves; in others it is almost impossible to locate ourselves or anyone else within the story. It isn't just the length of the parables that varies, the type, the subject matter and the focus change and change again.

As we reach the end of the book, having looked at so many of the parables that Jesus taught, it is that variety of styles, images and subject matter that is most striking. Those of us who look for illustrations to use find that, after a while, the ones we choose are somewhat predictable and cover only a few subject areas. The parables are not like this – it is this unlimited variety that makes them so challenging to read and understand, but also so inspiring. Jesus' parables are – unfailingly – surprising, and because they are they call us into deeper and deeper reflection about God, the world and ourselves.

Epilogue

There is a story told about a businessman who wanted to learn about jade – and, in particular, how to tell what is and what is not jade. So he went to a wise teacher to learn. When he arrived the teacher's servant met him, apologized that the master was busy, and gave him a piece of jade to hold while he waited. After an hour the servant emerged and apologized again, saying that the teacher could not see him that day but had arranged an appointment for the following week. The next week the same thing happened; as it did the next, and the next. Eventually the businessman, overcome with fury, burst into the teacher's room, shouting, 'How dare you treat me like this. Week after week I have come to see you, and week after week you have been too busy. And to cap it all, the piece of jade your servant gave me today is not even jade!' He had, of course, learnt all he needed to know by sitting with a piece of jade regularly.

Having spent many months living with the parables, I feel that they are a little like this. We can spend long hours discussing a definition of what is and what is not a parable, but after a while, just by 'sitting with them', you get a feel for this. For me, a parable opens a door and summons us through. It invites us to locate ourselves emotionally within it and to learn to see the world with new eyes. A parable of Jesus invites us into a world – one that is often, for us in the twenty-first century, bemusing and quite alien – in which surprises lie. It calls us to wrestle, to think and think again, and sometimes to emerge still not understanding it but none the less changed. Sometimes the message of a parable is incomprehensible. Sometimes it is partially clear. Other times a parable offers us its meaning *very* clearly, but in every case they challenge us to think again about ourselves, about those around us, about the world and about God.

Neuroscientists have observed that brain centres light up – which indicates the formation of new neural pathways – far more with metaphors than with any other form of communication. I am not aware of any specific research, but imagine this would be found to be no less true of parables. As I said in the Introduction, parables summon us into advanced-level interpretation skills, refusing to allow us to use the same method on each one. They demand that we take each parable on its own merits, not knowing when we start what we will learn from it.

Parables are tricky and often frustrating. They are intriguing and challenging. They are tantalizing and suggestive. They are stimulating and inspiring. In them we hear the voice of Jesus speaking to us through the centuries, asking us – as he did his first followers – 'Do you get it yet?' If our answer is, as theirs was, 'No, I don't think so', this does not make us 'bad' disciples any more than the first ones were. Instead, Jesus settles downs once more and says, 'Look! A certain person was ...' or 'The kingdom of the heavens is like ...'.

'Come and join me,' he says, 'see the world through my eyes ... now what do you see? ... And now? ... And now?'

The parables summon us on a journey of discovery. It is not always a comfortable journey; in fact quite often it is a distinctly uncomfortable one, but like no other. Once you set out on it you will never see anything in the same way again.

Biblical References Index

*References in bold indicate extended treatment
of the passages containing the Parables*

Old Testament

New Testament

CPSIA information can be obtained
at www.ICGtesting.com
Printed in the USA
BVHW031919290721
613197BV00006B/131